PERSPECTIVES ON SOCIAL MEDIA

Perspectives on Social Media presents the most current research on the effectiveness of social media across sectors. Progress in finding better applications for social media relies on the difficult task of integrating media technologies into fields such as engineering, marketing, health, learning, art, tourism and the service industry. This book is based on cutting-edge creative work among top international researchers and renowned designers and provides readers with a preview of the most visionary outcomes in the field of social media. Some of the major topics that the book discusses are:

- New social media design
- Sense of community in Web applications
- App design and development for mobile devices

Perspectives on Social Media uniquely builds on recent disputes among the top scholars around the world, thus including the dynamics of knowledge sharing and cross-fertilization that one would expect to happen on the Web but that are rarely found in a book.

Piet A. M. Kommers is Associate Professor at the University of Twente and Adjunct Professor at the University of Joensuu, Finland, and Curtin University, Perth, Australia.

Pedro Isaías is Professor of Information Management and Information Systems and Director of the master degree program in Electronic Commerce and Internet at the Universidade Aberta (Portuguese Open University), Lisbon, Portugal.

Tomayess Issa is a Senior Lecturer at the School of Information Systems at Curtin University, Australia.

PERSPECTIVES ON SOCIAL MEDIA

A Yearbook

Edited by
Piet A. M. Kommers, University of Twente,
The Netherlands

Pedro Isaías, Universidade Aberta (Portuguese
Open University), Portugal

Tomayess Issa, Curtin University, Australia

Routledge
Taylor & Francis Group

NEW YORK AND LONDON

First published 2015
by Routledge
711 Third Avenue, New York, NY 10017

and by Routledge
2 Park Square, Milton Park, Abingdon, Oxon OX14 4RN

Routledge is an imprint of the Taylor & Francis Group, an informa business

Library of Congress Cataloging-in-Publication Data
    Perspectives on social media: a yearbook/edited by Piet A.M. Kommers,
    Pedro Isaias, Tomayess Issa.
        pages cm
    Includes bibliographical references and index.
    1. Social media—Research. 2. Social media—Cross-cultural studies. I. Kommers,
    Piet A. M., editor of compilation. II. Isaias, Pedro, editor of compilation.
    III. Issa, Tomayess, 1965- editor of compilation.
    HM742.P48 2014
    302.23'10072—dc23   2014004051

ISBN: 978-0-415-85415-3 (hbk)
ISBN: 978-0-415-85416-0 (pbk)
ISBN: 978-0-203-74461-1 (ebk)

Typeset in 10/12 Bembo
by codeMantra

CONTENTS

FOREWORD

My online friends Tomayess Issa and Piet A. M. Kommers recently released their new book *Perspectives on Social Media*. We met through social media a year ago. Since then, we have worked together in a variety of projects and have become good friends along the way. As they were nearing the completion of this book, they asked if I would write the foreword. To be honest, I was flattered. I welcome this collection of papers on social media and commend the contributors for their valuable work.

As an instructor of Computer Education and Instructional Technology, I found *Perspectives on Social Media* refreshing. This book addresses social media across sectors in detail and presents the most current research on the effectiveness of social media. Many books have been published on social media recently, but this one gives a broader perspective from all over the world and from different sectors such as engineering, marketing, health, learning, art, tourism and the service industry.

While seeking to understand the use of social media, you can find much information on the Web, and there are lively discussion groups on LinkedIn, but what we have needed is an authoritative work based on real-world examples. And now we have that with this book, which is based on cutting-edge creative work among top international researchers and renowned designers.

Perspectives on Social Media will provide readers with a preview of the most visionary outcomes in the field of social media. *Perspectives on Social Media* is unique as it builds upon recent disputes among the top scholars around the world, thus including the dynamics of knowledge sharing and cross-fertilization that one would expect to happen on the Web but that are rarely found in a book. *Perspectives on Social Media* discusses new social media design, sense of community in Web applications and app design and development for mobile devices.

In summary, this book demonstrates that the social media environment is a work in progress. By exploring the functioning of social media from various angles in a thoughtful manner, these papers will speed up that process and enrich the community of practice.

Assistant Professor Sehnaz BALTACI GOKTALAY
Bursa, Turkey
December 2013

Bio:

Sehnaz BALTACI GOKTALAY completed her MSc on Instructional Design, Development and Evaluation at Syracuse University, New York, and PhD on Instructional Technology at SUNY, Albany, New York. She has been working at Uludag University, Turkey, as an assistant professor in the Department of Computer Education and Instructional Technologies. Her research interests are e-learning and integration of Web 2.0 technologies in education, social networking, clinical supervision model and best practices in teacher education. She is involved in several national, international and European Union projects on Web 2.0 technologies and new teacher education.

PREFACE

This yearbook emerged from selected papers from various conferences organized by the International Association for Development of the Information Society (IADIS). The editors requested that the authors modify the original papers to put into perspective the authors' proposals and predictive scenarios.

The result is this book, *Perspectives on Social Media*, that presents the most recent trends and future predictions on how social media will infiltrate societal sectors like education, information services, economy, entertainment, urban planning, management, design, gaming, transportation, farming, etc. In fact, these chapters convince us that no sector will remain untouched by social media.

Beyond the exemplary variety in sectors, this book makes us aware of what functions are affected primarily. This list allows you to extrapolate in a bit more systematic way what we may expect to happen now as well in the future.

In terms of prospected social media, the trends include collaboration, learning, (meta-) communication, social integration, collective awareness, microfinance, blending urban with rural life, bridging the digital gap, reflection, mindful recreation and philosophizing: these are the endemic trends of Web-based participation in the coming years.

In terms of implementation, the buzz expectations for 2014 are: (1) Smart environment; tracing persons' behaviour and deriving intentions. (2) Reconquering privacy; authorities will be forced to accept their greediness to collect data without focus. (3) Growing the presence of advertising throughout social media. (4) Cloud computing will become more common and aggressive in terms of competition; 200 GB has been offered for free already. (5) Ultra-dense cameras and screens, data glasses and smart watches will feed social media and open the gate to a real "virtual presence."

From a broad view, we expect an ever growing landscape of unforeseen, serendipitous integrations of social media in each sector of life and society. The introduction of the Google Glass and micro drones will fuel the privacy issue even more than in 2013. Feel welcome to dive into the underpinning chapters and think how it will affect your personal and professional life now as well as in the future.

Section I—Collaborative Learning and Social Network Systems

In Chapter 1, "Analysis of Computing Platforms as a Tool for Collaborative Learning of Secondary School Students in the Municipality of Guimarães in Portugal: New Perspectives," Durães & Lucena explore the usage of computing platforms by students and teachers in higher education schools in the city of Guimarães, Portugal. It is crucial to recognize the tools that truly can be used as educational tools and assess their performance in order to encourage meaningful, critical and effective learning. To collect empirical data, the authors used three means: questionnaires, interviews and discussion groups.

Chapter 2, entitled "Knowledge Exchange in Social Networking Sites," was written by Miralbell and focuses on the dynamics of knowledge interchange that can occur inside online social networks. The author studies how social media can enhance knowledge exchange and the opinion that users have of the efficiency of social networks as a mean of sharing and exchanging knowledge. The empirical data were gathered with the help of a survey that was posted in 28 diverse communities on the Internet (such as LinkedIn, Facebook, Ning, etc.).

Chapter 3, with the title "Social Networking as an Enabler to Recruit and Retain Students at the University of Pretoria (UP)," was composed by Lazenby & Lombard. It focuses on the use of social media as an embedded enabler in the successful "JuniorTukkie" approach (a program initiated in 2004 with the purpose of developing academic achievers from disadvantaged backgrounds) project at the University of Pretoria. The authors try to demonstrate that social networking tools can be used as a facilitator for the successful enrollment and retention of quality prospective students in a competitive environment.

Section II—Social Media

Chapter 4, "Toward Realizing Meta Social Media Contents Management System in Big Data," was written by Nakanishi, Uchimoto & Kidawara. They propose a new model of a meta social media contents management system that combines heterogeneous data from every type of social media system, repeatedly analyzes the data and provides visualizations for understanding. The authors also present an outline of their meta social media contents management system.

Chapter 5, "Social Media for, with, and by Professionals—Participatory Design through Reflexive Engagement," written by Pihkala & Karasti focuses on reflexivity and participation as crucial approaches in the development and research of social media-supported practices for professionals. The authors report their experience of reflexivity in the participatory design of a social media-supported collaboration model.

Chapter 6, by Giota & Kleftaras, is called "Cyberpsychology and Social Media: Online Social Support in Mental Health." This chapter explores how the employment of social networking sites in Greece influences online social interactions and interpersonal relationships. It focuses on how socio-demographic factors, personal characteristics and psychopathology indicators are connected to the search for social support online. The authors state that social networking sites are starting to play a role in important areas of mental health research such as anxiety, depression and suicide prevention.

Section III—ICT Communities

In Chapter 7, "Challenges in Promoting Digital Communities in Rural Coopetitive Settings," Cabitza & Simone report on the results of a project meant to develop rural organizations in northern Italy. This project examines a network of farmers and encourages the adoption of social computing technologies to manage their necessities. This chapter demonstrates the challenges the authors went through with the project and the strategy they used to introduce a community-oriented ICT. It also delineates the additional steps that must be taken to complete the process of ICT implementation.

Chapter 8, "Non-Users of ICT and Social Media—Marginal Voices," written by Talsi focuses on the notion that not using ICT can lead to exclusion in society and can make everyday life harder. The author argues that in a society where using information technologies is standard and society is more or less mediated by information technologies, to not use these technologies is considered to be a nonstandard activity. Not using ICT not only influences the life of non-users, but it also influences technology development. The empirical data were collected and analyzed with methods of multisited qualitative research.

In Chapter 9, "The Use of a Social Media Community by Multicultural Information Systems Development Teams to Improve Communication," Goede & Nhlapo present a participatory action research project to design and implement a social networking community to enhance informal communication between team members. This chapter proposes the usage of a social network community for a multicultural information systems development team in order to improve the quality of their communication.

Chapter 10, with the title "Using Social Media to Improve the Work-Integrated Learning Experience of ICT Students: A Critical Systems Approach," was written by Goede & Harmse. It provides an action research project using a critical social research perspective to improve the quality of experience of ICT students who must undertake a period of work-integrated learning as part of the academic course at universities of technology in South Africa.

Section IV—Social Media Technologies in Higher Education

Chapter 11, "Higher Education: The Incorporation of Web 2.0," authored by Miranda, Isaías & Pífano argues "for or against" approaches regarding the Education 2.0 debate. The chapter focuses on the significance of empirical research in measuring Web 2.0's educational importance. Not only have the authors argued for the importance of Web 2.0 in educational context, but they also explain that the employment of the social Web in an educational context must be personalized to the specificities of each situation. This chapter concludes that employing Web 2.0 in higher education requires indispensable changes when it comes to learning and teaching.

In Chapter 12, "Factors That Influence Acceptance of Social Web Technologies for Learning," Echeng, Usoro & Majewski explore the notion that use of social networking tools in teaching can be achieved by using motivational procedures to get the students involved in using Web 2.0 tools for professional and/or academic reasons. This chapter addresses the issue of full acceptance of these new tools by developing a model with the following variables: motivation to use, perceived usefulness, social factors, perceived ease of use, performance expectancy, facilitating condition and prior knowledge.

In Chapter 13, "Smart Media in Higher Education—Spread of Smart Campus," Choi, An & Le investigate various types of smart campuses that are currently being constructed in Korea and reflect on the impact that a smart campus can have on higher education. This research identifies a smart campus as "a system that improves efficiency and effectiveness of college administration and education using smart devices and information communication technology."

Section V—Security and Privacy in ICT or Social Media

Chapter 14, "An Investigation into Japanese University Students' Online Privacy Concerns," by Maruyama examines not only the connection between online privacy and information disclosure behaviour but also the aspects that influence this connection. This study focuses on Japanese university students' use of social media sites and on their online privacy apprehensions. The author develops a model of interrelationship between factors that can apply to various areas of social media research.

Section VI—Social Media and Smart Technologies

Chapter 15, "Connecting and Communicating with the Near Field: How NFC Services for Smartphones May Benefit Consumers/Citizens Through Social Media Integration and Augmentation," composed by Slettemeås, Evjemo & Akselsen investigates how a large socio-technological system, in this case a piloted NFC ecosystem developed for smartphones, is experienced, consumed and communicated among its users.

Chapter 16, "Biasomic Future," composed by Širbegović explores the notion of biasomic method as "a visual analytics method for the research of media bias in news that applies automated text analysis methods, information visualization and human gamers as annotators." The main purpose of this study is to facilitate cooperation between social science and computer science by developing a visual analytics approach as an interdisciplinary solution using the best approaches from text mining, the best approaches from social sciences and information visualization disciplines.

Chapter 17, "Mobile Solutions for the New Ways of Working Era," by Ylikaup-pila, Väätänen, Laarni & Välkkynen, presents the idea that new mobile solutions facilitate working without traditional personal workstations. The authors developed and tested a New Ways of Working mobile demonstrator in the Finnish national NewWoW (New Ways of Working) project that focuses on developing understanding regarding the changing needs of knowledge workers. The authors examined multilocational mobile work and configurable workspaces on-site.

Section VII—Gaming

Chapter 18, "The Role of Interactive Technology in Prosocial Mobile Games for Young Children," was written by Humphries. Humphries has a goal to plan and develop a game to test emotion recognition that can also be used as an entertaining, touch screen tablet game for cooperative play among preschool children.

In Chapter 19, "Location-Enabled Stamp-Rally System for Local Revitaliza-tion," Hattori, Hayami & Kobayashi describe a system for conducting a stamp-rally (orienteering type game in Japan) and propose a combination of the system and location-based systems. This chapter presents the results and findings from field trials using the authors' prototype system for conducting a stamp-rally combined with a bingo game.

In Chapter 20, "Technology Enhanced Literacy Learning in Multilingual Sub-Saharan Africa: The Case of GraphoGAME Kiswahili & Kikuyu Adaptations in Kenya," Puhakka, Lyytinen & Richardson present an adaptation to Kenya of a digital training game called GraphoGAME[TM] that was developed by the Jyväs-kylä Longitudinal study of Dyslexia. This game helps children with problems in reading. The authors conclude that since the Kenyan education situation is very complex due to its multilingual nature it is vital to understand how a tool such as GraphoGAME can proficiently supply learners and teachers the necessary learning support in a context where children speak various mother tongues.

The editors,
Piet A. M. Kommers, University of Twente, The Netherlands
Pedro Isaías, Universidade Aberta (Portuguese Open University), Portugal
Tomayess Issa, Curtin University, Australia

1

ANALYSIS OF COMPUTING PLATFORMS AS A TOOL FOR COLLABORATIVE LEARNING OF SECONDARY SCHOOL STUDENTS IN THE MUNICIPALITY OF GUIMARÃES IN PORTUGAL

New Perspectives

Dalila Alves Durães & Francisco Javier Hinojo Lucena

SECONDARY SCHOOL OF CALDAS DAS TAIPAS, PORTUGAL AND UNIVERSITY OF GRANADA, SPAIN

1. Introduction

In the 21st century, technologies are beginning to be viewed in a new perspective in the educational process. They are no longer regarded as mere tools, which made old educational models more efficient and effective, but they are now considered to be structuring elements of a new form of education, with the aim of expressing the diversity of cultures and pedagogical processes. In this sense, TV, video, radio, the Internet and printed materials make it possible to articulate new languages and new rationales in schools. More and more schools and education centers are using online tools for collaborative learning and to search for information.

The teacher's role is irreplaceable; it is essential in the presentation of ideas, building working relationships and creating an effective learning environment. However, even when motivated to use new technologies, particularly computers and the Internet, teachers are confronted with a great difficulty, either because they don't have specific and appropriate training or resources are limited. It should be stressed that innovative technology is an auxiliary resource for learning; however, the teacher must have technological knowledge and a holistic vision (i.e., a global vision capable of overcoming the fragmentation of knowledge). A teacher must also have a progressive approach to social change through dialogue and base his or her teaching on research so that students can acquire knowledge with criticality.

It is also important to identify tools that can be used for educational purposes and evaluate their implementation in order to promote meaningful, critical and effective learning.

Communicating and learning are the key points for the design and development of new approaches and learning. It is also important to identify the potential for using social media in education, whether by students or between teachers and students.

In this article, I want to show the use of computing platforms by students and teachers in higher education schools in the municipality of Guimarães, Portugal.

2. Your Proposal

The municipality of Guimarães is located in north Portugal, about 60 km from Oporto. Guimarães has 69 parishes and is one of the most densely populated boroughs with around 160,000 inhabitants who reside mainly in the peripheral areas of the city. Its population is one of the youngest in Europe. This borough is one of the most highly industrialized regions of the country and, consequently, provides a higher rate of employment. Manufacturing and textiles are the most common industries, and it has a young manpower available, particularly women with low skills.

In Portugal, the Basic Law of the Education System determines that basic education is universal, compulsory and free. The same law organized the educational system into preschool education, school education and extracurricular education. The latter covers activities of literacy, basic education and professional training and initiation.

Higher education lasts for three years and is organized into courses that are mainly geared to working life (technological and professional courses) and those for continued studies (scientific-humanistic courses).

The scientific-humanistic courses, aimed at those pursuing higher studies (university or polytechnic), have a term of three academic years, corresponding to the 10th, 11th and 12th years of schooling. The courses are intended for students who have completed a basic education (nine years or equivalent qualification) and who wish to obtain a higher education. The formative offer comprises four courses: Science and Technology, Socioeconomic Sciences, Languages and Humanities and Visual Arts.

Technological and professional courses are one of the higher-level courses of education, characterized by a strong link with the professional world. These courses take into account the student's personal profile and focus on skills development for the exercise of a profession, in conjunction with the local business sector. The professional courses meet several objectives: develop personal and professional skills for the exercise of a profession; focus on training offerings that match the needs of local and regional work and prepare to enter post-secondary training or higher education, if that is the wish of the pupil.

2.1. Proposal Aims

All my research interest revolves around a general objective and specific objectives that derive directly from the general objective:

"To describe the influence of variables present in computing platforms as a tool for collaborative learning in the municipality of Guimarães and the influence of social media in schools."

For that, I apply several specific objectives:

> *Identification of the school's location, identification of school resources, courses existing in these schools, identification of computing platforms used, identification of collaborative learning communities, satisfaction and students' training needs and the enhancement of the use of this type of technology in the future.*

In my case, the universe that has directed this research work is higher school students in the municipality of Guimarães. In this municipality, there are three secondary schools: Caldas das Taipas (ESCT), Martins Sarmento (ESMS) and Francisco de Holanda (ESFH). In the three academic years of higher school, there are several classes that belong to some training courses. These options depend on courses offered by higher schools. The sample can be considered as groups or subsets of groups of a population that represent the same, where the phenomenon is studied. All the population individuals should have the same opportunity to be included in the sample.

In school year 2009, the secondary schools ESFH, ESCT and ESMS had 1614, 1067 and 1119 students, respectively. These students were allocated among various degrees of education. In addition to general courses, technological and professional courses were offered. All courses were diurnal in nature, with the exception of those offered at ESFH, where technological and professional courses were diurnal or nocturnal. In the year 2012, the number of students was 1503, 1271 and 1206 in secondary schools ESFH, ESMS and ESCT, respectively. All the technological courses ceased to exist in these three schools.

2.2. Methodology

In keeping with the descriptive, eclectic nature of my research methodology, data collection was carried out through the use of three different types of instruments: questionnaires, interviews and discussion groups.

The questionnaires integrated 194 variables, which are found in 49 issues and were grouped into three parts: characterization of the student, the school and computing platforms, whose aims are to respond to all the objectives set out above. The questionnaires were applied to 666 students between February and June 2009 and to 320 students between February and March 2012. This new application makes it possible to compare the two samples and to identify what types of changes have occurred.

The interviews and discussion groups were also conducted in two distinct phases in 2009 and 2012.

2.3. Key Findings

The main conclusion obtained is that, in general, most students don't study. Those few who do study prefer studying alone and without the use of information and communication technology (ICT).

Comparing the two phases, it turns out that the resources have improved and increased in three schools. In the first phase, the ESMS high school only had Internet access in the ICT rooms; the other schools only had Internet access in ICT rooms, the school library, and the main building. In the second phase, all the schools had Internet access and Wi-Fi network.

In the first phase, the new technologies and computer platforms were not used due to the low speed of access to the platform and the Internet itself. Other reasons include the low usage by teachers of those platforms and the fact that students often become more distracted on those computer platforms.

The second phase yielded similar results: non-use of computer platforms by the teachers, students not preparing themselves yet for this form of learning and students being more distracted with other contents.

Both phases verified that scientific-humanistic courses use more computing platforms and technologies than the other courses. However, in the last phase, this difference was toned down, with its increased use by professional courses. Within scientific-humanistic courses, the science and technology course uses the platforms and technologies in collaborative learning more often than other courses.

The computing platforms students used most are Moodle, blogs, YouTube, wikis, MSN, Google and the School Page. Those computing platforms are used primarily for students to study. Students also used computing platforms to chat with friends, seek information, have fun and work. Students used the computers for entertainment: they played games, listened to music, downloaded music and movies and watched movies. The main virtual learning communities used by students were Moodle, wikis and blogs. Such computer platforms now offer a portal for entertainment and communication, and they have grown exponentially in recent years. Thus, students are attracted to these platforms to communicate, have fun and meet new people. Nevertheless, the aim of browsing for information and acquiring new knowledge is just a residual outcome.

3. Predictive Scenario

The dilution of distance establishes a form of openness and promotion of access to and participation in the activities of communities. However, you might want to distinguish three forms of distance: geographical, social and technological.

Geographical distance becomes irrelevant with the creation of virtual learning environments, since there is a common language in the individuals' access to the network and participation in the sharing of knowledge and practices. Since language is a criterion of access defined initially in the creation of these environments, this type of distance is no longer a factor.

Technological distance can affect access since the speed and access mode may create some restrictions for users with less-developed technological means. However, the promotion of fluency of multiple media is a strategy for the digital inclusion and the appropriation of the net as a means of information and communication.

Regarding social distance, the problem focuses on processes of participation and integration in the activities of the community, since in the era of globalization, all individuals (whether working in groups or alone) may participate in the processes of education and training, even social and cultural minority groups. In this kind of distance, it is necessary to promote the reconstruction of social interaction processes in the network, through which one can learn how to become a member of the community (Castells, 2004).

The boundaries and borders of face-to-face education were dimmed through the creation of virtual communities, since time and space increased learning, encouraging the development of new perspectives for initial training and lifelong learning.

For the generation of my research student sample, technology, particularly the Internet, assumed a substantial stake in students' social and educational lives.

In this sense, schools now have opportunities to apply ICT that are so effective outside the classroom for educational purposes. Taking advantage of these technologies will require profound changes in the roles of teachers, students and schools.

For students to gain the most benefit from school, the distance between the school and the students should be shortened as much as possible. To accomplish this, schools ought to create a group of platforms so that students, when they are at school, can access and communicate with their peers and, under teachers' guidance, produce works and experience collaborative learning. The geographic distance is thus faded, allowing all to profit from the same learning. The technological distance in schools within the same borough fades when students have access to the Internet.

Communities and government should account for technological change when setting the agenda for systemic change in education. The evaluation of high school curricula and how they integrate collaborative learning through computer platforms and ICT is important. In this context, learning assessments, which have a huge influence on education policies, should be revised so that teachers can use collaborative learning in the teaching-learning process. It is also necessary for education policies to promote the use of computer platforms and ICT.

Rather than being repositories of knowledge, teachers are guides who help students navigate through electronically accessible information. For this reason, teachers must receive extensive training in how to use emerging information technologies.

Industry must develop educational devices from comparatively low-price games hardware and software. Software manufacturers should build educational games for use in learning, because children typically enjoy and find excitement in interacting with new technologies. These games must include both cognitive and non-cognitive skills, such as critical thinking, problem solving, collaboration, effective communication, motivation, persistence and willingness to learn. These skills also include creativity, innovation and ethics, which are important to later success, and may be developed in formal or informal learning environments.

The new virtual learning environments must create the possibility for the development of social and cognitive interactions, that are organized around the activities and contexts, which will play an increasingly important role in understanding the knowledge society's processes of learning and training.

However, there must be collaborative and technological mediation of the processes of interaction (i.e., it is necessary to organize around goals, contexts and mediating collaborative learning activities in order to develop the sharing of objects of study in the community). Through collaborative mediation, the virtual learning community springs up from group and individual activities in the representation of distributed knowledge. Mediation is the way as there will be participation and collaboration (i.e., the media where the process of cognitive and social interactions is conducted will be the key factor for the sustainability and mobilization of the virtual community).

I propose that educational systems gradually will incorporate Semantic Web technologies, with the goal of providing a more flexible learning environment. The Semantic Web must provide an environment where software agents can browse through Web documents and perform sophisticated tasks. These systems allow for numerous improvements in the context of Web-based educational systems that improve the quality of learning.

When students are studying and using the World Wide Web (WWW), there is much interference in their field of study, as they can be easily distracted by other issues. It is, therefore, necessary to provide a system that filters and interprets the content available and presents the student only what is relevant for learning.

Similarly, it is necessary to create a system for teachers that allows them to direct students in their learning. Teachers need a set of systems that may detect various reactions from students, including fatigue and possible indifferences.

When students, for various reasons, may not be predisposed to learning and in classes with a high number of students, the teacher needs instruments that can indicate whether a particular student is using other applications or is not predisposed to learning. In this sense, the Semantic Web technologies work well since they use intelligent systems that can detect a student's lack of attention.

These mechanisms applied in the context of collaborative learning in e-learning can be used to detect changes in students' behavior and provide instant feedback to the teacher who can better supervise students and prevent them from being distracted.

4. Conclusions

The Semantic Web has great potential for improving technology-enhanced learning in many ways. However, it is still in its infancy.

The Semantic Web-based educational applications in the next generation are expected to be more adaptive and offer a personalized learning environment; pedagogies to enhance instruction/learning; effective information sharing, storage and retrieval; new forms of collaboration with peers and many other characteristics that enable the performance of a better use of Anytime, Anywhere, Anybody Learning using most of the WWW resources as reusable learning objects supported by standard technologies.

It is also convenient to show that many times schools mainly regard ICT platforms and social interaction sites as a form of entertainment for students and not a vehicle for learning. Therefore, it is necessary to overcome this stigma and use this form of communication to enrich students' learning.

5. References

Anderson, P. (2007). What is 2.0. Ideas, technologies and implications for education. 60.

Anderson, T., & Whitelock, D. (2004). The educational semantic web: Visioning and practicing the future of education. *Journal of Interactive Media in Education (JIME)*, 7(1), 1–15.

Berners-Lee, T. (2001, May 17). The semantic web. *Scientific American*.

Castells, M. (2004). A galáxia internet, reflexões sobre internet, negócios e sociedade. *Lisboa: Fundação Caloustre Gulbenkian*.

Costa, F. A., Peralta, H., & Viseu, S. (2007). As tic na educação em portugal—concepções e prácticas. *Porto Editora*.

Dieuzeide, H. (1994). Les nouvelles technologies. *Outils D'enseignement*. Paris: Nathan.

Giannakos, M., & Lapatas, V. (2010). Towards web 3.0 concept for collaborative e-learning, In *Proceedings of the Multi-Conference on Innovative Developments in ICT* (147–151).

Hwang, K. A., & Yang, C. H. (2009). Automated inattention and fatigue detection system in distance education for elementary school students. *Educational Technology & Society*, 12(2), 22–35.

Jonassen, D. (1998). O uso das novas tecnologias na educação à distância e a aprendizagem construtivista. *Em Aberto: Educação à Distância*, 16(70), 70–78.

Jonassen, D. (2000). *Computers as mindtools for schools: engaging critical thinking 2nd*. Upper Saddle River, N.J.: Merrill [trad. Portuguesa: Computadores, Ferramentas Cognitivas: Desenvolver o Pensamento Crítico das Escolas. Porto: Porto Editora].

Meetoo-Appavoo, A. (2011). Constructivist-based framework for teaching computer science. *International Journal of Computer Science and Information Security (IJCSIS)*, 9(8), 25–31.

Papert, S. (1994). A máquina das crianças: Repensando a escola na era da informática. Porto Alegre: Artes Médicas.

Papert, S. (2000a). Change and resistance to change in education. Taking a deeper look at why school hasn't changed. In A. D. de Carvalho (Ed.), *Novo Conhecimento. Nova Aprendizagem* (pp. 61–70). Lisboa: Fundação Calouste Gulbienkian.

Ponte, J. P. (1994). *O Projecto MINERVA: Introduzindo as NTI na Educação em Portugal: Introducing NIT in Education Potugal.* Lisboa: ME/DEP GEF.

Richardson, W. (2005). The educator's guide to the read/write web. *Educational Leadership, 63*(4), 24.

Rubens N., Kaplan, D., & Okamoto, T. (2011). E-Learning 3.0: anyone, anywhere, anytime, and AI. In *International Workshop on Social and Personal Computing for Web-Supported Learning Communities* (SPeL 2011).

Salomon, G. (2002). Technology and pedagogy: Why don't we see the promised revolution? *Educational and Technology,* 71–75.

Turkle, S., & Papert, S. (1992). Epistemological pluralism and revaluation of the concrete [versão electrónica]. *Journal of Mathematical Behavior, 11*(1), 3–33.

2

KNOWLEDGE EXCHANGE IN SOCIAL NETWORKING SITES

Oriol Miralbell

OPEN UNIVERSITY OF CATALONIA, SPAIN

1. Introduction

Since the last decade of the 20th century, substantial changes in global communication (Castells, 1996) have fostered the emergence of the information and global economy where productivity and competitive advantage of agents (enterprises, regions or nations) depend on their capacity to generate, process and apply information based on knowledge. In this networked society, knowledge is in the center of all the processes and the Internet has become the place where most information flows (Wellman, 2001).

The dynamics of knowledge exchange that happen inside online social networks and their structure have a direct influence on the characteristics of knowledge exchange. The generation of new knowledge and innovation arise more easily in sparse and unbounded networks with a structure characterized by many nodes representing members of the network who receive few connections: only a few members receive many connections (Wellman, 2001). The most common structures of personal networks in social networking (SN) sites are flexible and open structures based on selective contacts of their members that change often role. Relationships are diffused and scattered while network members that have a high level of autonomy of action keep weak, diverse and changing relations between them. In summary, these networks work better when used for the diffusion of innovation and for knowledge generation (Wellman, 2001).

As an improvement to Web 1.0, Web 2.0 is a network service that allows multiple access and provides greater mobility (DiNucci, 1999), harnesses the collective knowledge of users (O'Reilly & Battelle, 2009; O'Reilly, 2006) and permits users to control the edition and diffusion of their information (O'Reilly, 2006). SN sites have become one of the most successful services of Web 2.0 as evidenced by a huge increase in the number of users in the last few years. Among the major SN sites today are Facebook (founded in 2005), Twitter (started in 2006), LinkedIn (founded in 2003) and YouTube (created in 2005). Professionals use the first three of these most often for knowledge exchange. SN sites allow individuals to cooperate and interact inside sparse and unbounded social networks of knowledge with flexible and open structures. SN sites promote **interactivity** among users/members who can exchange knowledge and manage their relationships. These sites also facilitate users' **autonomy** by allowing them (1) to create a public profile to share among a list of contacts, (2) to manage their activity with intuitive tools and processes and (3) to cross contact lists with other users in an **open environment** that fosters **diversity** among members. These factors make connective networks successful in the area of knowledge exchange (Downes, 2006; Siemens, 2006).

2. Factors for Successful Knowledge Exchange in Social Networking Sites

In order to determine how social media can increase knowledge exchange, we have looked at the factors inherent to SN sites to achieve a successful knowledge exchange. We also have studied the perception that users have of the efficiency of SN to share and exchange knowledge.

3. Methodology

Considering the factors of success for connective networks of knowledge we have worked on designing a new acceptance model of the SN sites (Figure 2.1) based on the TAM - Technology Acceptance Model (TAM) (Davis, 1989), one of the most diffused theories of technology adoption extensively used in studies on conventional information systems (Wiedenbeck & Davis, 1997), on the Internet (Luarn & Lin, 2005), or in the learning (Ma, Andersson, & Streith, 2005) and in e-learning (Ndubisi, 2006) domain.

To determine how knowledge exchange occurs inside SN sites, we organized specific virtual communities of tourism professionals inside SN sites and analyzed their exchange of information and knowledge.

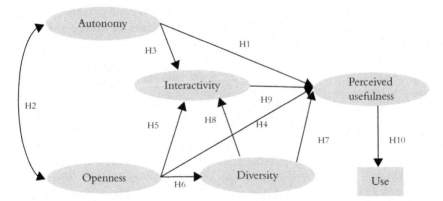

FIGURE 2.1 Acceptance model for social networking sites.

These professional members of virtual communities are especially interested in the exchange of knowledge for the purpose of strengthening their skills, achieving personal development and improving their careers. Informal learning often occurs when members interact and exchange knowledge with peers (Buysse, Winton, & Rous, 2009) inside virtual communities.

In our research, we focused on virtual communities of professionals in tourism: there is an endemic high level of mistrust between tourism companies and tourism professionals which hinders cooperation between them, but we knew about their high level of interaction inside online social networks. This made this case especially interesting. Through an Internet search, we found 28 virtual communities with 85,612 members, distributed among the following SN sites: LinkedIn (13 groups with 65,000 members), Facebook (8 groups with 3,133 members), Ning (6 communities with 14,136 members) and Hosteltur (with its own platform and 3,343 members).

To gather data for empirical research, we designed a survey that we posted in these 28 different communities on the Internet (LinkedIn, Facebook, Ning, etc.), inviting their members to respond through a questionnaire. The survey questions corresponded to the variables we had previously identified. We grouped the questions in four sections: (1) socio-demographic data, (2) information on Internet behavior and the use of technological resources, (3) information on perceived factors that influence knowledge exchange in SN sites and (4) information on features influencing the adoption of SN sites. To validate the model, the questions in the fourth section were set up on Likert scale.

We obtained 363 voluntary responses over Google Docs between December 2009 and July 2010. This information was integrated into a database with 81 variables, which helped us perform a descriptive analysis of the behavior of these community members using SN sites for knowledge exchange.

The acceptance model of these SN sites was tested using SPSS v.19 AMOS through an exploratory factor analysis first and then a confirmatory factor analysis through the structural equation model (SEM) which checked the validity of the measurement model and the structural model.

4. Key Findings

By analyzing the data collected in the survey, we found that professionals believe that SN sites are efficient for exchanging knowledge but they did experience some limitations.

4.1. Users Prefer Socialization to Commitment

About 63.3% of the members of virtual communities of tourism professionals think that SN sites are useful to them, and 56.7% view them as good environments for learning and for knowledge exchange.

Nearly 79.3% of these professionals have a high level of participation, but only 56.8% interact with other members and just 42.5% get involved in generating new ideas.

Professionals are more motivated to improve relations (62.5%) than to generate new knowledge. In general, we observed that SN sites are especially used for socialization and gaining relationships and less for generating knowledge, though participation is high.

Even though professionals are using SN sites to maintain relationships with friends and other professionals, only 53.7% feel trust, about 47.1% feel committed to their networks while 44.9% feel loyalty to other members. The low percentages of members that feel trust, commitment and loyalty with their networks can be seen as a hindrance to interaction and knowledge exchange (Brandtzaeg & Heim, 2008; Chow & Chan, 2008; Garbarino & Johnson, 1999; Gefen & Straub, 2004).

We concluded that virtual communities inside SN sites are very much appreciated and used to socialize, but the level of commitment in exchanging professional knowledge seems less significant.

4.2. Autonomy of Users and Openness Are Beneficial for Knowledge Exchange

The acceptance model shows that the success factors of connective networks influence the perceived usefulness and use of SN sites.

Regarding the factors that impact knowledge exchange inside SN sites, the perceived levels of autonomy influence the perceived usefulness of the sites, which in turn influences the level of usage. Also the perceived level of interactivity has a positive influence on the perceived usefulness of the sites.

On the other hand, there is a strong correlation between the perception of openness that users have of SN sites and their sense of autonomy. That is, the more users feel that communication is easy and free from internal and external limits, that they can enter and exit the community with no difficulty, and that there are no limits to their participation, the more they believe their autonomy will increase and the more useful they will find such sites to be in cultivating relationships.

Finally, there is a direct link between perceived openness of SN sites and the perceived diversity of members and ideas within such sites. Consequently, a site's openness will increase the probability of its members' diversity which, in turn, will foster interactivity and improve knowledge exchange.

4.3. Predictive Scenario and Conclusions

SN site users are increasingly interacting for different purposes. While they do exchange knowledge, users are especially interested in socializing and keeping relationships with peers, family and friends. These relations in the virtual world are not replacing traditional physical relationships, but they are complementary. In the business world, SN sites are used more and more for exchanging knowledge between customers and among professionals, which is transforming these sites into new strategic communication spaces for business.

Organizations and developers must review the ways SN sites are used, reconsider existing services and identify new solutions to integrate, especially to facilitate more autonomous but also coordinated processes of interaction that make knowledge exchange and knowledge generation more efficient. We believe that changes occur mainly in two directions: gaining autonomy and openness of the systems and facilitating better coordination with easy-to-use administration tools.

4.4. Making SN Sites More Accessible and Open to Facilitate Autonomy and Diversity

The benefits of SN sites depend on their features which allow users to manage their relationships more efficiently because they can track their activity, to interact easily with others without any constriction of time or distance, to enjoy social activity through different services that are easy to use, such as an informing environment, a delivery system for sharing information, and a task completion system, and to "act upon the information received" (Magro, Ryan, & Prybutok, 2013).

The ease of use is strongly related to the perception of self-efficacy that users have (i.e., their autonomy) (Bandura, 1997; Compeau & Higgins, 1995). This is one of the factors of acceptance of information systems in general because they influence the perceived usefulness and motivate the use (Davis, 1989; Miralbell Izard, 2013).

From the perspective of activity inside networks, we know that social capital (i.e., the expected benefits of interacting inside a network) (Adler & Kwon, 2000; Bourdieu, 1980; Burt, 1999) and satisfaction (strongly related to perceived usefulness) influence continuance intention in using SN sites such as Facebook. Two factors influence the continuance intention to use of Facebook: the user's attitude and hedonic enjoyment. For users to continue to visit SN sites, they must feel comfortable and have a pleasant experience (Magro et al., 2013).

A larger number of members will affect positively the level of participation and interaction on an SN site. A high level of user participation and interaction inside the network are necessary for knowledge exchange (Ardichvili, Page, & Wentling, 2003; Lave & Wenger, 1990), while a large diversity of ideas and profiles of the members affects the generation of innovative ideas positively (Wellman, 2001). The openness of SN sites helps attract more interested and diverse users to them.

Compared to preexisting virtual communities' platforms, SN sites have increased the capacity for autonomy of the users and the openness of the systems facilitating the interaction, connecting cross-platforms that allow the exchange of contacts and relationships between social networks without technical barriers. Owners and developers of SN sites must keep working to increase autonomy for users and to create a high level of connectivity with other SN sites, to foster interaction, to increase use and promote innovative knowledge generation.

4.5. Facilitating Knowledge Exchange with Powerful Administration Features

The process of knowledge generation inside social groups is cyclic (Nonaka & Takeuchi, 1995): through ongoing recodification, tacit knowledge is transformed into explicit knowledge and back again. From an individual approach in connective networks of knowledge, members can learn by exchanging knowledge freely and independently (Downes, 2006, 2007a, 2007b; Siemens, 2005, 2006, 2007) in environments such as personal learning environments (PLE) (Haskins, 2007) though the cognitive dimension in a group dedicated to exchange information and knowledge is focused on common meanings and the understanding that individuals and the group have (Boisot, 1998; Boland Jr. & Tenkasi, 1995). To achieve successful collective knowledge exchange on SN sites, it is necessary to facilitate a common ground and a higher level of commitment and trust that help increase interaction and knowledge exchange in virtual communities of practice (CoP), a type of virtual groups that integrate four key elements to succeed: (a) mutual commitment of members; (b) the joint venture of the group; (c) a shared repertoire of all members in the topics, culture and language and (d) the peripheral participation of the noncore members of the group (Lave & Wenger, 1990). SN sites facilitate peripheral participation (d) and the visibility of shared repertoires (c), though users have perceived inside SN sites a lack of mutual commitment (a) and joint venture of the group (b).

As we have seen earlier, autonomy is important for users of SN sites though coordination and flexible leadership in CoPs are also needed to facilitate knowledge exchange and foster knowledge generation. This requires SN sites to provide adequate services that make coordination possible. Leaders should be able to help group members interact dynamically, coordinate discussions and add knowledge to discussions in a planned and organized way. This would foster the emergence of new ideas inside the group. These groups need specific collaboration tools such as a calendar to schedule tasks inside the group, a collaborative system of file administration, organized discussion scenarios, etc. (Llorens & Capdeferro, 2011). Professionals are willing to share knowledge in virtual communities such as LinkedIn or Facebook, but they dedicate more effort to personal and professional relations. To increase the level of knowledge generation and the emergence of new ideas inside virtual communities, a higher level of trust and a greater sense of commitment among professionals are necessary. With coordinated and dynamic processes of knowledge exchange, CoPs can afford the adequate conditions for this change of attitude of the members of virtual communities.

In summary, to achieve a successful knowledge exchange, communities of knowledge inside SN sites must meet certain characteristics in order to become fully operational (von Friedrichs Grängsjö, 2003). First, they need standards and values formed by factors such as oral and ethical attitudes and norms that are of primary importance to the organization. Second, there must be a dynamic and flexible leadership, so that social networks are not characterized by a hierarchy that would constrain the liberty of members. Third, borders (both internal and external) must be flexible so that members from outside the group feel free to enter and members can freely manage their relations and activities between the clusters of the network. Finally, knowledge communities should have a high mutual dependence in which all members recognize their interdependence, both internally and externally.

In a connective knowledge network scenario, new solutions (via apps of the existing SNs or with new social medias) must be created that make knowledge exchange more efficient through coordination of activity inside the groups and tutoring the initiatives, helping to codify common meanings, creating new ideas and exchanging knowledge, since they will increase trust, commitment and loyalty of the participants, which are essential to cooperative knowledge generation and exchange.

5. References

Adler, P. S., & Kwon, S. W. (2000). Social capital: The good, the bad, and the ugly. *Knowledge and Social Capital*, 89–115.

Ardichvili, A., Page, V., & Wentling, T. (2003). Motivation and barriers to participation in virtual knowledge-sharing communities of practice. *Journal of Knowledge Management*, 7(1), 64–77.

Bandura, A. (1997). *Self-efficacy: The exercise of control*. New York: W.H. Freeman.

Boisot, M. (1998). *Knowledge assets: Securing competitive advantage in the information economy*. Oxford University Press, USA.

Boland Jr., R. J., & Tenkasi, R. V. (1995). Perspective making and perspective taking in communities of knowing. *Organization Science*, 350–372.

Bourdieu, P. (1980). Le capital social. *Actes de La Recherche En Sciences Sociales*, 31(1), 2–3.

Brandtzaeg, P. B., & Heim, J. (2008). User loyalty and online communities: Why members of online communities are not faithful. In *Proceedings of the 2nd International Conference on Intelligent Technologies for Interactive Entertainment* (p. 11).

Burt, R. S. (1999). The social capital of opinion leaders. *The Annals of the American Academy of Political and Social Science*, 566(1), 37–54.

Buysse, V., Winton, P. J., & Rous, B. (2009). Reaching consensus on a definition of professional development for the early childhood field. *Topics in Early Childhood Special Education*, 28(4), 235–243.

Castells, M. (1996). *The rise of the network society* (Vol. 1). Malden, MA: Blackwell.

Chow, W. S., & Chan, L. S. (2008). Social network, social trust and shared goals in organizational knowledge sharing. *Information & Management*, 45(7), 458–465.

Compeau, D. R., & Higgins, C. A. (1995). Computer self-efficacy: Development of a measure and initial test. *MIS Quarterly*, 19(2), 189–211.

Davis, F. D. (1989). Perceived usefulness, perceived ease of use, and user acceptance of information technology. *MIS Quarterly*, 13(3), 319–340.

DiNucci, D. (1999). Fragmented future. *Print*, 53(4), 32.

Downes, S. (2006). Learning networks and connective knowledge. In *Instructional Technology Forum* (Vol. 28).

Downes, S. (2007a). An introduction to connective knowledge. In *Media, Knowledge & Education—Exploring New Spaces, Relations and Dynamics in Digital Media Ecologies. Proceedings of the International Conference Held on June 25–26, 2007.* Innsbruck: Innsbruck University Press.

Downes, S. (2007b). Learning networks in practice.

Garbarino, E., & Johnson, M. S. (1999). The different roles of satisfaction, trust, and commitment in customer relationships. *The Journal of Marketing*, 70–87.

Gefen, D., & Straub, D. W. (2004). Consumer trust in B2C e-commerce and the importance of social presence: Experiments in e-products and e-services. *Omega, 32*(6), 407–424.

Haskins, T. (2007, June 4). PLEs are power tools. Blog. Growing changing learning creating. Retrieved from http://growchangelearn.blogspot.com.es/2007/06/ples-are-power-tools.html

Lave, J., & Wenger, E. (1990). *Situated learning: Legitimate peripheral participation.* Cambridge University Press.

Llorens, F., & Capdeferro, N. (2011). Facebook's potential for collaborative e-learning. *Revista de Universidad y Sociedad Del Conocimiento, RUSC, 8*(2), 197–210.

Luarn, P., & Lin, H. H. (2005). Toward an understanding of the behavioral intention to use mobile banking. *Computers in Human Behavior, 21*(6), 873–891.

Ma, W. W., Andersson, R., & Streith, K. O. (2005). Examining user acceptance of computer technology: An empirical study of student teachers. *Journal of Computer Assisted Learning, 21*(6), 387–395.

Magro, M. J., Ryan, S. D., & Prybutok, V. R. (2013). The social network application post-adoptive use model (SNAPUM): A model examining social capital and other critical factors affecting the post-adoptive use of Facebook. *Informing Science: The International Journal of an Emerging Transdiscipline, 16.* Retrieved from http://www.inform.nu/Articles/Vol16/ISJv16p037-069Magro0629.pdf

Miralbell Izard, O. (2013). Social networking sites and knowledge exchange. The proposal of an acceptance model. In *Proc. of IADIS Internation Conference Web Based Communities and Social Media.* Prague, Czech-Republic.

Ndubisi, N. (2006). Factors of online learning adoption: A comparative juxtaposition of the theory of planned behaviour and the technology acceptance model. *International Journal on E-Learning, 5*(4), 571.

Nonaka, I. A., & Takeuchi, H. A. (1995). *The knowledge-creating company: How Japanese companies create the dynamics of innovation.* Oxford University Press.

O'Reilly, T. (2006). Web 2.0 compact definition: Trying again. OReilly Radar.

O'Reilly, T., & Battelle, J. (2009). Web squared: Web 2.0 five years on. *Web 2.0 Summit.*

Siemens, G. (2005). Connectivism: Learning as network-creation. *ASTD Learning News, 10*(1).

Siemens, G. (2006). *Knowing knowledge.* Lulu.com.

Siemens, G. (2007). Connectivism: Creating a learning ecology in distributed environment. *Didactics of Microlearning: Concepts, Discourses, and Examples*, 53–68.

von Friedrichs Grängsjö, Y. (2003). Destination networking: Co-opetition in peripheral surroundings. *International Journal of Physical Distribution & Logistics Management, 33*(5), 427–448.

Wellman, B. (2001). Computer networks as social networks. *Science, 293*(5537), 2031.

Wiedenbeck, S., & Davis, S. (1997). The influence of interaction style and experience on user perceptions of software packages. *International Journal of Human-Computer Studies, 46*(5), 563–588.

3

SOCIAL NETWORKING AS AN ENABLER TO RECRUIT AND RETAIN STUDENTS AT THE UNIVERSITY OF PRETORIA (UP)

Karen Lazenby & Petrus Lombard

UNIVERSITY OF PRETORIA, SOUTH AFRICA

1. Introduction

Traditional communication methods such as the telephone, fax, letters and the lack of infrastructure easily lead to slow response time and insufficient and outdated information. These methods are no longer the best way of communication for school learners. It is also expensive to communicate frequently to thousands of students and parents who want to be contacted and given information quickly. The fast pace of technological change increases competitive pressure between institutions to successfully communicate with quality students.

This article focuses on the use of social media as an embedded enabler in the successful JuniorTukkie (JT) programme at the University of Pretoria. The JT programme was initiated to empower academic achievers to bridge the gap between school and university and to succeed at university. The JT programme is based on relationship building; therefore, effective communication with learners and their parents is essential. Barnes & Lescault (2012) define social networking as "a web-based service which allows individuals to construct profiles for themselves in a system, connect with others and view and transverse their list of connections within the system." Social networking has become the most effective method of communication between the university and prospective students and helps retain students in the recruitment (from application to admission) process. The role of trust in the use of social media in the recruitment process is crucial.

2. Customer Relationship Management at the University of Pretoria

Bajou & Bajou (2013) map the educational value chain onto the four customer relationship management (CRM) stages: exploration (recruitment), expansion

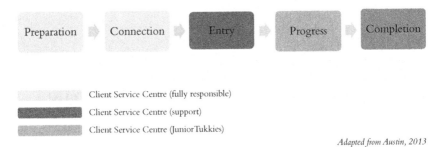

FIGURE 3.1 Value chain.

(enrollment management), commitment (retention and persistence), continuation (graduation, placement, and alumni affairs) or dissolution (discontinuation/drop out). They make a strong case about the importance of quality communication during these different stages.

The Client Service Centre (CSC) was established in 2002 to connect students and other clients of the University of Pretoria. It is the driver of the university's CRM strategy. As pointed out by Bajou & Bajou (2013, p. 250), "from the service side of an institution, students are customers who expect to receive high-quality and prompt service." The CSC services cover the value chain in the life cycle of the student as illustrated in Figure 3.1. The CSC is responsible for student recruitment, produces publications for students and also serves as the information hub of the university (general enquiries via phone, walk-in, e-mail and Web). Other services include application for study support, information about admission and registration, financial aid, student accounts and payments, access cards and parking, application for residence/accommodation support, the international student division and the graduate career office. The CSC also maintains information governance and the university website and intranet.

2.1. The JuniorTukkie Programme

The JT programme was launched in 2004 with the vision of developing academic achievers from students with disadvantaged backgrounds (regardless of whether they eventually apply to study at the University of Pretoria). The name is derived from the informal name of the University of Pretoria (Tuks). It has evolved from sending two school learners to the National Aeronautics and Space Administration (NASA) Agency in Houston, Texas, to a membership of 3,052 learners in southern Africa (grades 10–12). Individual learners are identified in grade 10 and have to maintain their marks to remain a JT. It is a fair and transparent system, and any learner can access the JT website, apply online for membership and access the JT magazine.

Considerable time is spent on providing JTs with information and on streamlining their administrative processes to facilitate retention up to registration. Equity learners, especially, are selected for empowerment courses on campus that are sponsored by external companies (Investec, Dimension Data and Johnson & Johnson). Bursaries are available for these learners if they register at the university. The empowerment courses aim to equip learners for the transition to university, and research has been conducted to ensure that the courses are designed to achieve the desired impact. The courses include career guidance, emotional intelligence (Clark, 2005; Norton, 2010; Zepke & Leach, 2010), mathematical reasoning (Pasensie, 2012), computer skills and reading and comprehension (including a free eye test and prescription glasses). Social activities are designed to foster networking and relationship building (Morosanu, Handley, & O'Donovan, 2010).

The JT programme has proven to be sustainable, scalable and actionable. Its success is ascribed to the integrated strategy (as part of the Client Service Centre) and use of social media, funding from external companies, institutional buy-in and the passion of the JT staff. For the 2013 student first-year intake, some 77% of JT learners registered for study at the University of Pretoria. Since the inception of the programme, less than 5% of the students have discontinued their studies. Currently, more than 2,200 registered JTs are on campus. Their academic progress is monitored where possible, and interventions with academic staff and other support departments are arranged when needed to ensure that they graduate. Many of them belong to the JT Student Society that was established in 2010. Members of the society assist with JT events in order to give back of their time and skills. These students are invaluable as mentors for the JT learners who attend the events. The JTs who graduate become part of the JT Alumni and contribute some of their time in their workplace and their communities to assist other JTs.

2.2. The Use of Social Media in the JuniorTukkie Programme

Hayes, Russchman, & Walker (2009) emphasize a high degree of human interaction, behaviour and personalization in the successful use of social media. In 2009, the JT office started to make use of social media technology (Web-based and mobile applications) to communicate with top academic achievers. The use of social media helps bridge the digital divide because about 97% of learners have cell phones, but they do not necessarily have access to computers.

Learners receive communication via e-mail and SMS if any new information is loaded on the Web. Through the use of Facebook, Twitter and WhatsApp short messages are sent to learners and they are referred to the JT website, UP Blog, the JT e-magazine as well as the e-newsletter. They can reply by short message service (SMS), e-mail or on the JT Web Comments page as well as via the social network tools. Response handling is time consuming and requires a dedicated person to answer enquiries and requests.

The JT website (www.up.ac.za/juniortukkie) includes information on career courses, application and admission information, residences, faculties, sports, and the social networks that form part of the university's diverse community. The availability of videos on YouTube also plays a significant role in the distribution of information about activities. The website can be easily explored via cell phones and serves as a quick link to most of the information and self-help resources such as study guides and matric[1] exam papers. Online applications, information changes and the upload of documents are made easier and lower the administration burden on scanning of documents and typing of data. The JT online membership tool gives prospective students easier entrance to access at the university from an early stage (in addition to the student portal). Data can be entered via a cell phone and are immediately available in a database. These data assist the recruitment division in supporting prospective students who need to make correct career choices and streamline their application process. The JT website shows a tremendous growth in site visits due to the use of social media. Monthly visits vary between 40,000 to 131,000 hits depending on the actions taking place in the JT office.

2.3. Key Findings

In a survey administered to undergraduate University of Pretoria students (66.5% response rate), a question asked: "Which forms of communication do you wish your instructors used more?" Some of the results were as follows: social studying sites, 29.5%; Facebook, 26.2%; Twitter, 13.4%; instant messaging/online chatting, 29.6%; text messaging (SMS), 40.4% and e-mail, 70.4% (Educause, 2013). These results provide a general idea of the preferred social media methods in the teaching and learning environment.

In an attempt to identify the effectiveness of the different social media tools that are used by the JT office, a survey was conducted over a few days in July 2013. The survey results indicate a preference for WhatsApp (Table 3.1).

During the grade 12 Preparation conference for top provisionally admitted/selected students that took place in September 2013, a survey was conducted on their preferred communication channel with the JT office.

TABLE 3.1 Social Media Survey (Snap Shot Taken Over Five Days in July 2013)

Media	Respondents	Satisfaction			
		Excellent	Good	Average	Poor
Facebook	427	251 (58.78%)	144 (33.72%)	30 (7.03%)	2 (0.47%)
Twitter	102	74 (72.55%)	24 (23.53%)	3 (2.94%)	1 (0.98%)
WhatsApp	61	49 (80.33%)	9 (14.75%)	3 (4.92%)	0 (0.00%)

1 Matric - the same as Grade 12 (last year of high school).

Seventy-three percent of the respondents indicated that they prefer SMS, while 67% also prefer e-mails. Seven percent of the respondents indicated that they prefer communication via the JT website, another 13% prefer Facebook and 15% prefer Twitter as communication tool. Some of the respondents indicated that they prefer one or more of the social networking tools for communication.

More substantial and longitudinal research would need to be conducted in order to obtain reliable data to identify trends. However, cognizance should be taken of the transient nature of social media, and due to the dynamic nature of technology, its use should be monitored and adapted continuously.

Although no conclusive evidence is available, the JT students seem to prefer personalized communication (such as SMS, e-mail and WhatsApp). This could be attributed to the uncertainty associated with the application, admission and registration process (including financial aid and accommodation matters). Facebook and Twitter are mass communication methods that are more appropriate for general information and marketing.

3. Predictive Scenario

Despite the widespread use of social media technology, little is known about the benefits of its use in higher education in recruitment and retention. Since social media has become more integral to students' lives, more research is required to understand its various applications in the areas of research, teaching and learning, recruitment and student support.

Approximately 80% of all responses from JTs and their parents include positive feedback. Since 2009, more than 70,000 e-mails have been sent by parents and students in which they express their gratitude (stored on a database). This is indicative of its success and effectiveness in communications with JTs and their parents. The fact that such a large percentage of JTs register at the University of Pretoria and succeed at the university provides more tangible evidence.

The current JT strategy revolves around the JT coordinator. Although parents and learners are reluctant to engage with anyone else, contingency plans are necessary to ensure future scalability. As enrollment numbers grow, it will become impossible for the JT coordinator to sustain the quality of communication and support. Administrative support is available, and registered JT students assist with communication to prospective students. Learners relate to the JT coordinator like they would to a respected and trusted father or grandfather. Parents also trust the JT coordinator and prefer to contact him or her throughout the first part of the value chain (recruitment and enrollment management). The consistency, reliability, accuracy, personalization and caring provided by the JT coordinator significantly reduce anxiety and provide for quicker response times compared to the contact center which deals with almost 36,000 calls and 12,000 e-mails a month.

A survey in 2013 showed that prospective students rate the call center and the faculties (academic departments) 2.9 and 2.7, out of 4, respectively. The abandonment rate in the call center is high, namely an average of 14%, which means that 14% of clients cannot even get through to the university when they call. This is because of capacity constraints: a decision has been made to pilot a project in which other divisions in the CSC assist with e-mails during peak periods so that call center staff can prioritize calls. In the survey, prospective students rate the information in the publications and on the website 3.2 out of 4. From a governance and fairness perspective, it is not ideal for two communication models to exist—namely the JT office that primarily uses social networking for JT students and their parents and the contact center that services more than 100,000 students and their parents (mostly through voice and e-mails). The JT programme could be criticized as being elitist, but it provides a competitive advantage to attract and retain academic achievers because of its personalized strategy.

The student recruitment team has been restructured to support the JT programme—as opposed to their former strategy of school visits and exhibitions. If other colleagues are introduced to build relationships with JTs, it would warrant research on personality, cultural and gender influences and whether the model would be transferable to other cultures outside of South Africa. A question could be posed about the way in which the value of trust influences the effectiveness of social media across cultures within a recruitment and retention process. The importance of the JT coordinator's relationship with students and parents should not be underestimated because it forms the foundation of the programme's success—probably irrespective of the social media tools that are used. Due to the highly competitive nature of higher education in South Africa and the financial constraints faced by many students and parents, anxiety levels are high between the point of application and registration.

4. Conclusions

Social networking tools enable interactive and timely communication with prospective students via their cell phones. Therefore, it is of utmost importance that several social networking tools are used because different people prefer different communication methods. This article has attempted to show that social networking tools can be used as an enabler for the successful recruitment and retention of quality prospective students in a competitive environment. It has also highlighted the role that trust plays in the relationship between a parent or learner and the university contact person, particularly in the recruitment and retention process. In addition, social media tools such as Facebook and Twitter seem to be more appropriate for general information and marketing. JT learners have indicated a preference for communication methods that allow for privacy such as WhatsApp, e-mail and SMS. A question is posed about the governance implications of using two communication models.

5. References

Austin, L. (2013, January). *Keynote Address at Student Access and Success Conference,* University of Pretoria.

Bajou, D., & Bajou, A. (2013). Shared governance and punctuated equilibrium in higher education: The case for student recruitment, retention, and graduation. *Journal of Relationship Marketing, 11*(4), 248–258.

Barnes N. G., & Lescault, A. M. (2012). *Social media adaption soars as higher-ed experiments and reevaluates its use of new communications tools.* University of Massachusetts, Dartmouth.

Clark, M. R. (2005). Negotiating the freshman year: Challenges and strategies among first-year college students. *Journal of College Student Development 46*(3), 296–316.

Educause Student and Information Technology Survey, ECAR (2013). University of Pretoria Data.

Hayes, T. J., Russchman, D., & Walker, M. M. (2009). Social networking as an admission tool: A case study in success. *Journal of Marketing for Higher Education, 19*(2), 109–124.

Kuzma, J. M., & Wright, W. (2013). *Using social networks as a catalyst for change in global higher education marketing and recruiting.* Retrieved from http://0-inderscience.metapress.com.innopac.up.ac.za

Morosanu, L., Handley K., & O'Donovan, B. (2010). Seeking support: Researching first-year students' experiences of coping with academic life. *Higher Education Research and Development, 29*(6), 665–678.

Norton, J. (2010, April). Retention and personal development: Assessing the role of universities in assisting students to navigate psychological demands of higher education. *Journal of the Australia and New Zealand Student Services Association, 35.*

Pasensie, K. (2012, September). *Barriers to access in higher education.* Briefing Paper 299. Southern African Catholic Bishops' Conference: Parliamentary Liaison Office.

Zepke, N., & Leach, L. (2010). Improving student engagement: Ten proposals for action. *Active Learning in Higher Education, 11*(3), 167–177.

SECTION II
Social Media

4

TOWARD REALIZING META SOCIAL MEDIA CONTENTS MANAGEMENT SYSTEM IN BIG DATA

Takafumi Nakanishi, Kiyotaka Uchimoto, & Yutaka Kidawara

NATIONAL INSTITUTE OF INFORMATION AND COMMUNICATIONS TECHNOLOGY, JAPAN

1. Background

Even though the amount of social media data is increasing explosively, we understand very little from them and only become saturated by reading each SNS timeline. In addition, each piece of data is too fragmented. For example, a tweet is a mere sequence of less than 140 words. We often obtain news updates or notices from one tweet without understanding the perspective of a focused issue. In the current method, most search or retrieval methods are done per data. For example, the current systems retrieve data that correspond to a user's query to a bit of appropriate data and focus on each piece of data. We cannot understand an issue by just focusing on one bit of data. Current search or retrieval systems do not correspond to the current social media situation. Since there are many types of social media on the Web, we must realize a new analysis and visualization method that interconnects various massive heterogeneous social media contents.

Based on the above background, we have to focus on Big data analytics, which is completely different from such current data analytics as data mining technology. The key issues of Big data analytics are heterogeneity, continuity and visualization.

In this chapter, we introduce Big data analytics and describe its features: heterogeneity, continuity and visualization. We also show one application example, called "Topic-Based Browsing of Conversation Tendencies in Twitter," and propose and represent an overview of our meta social media contents management system.

2. What Is Big Data Analytics? How Is It Related to Social Media?

Recently, not only businesspeople but also researchers are focusing on Big data, which is defined by three Vs (Berman, 2013):

Volume: Large amounts of data

Variety: Different forms of data, including traditional database, images, documents and complex records

Velocity: Data content constantly changing through the absorption of complementary data collections and from streaming data from multiple sources

Current research on Big data focuses on high performance computing and parallel distributed processing. However, we have to focus on another aspect, the schemaless data processing issue, which is different from very large database (VLDB). Schemaless means that schemas cannot be designed for systems because most current systems have goal-oriented designs. However, systems for Big data environments are not allowed to decide any goals without user queries.

It is important to discover answers or clues for users in real time. A system has to create appropriate schema from the data themselves given by user queries. Until now, data have been organized based on database schema. Currently, only various fragmentary data exist on the Web.

This is a huge paradigm shift. We must create schema and data structures that correspond to the processing required by users after they input queries. We have to shift the system from designing closed assumptions to open assumptions.

Heterogeneity, continuity and visualization are the most critical features of Big data analytics, which provides scale and connection merits based on them. No current data analysis methods are based on open assumptions. Big data analytics provides a new data analysis method based on open assumptions. Below, we discuss the inconsistencies caused by continuing to use the current methods. Figure 4.1 shows the relationship among the three elements (volume, variety and velocity) of Big data's definition and its analysis features (heterogeneity, continuity and visualization).

Big data analytics is related to the analysis of social media contents because they are one example of Big data. In Big Data Planet (2013), Hewlett-Packard claims that every 60 seconds, social media users generate more than 98,000 tweets on Twitter, 695,000 status updates on Facebook, 11 million instant messages and 217 new mobile Web users.

To analyze all social media, we have to consider and integrate various heterogeneous social media contents, including Facebook, Twitter, LinkedIn, etc. Social media contents can be regarded as human sensors. Each user in a social media generates fragmented data about feelings and emotions and gives updates about attending events like concerts and baseball games. When discrete social media contents are approximately continuous, we can identify each human's moving trajectory. We do not want to show every single piece of data like current search engines; rather, we want to identify the trends of human actions. Our system has to provide a visualization of the overview. Social media analytics includes Big data analytics.

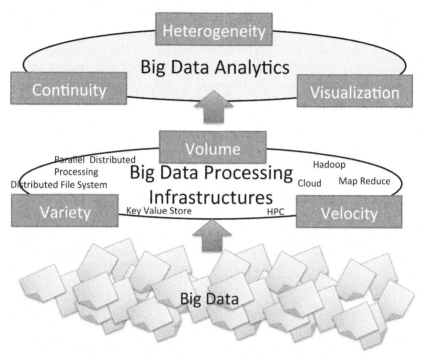

FIGURE 4.1 Relationship among three Vs of Big data definition and Big data analytics definition: heterogeneity, continuity, and visualization.

3. Heterogeneity: Big Data Analytics Features

In Big data analytics, heterogeneity is different than it is in the Big data definition. The variety of Big data definitions includes such content as images, sounds, documents, etc. Its heterogeneity includes such data fields as news, entertainment, technology and science, all of which are semantic aspects.

In Big data analysis, reasonable correlations must be discovered between heterogeneous fields. Currently, semantic Web technologies (Berners-Lee, 2006; Bizer, Heath, & Berners-Lee, 2009; Greaves & Mika, 2008) or association rule extraction technologies (Gonzales, Nakanishi, & Zettsu, 2011) are generally used. However, in Big data analytics, there are three inconsistencies because the Big data environment is an opened assumption not a closed assumption (Nakanishi, Uchimoto, & Kiadawara, 2013).

4. Example of Three Opened Assumptions' Inconsistencies

We focus on human relationships to represent our example (see Figures 4.2 and 4.3).

First, in Figure 4.2, we present an example of human relationships between AI and DB communities that share fields. ai and bj are researchers. The edges indicate relationships that represent the similarity of their research and the symmetric and transitive relationships. When someone adds symmetric and transitive relationships to a_3 and b_4, a_1 is related to b_5 because a_1 is related to a_3, a_3 is related to b_4 and b_4 is related to b_5. Realistically, a_1 may also be related to b_5.

Next, in Figure 4.3, we illustrate another example of personal relationships between workplace and music communities by assuming that no common fields exist. The edges represent the relationships of friendships and coworkers or co-session members, and the edges indicate symmetric and transitive relationships. For example, a_3 met b_4 at a party and they became friends. In this case, we add symmetric and transitive relationships between a_3 and b_4. Is it true that a_1 is related to b_5 when we add such relationships between a_3 and b_4 in the graph structure? Here, a_1 is related to b_5. However, realistically, a_1 and b_5 do not

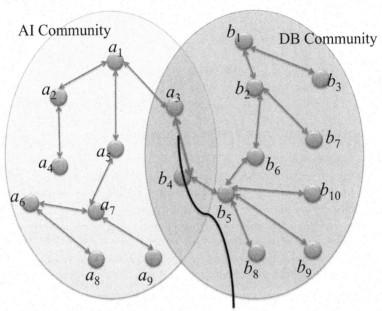

Someone adds relationships between a_3 and b_4

FIGURE 4.2 Relationships among persons in communities AI and DB. ai and bj are researchers. When someone adds symmetric and transitive relationships between a_3 and b_4, it is true that a_1 is related to b_5 because a_1 is related to a_3, a_3 is related to b_4, and b_4 is related to b_5.

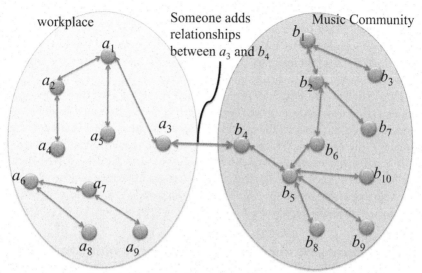

FIGURE 4.3 Relationships among persons in workplace and music communities. ai are co-workers and bj are musicians. When someone adds symmetric and transitive relationships between a_3 and b_4, it is not true that a_1 is related to b_5. In the graph structure, it is true that a_1 is related to b_5. However, realistically, a_1 and b_5 do not share common ground without other definitions or analysis.

share any common ground without other definitions or analysis. In this case, inconsistencies are caused by the previous methods.

The difference between the first and second examples is community positioning. Here, we consider a community to be a set and the persons are its elements. For the first example, the AI community is set A and the DB community is set B. The following is the relation of sets A and B:

$$A \cap B \neq \varnothing.$$

For the second example, the workplace community is set A and the music community is set B. The following is the relation of sets A and B:

$$A \cap B = \varnothing.$$

We represented the inconsistencies of these examples and applied it to various fields. However, we used the results of these methods for cooperation within cases where the near fields are linked or in the same fields. They do not completely apply to linking heterogeneous fields. The second example may also be applicable to the previous method. In this case, any relation between sets is only implicit.

When elements are added to heterogeneous sets, their elements have the same order relation. In this case, it is implicitly true that $A \subset B, B \subset A$, or $A \cap B \neq \varnothing$.

When it is true that $A \cap B \neq \varnothing$, we use the previous methods. However, we do not make real-world inferences for $A \cap B = \varnothing$ because set theory is limited. In set theory, we have to define the transitive and order relationships in each attribute based on the relationships in each new scene. Such outdated computer schemes as database and rule-based systems were designed by closed assumptions. New scenes do not appear. However, current systems interconnect heterogeneous systems or the data for heterogeneous fields, which are not closed assumptions.

In the Big data era, we must discover the relations for $A \cap B = \varnothing$. We believe that discoveries lead to knowledge. Computers are discovering new relations based on opened assumptions overlooked by humans. We must create a system that discovers relationships when $A \cap B = \varnothing$.

5. Three Opened Assumptions' Inconsistencies with Two Easy Mathematical Proofs

First, we provide proofs of the inconsistency of order relations between two certain sets.

The preconditions of the proofs are as follows. There are two sets, $A = \{a_1, a_2, ..., an\}$ and $B = \{b_1, b_2, ..., bm\}$, where $A \cap B = \varnothing$. Each set defines the order relations differently.

We prove that we cannot determine the relationship between sets A and B or other relationships when we get relationship f between $a_1 \in A$ and $b_1 \in B$.

Proof: We prove by induction that it is satisfied when $b_i = f(a_i)$ is not true.

When $i = 1$, $b_1 = f(a_1)$ is true by the above condition.

We assume that bk = f(ak) is true when $i = k$.

When $i = k + 1$, bk + 1 = f(ak + 1) is not true because set A has an order relation. However, set B has another order relation. bk $\leq$ bk + 1 may not be true if ak $\leq$ ak + 1 is true and vice versa. Furthermore, both ak $\leq$ ak + 1 and bk $\leq$ bk + 1 may not be true and although $b_1 = f(a_1)$ is true, $b_i = f(a_i)$ is not.

[Q.E.D]

We cannot uncover the relation between each heterogeneous set when we discover or link between heterogeneous elements. It is also difficult to identify other relations with clue $b_1 = f(a_1)$.

Next, we prove the inconsistency of the order relation when someone links to elements of a heterogeneous set. Using the same sets A and B as in the former case, set B has order relation $b_1 \leq b_2 \leq b_3 \leq b_4$. ... Set B has a transitive relation; if $b_1 \leq b_2$ and $b_2 \leq b_3$ are true, then $b_1 \leq b_3$ is true. Set A has its own order relation.

Proof: We prove that $a_1 \leq b_3$ is true when we obtain relation $a_1 \leq b_1$. To reveal the conclusion, $a_1 \leq b_3$ may not be satisfied. We thus show a counterexample: Assume $a_1 = (1, 5)$, $b_1 = (2, 1)$, $b_2 = (3, 2)$, and $b_3 = (4, 3)$.

The relationship of a_1 and b_1 focuses on each first element.

Then $a_1 \leq b_1$ is true.

The order relation of set B focuses more on the values of each second element. Then $b_1 \leq b_2 \leq b_3$, and if $b_1 \leq b_2$ and $b_2 \leq b_3$ are true, then $b_1 \leq b_3$ is true.

However, $a_1 \leq b_3$ is not true in the order set of set B.

Like the relation of a_1 and b_1, an inconsistency occurs whose order and transitive relations of set B are not guaranteed.

[Q.E.D]

Although we strictly define the order and transitive relations in a certain set, an inconsistency occurs with a relation with elements outside of it.

6. The Three Opened Assumptions' Inconsistencies

Until now, computer science researchers have based their ideas on closed assumptions by freely linking and interconnecting each object. For example, the interconnection between element ai in set A and element bj in set B for $A \cap B \neq \varnothing$ remains a closed assumption. However, users, especially data-intensive scientists, do not require such knowledge. They have to consider new discovery methods in opened assumptions, where $A \cap B = \varnothing$.

Note that such inconsistencies only occur when extending the current methods introduced in Section 2. We call these inconsistencies the Three Opened Assumptions' Inconsistencies:

A relation does not guarantee the future.

For example, we can identify relationships among each set through data mining technology. Note that the results only represent the relationships of the present data. These relationships are not guaranteed if the system adds new records (data). Occasionally, researchers and users anticipate an uncertain value of a new record using extracted relationships. However, such usage is incorrect. Due to the insignificance of predicting uncertain values by data mining, we assume that sets A and B are attributes in the relational database and that ai and bi are the attribute values of each set. The data mining result is guaranteed if no updates occur. However, most tables undergo many updates. We assume k records in the database and that the numbers of each attribute value are k. The system performs data mining and extracts bi = f(ai). This relation f is only guaranteed when there are k records in the database. If the number of records is k + 1, relation f is not guaranteed. Indexing relations, which are extracted by various methods, is meaningless for predicting uncertain or missing values.

A transitive relation is not true when a user connects links for heterogeneous fields.

With closed assumptions, we create or extract relationships in a set. In this case, the transitive and order relations are true. However, they are not true when we create or extract relationships over the sets. This phenomenon occurs when we use bridge ontology, semantic webs, linked data, etc. Each ontology in specific fields is unconsciously created in closed assumptions. These techniques connect ontologies in specific fields that are changed from closed to open assumptions. Therefore, it may become possible to use these ontologies only by connecting each element of each set. On the contrary, is the determinant possible when trying to create bridge ontology? Such determination is difficult.

No relations in heterogeneous fields can be discovered in set theory.

Should such relationships be indexed or aggregated? We might semantically discover new relationships, but how to discover them is not understood. Even if part of the relations of each element of the sets is known, the relations of all of the sets are not guaranteed. Moreover, the relation is not guaranteed when a new record is entered, even if the relation of the sets was previously guaranteed. Therefore, even if we can retrieve the relationships, their discovery is impossible by inference and reasoning because only the relationships that we have discovered are effective; transitive and order relationships are not guaranteed. The transitive and order relations are not true when we create or extract relationships over the sets. This result is disappointing. However, it represents a paradigm shift from closed to opened assumption systems.

By connecting each element of each set, it may become impossible to use these ontologies. Computing some systems is very inefficient with bridge ontology and linked data. On the contrary, is the determinant in the case of trying possible for the author of bridge ontology? Determining this is very difficult. Of course, schema mapping has the same problem, since Relational Database (RDB) has a relation. Discovering new relations by inference and reasoning is difficult.

7. Continuity: Features of Big Data Analytics

Most Big data come from sensors. For social media, each human action is part of the Big data from each human sensor. It is important to aggregate every second such massive and various sensor data in the Big data processing infrastructures. However, there is a restriction on the sampling rate. For more realistic analysis, we must approximate the aggregated discrete data to continuous value data, because the real world is continuous.

For example, for listening to music, CDs and a CD player can be used. CDs have discrete sound data from the real world. Their music cannot be recognized without digital/analogue conversion by a CD player. This example shows us one important feature of Big data. Each piece only represents an instance of a certain state. Of course, higher sampling rates produce more correct data. However, the real world is a continuous place. Unless the data are continuous, many things cannot be discovered, like the example of a CD's music.

Other issues include which axis to interpolate. In the example of a CD's music, we can interpolate the time axis by a digital/analogue converter. Depending on the information provided by the data, we do not know which interpolation uses place information or which uses temperature of air/water information.

Finally, even though computer science researchers have researched approximation method from discrete to continuous values, they have never researched the selection or the creation of appropriate axes for continuous discovery. This is a critical theme of Big data analytics.

8. Visualization: Big Data Analytics Features

Visualization is important for Big data analytics for many different reasons. For example, a Google search provides a list that represents an appropriate dataset. Is such a list of representations satisfactory? In Big data environments, not every piece of data can be clicked on and checked because we are not interested in such details. Since we want to identify the trends of the whole dataset, visualization is a crucial issue for Big data analytics. We can use various visualization methods created by researchers.

However, another issue remains. What kinds of visualization provide better correspondence to user queries? A system has to select, create and provide appropriate visualization for users. To choose visualization, a system has to know which axis to focus on. For example, a graph that designates time on the x-axis is good for seeing the changes of a value by time. Therefore, realizing the creation or a selection method of axes that correspond to user queries is important. When we realize systems with such methods, they can select appropriate visualization. In Big data analytics, visualization changes are based on user purposes.

9. Discovery by Deviation of Dataset in Selected Axes

9.1. Constructing Big Data Analytics for Heterogeneity, Continuity and Visualization

We have to consider how to construct Big data analytics for heterogeneity, continuity and visualization features. One critical issue is from what point Big data should be viewed. We have no axes that measure whether data are appropriate. In Big data environments, systems have to provide not only appropriate datasets but also axes as viewpoints that solve user queries. How does the system extract axes? We proposed a method called global information extraction (GIE) (Nakanishi et al., 2013).

9.2. Global Information Extraction

In this section, we introduce our previously proposed analysis method: global information extraction. GIE is a very simple idea that is crucial for an appropriate axis discovery method. We ensured that our browsing style will change because our focus points change from watching or reading each bit of data to overviewing datasets. This is a big paradigm shift for users.

Figure 4.4 overviews our GIE assumptions. This research's focus point shows that the relations between terms after or at the same time as clustering have higher precision than directly driving them. The term distribution of the entire content set is different from the feature (attribute value) distribution of a content set clustered for a particular purpose.

Moreover, each feature appearing in a content set clustered for a particular purpose has certain relations. Their clustered contents represent the same purpose. Content authors are expected to use similar or identical features. As shown above, it is relatively important to compare the ratios of the content frequency (CF) of each term in the content set of the whole Web and in a content set clustered for a certain purpose. When the CF ratio of a certain term in the content set of the whole Web exceeds a content set clustered for a certain purpose, the term does not represent the characteristics of a content set clustered for a certain purpose. It is also the same when the rate is the same. When the CF ratio of a certain term in the content set of the whole Web is smaller than the content set clustered for a certain purpose, the feature represents the characteristics of a content set clustered

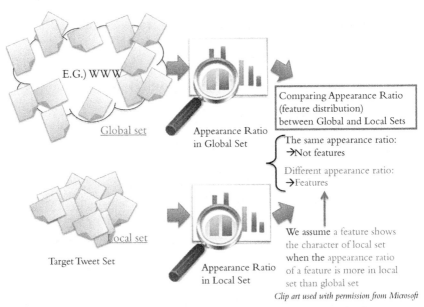

FIGURE 4.4 Overview of Glocal Information Extraction. Important point is comparison of feature appearance frequency between global and local sets. We assume that a word shows the local set characteristics when a feature's appearance frequency in it exceeds that in the global set.

for a certain purpose. We define the content set of the whole Web as a global set and a content set clustered for a certain purpose as a local set.

9.3. Example Application: Topic-Based Browsing Tendencies in Twittersphere

In the Twittersphere, our browsing method, which is called topic-based browsing tendencies (Takafumi et al., 2013), organizes the contents of Twitter topics into layers of hot topic words, feature words and actual tweets. Such organization shows a tweet's detailed structure and its sentiment and the overall view of the hot topics in the Twittersphere in real time. The feature words and their sentiments are extracted by GIE and a sentiment classification tool (Nakagawa, Inui, & Kurohashi, 2010).

Next, we show an example from December 25, 2012, at 14:17. When our system is accessed, it shows the Twitter timeline and hot topic words. Figure 4.5 shows "Christmas," "Present" and "New Year's card" as hot topic words.

On the other hand, we can also see "demise," which appears meaningless. But it also suggests anxiety. Therefore, we click on it to view the system's next screen

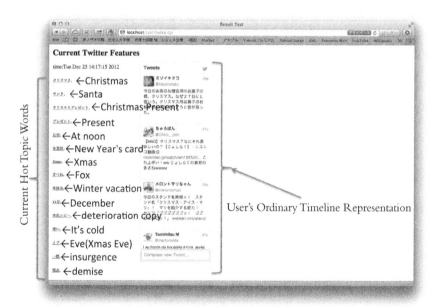

FIGURE 4.5 Opening system screenshot of Topic-Based Browsing of Conversation Tendencies in Twitter, on December 25, 2012. "Christmas" and "Present," etc. are hot topic words; we can also see "demise," which seems meaningless; yet it also causes unease.

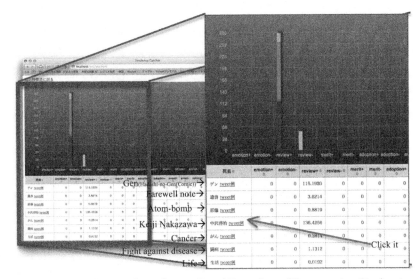

FIGURE 4.6 Second screenshot of Topic-Based Browsing of Conversation Tendencies in Twitter, on December 25, 2012, shows results of clicking "demise" from the first screen. This screenshot shows what feelings are expressed by topic "demise" for what kind of feature words. We can also see "Gen," "Atom bomb," "Keiji Nakazawa," etc.

(Figure. 4.6), which presents feature words and sentiments related to "demise." This screen shows the feelings expressed about the topic based on feature words. We also see "Hadashi-no-Gen" (comic book about the Hiroshima atomic bomb), "Atom-bomb," "Keiji Nakazawa," etc. We infer that Keiji Nakazawa has died. Nakazawa is a well-known comic author in Japan, and *Hadashi-no-Gen* is a particularly famous work of his. The system next presents the screen shown in Figure 4.7, which lists tweets related to "demise" and "Keiji Nakazawa:" "May his soul rest in peace," "Hadashi-no-Gen" and "peace."

10. Key Findings

The effective use of Big data does not analyze all the data; effective use identifies new observing points: axes. Our application, which does not represent a new computation method, includes a new concept of axis creation and an overview in the created or selected axes. In our application, we create a new browsing style by a system that provides axes using our GIE technique.

However, problems remain in our application that must be solved to realize Big data analytics. First, there are too few interoperation functions. When we realize them, we can do high-quality and high-level topic trajectory analysis by various viewpoints, such as time-sequence, area, communities, etc.

FIGURE 4.7 Third screenshot of Topic-Based Browsing of Conversation Tendencies in Twitter, on December 25, 2012. This is result of clicking "Keiji Nakazawa" on the second screen and shows actual tweets related to "demise" and "Keiji Nakazawa." Many tweets were similar to "May his soul rest in peace," "Hadashi-no-Gen," and "peace."

Our application only targets the Twittersphere. There are many social media, such as Twitter, Facebook, LinkedIn, Foursquare and Google+. End users have many IDs and passwords for each social media site. They want to control their own data at each site. In the near future, not only human sensors but also physical sensors will exist. Under this situation, the IDs and passwords of end users will continue to increase. The data generated by end users are also increasing. End users cannot remember so many IDs and passwords. Some applications provide cooperative functions among social media sites for mobile terminals. However, such structure is odd, because the operation of such functions is very heavy. Therefore, cloud systems must manage this operation.

Note that end users will also be Big data providers, because they will have many terminals and sensors in the near future. Of course, all social media are also providers to Big data, which are scattered over various places. It is necessary to realize a meta-system that aggregates Big data on various sites, discovers relationships among heterogeneous Big data, controls its data by unifying operations and provides visualization to understand trends corresponding to user queries. We call this a meta social media contents management system.

11. Predictive Scenario for Realizing a Meta Social Media Contents Management System

11.1. Future Scope of Our Method

All social media sites are Big data providers. All users are also Big data providers. In addition, each specific social media site and each individual user use their Big data for analytics. In the near future, end users will have many pairs of IDs and passwords. At the same time, their data will be scattered among social media sites. Each type of social media will provide a space for corroborative works and discussion. In the next step, each social media site will provide a new marketing model using Big data. However, since most users employ different roles for social media, analysis is required that mixes various social media to infer a user's true demand.

Both social media and user sides need a meta-cloud system that aggregates Big data from various sites and analyzes, operates and controls them. In this chapter, we are designing a meta social media contents management system that solves two big problems: explosion of IDs and passwords (all sites provide Big data) and heterogeneous social media contents interconnection. We must explain the Big data analysis features: heterogeneity, continuity and visualization. However, to realize Big data analysis, we have to solve the opened assumption inconsistencies and the privacy problem, which includes the explosion of IDs and passwords. We have to solve them and control all Big data by user queries with access authority. The opened assumption inconsistencies are a large problem.

11.2. IDs and Passwords Explosion: All Sites Have Big Data

One big problem is the scattered contents in each social media site. In the near future, not only text, images, sound and movies but also lifelog sensor data will be stored at each social media site. Therefore, a user who wants to use new social media or a lifelog sensor has to create a new account for each SNS. A user with many social media sites and lifelog sensors will also have many IDs and passwords. The explosion of the number of IDs and passwords is raising the opportunity threshold to begin lifelogs and new social media. Since users cannot remember all of them, we must realize a system that systematically and appropriately manages the data and access control.

Finally, users have Big data everywhere. They want to aggregate and confirm their own data. However, it is hard to get all of them and visualize them with the current systems, where end users have to input IDs and passwords at each social media site and separately access each. This is a heavy burden on end users. We can solve these problems by creating a meta social media contents management system.

11.3. Heterogeneous Social Media Contents Interconnection

Heterogeneous data must be interconnected among two or more heterogeneous social media. For example, users can currently interconnect data in heterogeneous social media by name-based aggregation to access friends in various ways, including a smartphone's address book. The current techniques cannot solve the following questions: What is the relationship between Persons A and B? Why do they have a relationship? In the case of the same social media, the current systems can probably solve these questions. However, with heterogeneous social media (Person A only has an account with social media X and Person B only has an account with social media Y), the system must compare heterogeneous data. Linked data (Berners-Lee, 2006; Bizer et al., 2009) guidelines facilitate ad hoc reuse and the integration of semi-structured data by consumer applications. However, among heterogeneous datasets, we found and proved the three inconsistencies shown above.

We freely link and interconnect each object. For example, the interconnection between element ai in set A and element bj in set B for $A \cap B \neq \varnothing$ remains a closed assumption. However, users, especially data-intensive scientists, do not require such knowledge. They have to consider new discovery methods under an opened assumption, where $A \cap B = \varnothing$. Here are the three inconsistencies for linking heterogeneous resources: (1) when the relation does not guarantee the future, (2) when no transitive relation is true when anyone connects to links for heterogeneous fields and (3) when no relation in the heterogeneous fields can be discovered in set theory. Closed assumption systems have already reached their limits. We call this problem the Three Opened Assumptions' Inconsistencies, which is the limit through which we consider the relation between heterogeneous fields in set theory. The paradigm shift is necessary.

We proposed solutions to these inconsistencies. Our model maps set theory and the Cartesian coordinate system by defining the function predicate. We can detect various differences and relative relationships by such a comparison. Using the old function family on databases designed by set theory is important to achieve mutual mapping. By actualizing this framework, we can discover new relationships in the Cartesian coordinate system, retrieve current relationships in set theory and create new predicate functions. See Takafumi et al. (2013) for details.

In this model, a system discovers relationships in the Cartesian coordinate system, not in set theory. The axes are necessary to discover such relationships. This model solves the following questions: What is the relationship between Persons A and B? Why do they have a relationship? In this model, axes answer "why" and the behavior of the two datasets answers "how." Our meta social media contents management system solves the above queries, because it can aggregate and analyze various social media contents on meta-layers.

11.4. Next-Generation System: Meta Social Media Contents Management System

Figure 4.8 shows our entire concept of a next-generation system—a meta social media contents management system that has three types of users: developers, end users and analysts.

Currently, many social media services exist separately and have such Big data about their users as profiles, locations, comments, image data, sound data, etc. Since each social media service has a data structure for its own services, systems must mediate, integrate and organize these heterogeneous data. Our meta social media contents management system considers the above questions concerning how and why Persons A and B are related. Usually, we compare the data of two people. However, Person A is a Facebook and a Foursquare user, and Person B is a Twitter and a Google+ user. In this case, the system has to aggregate Person A's data from Facebook and Foursquare and Person B's data from Twitter and Google+. First, it aggregates the data in each social media service by gaining permission from the end user, meaning that the end user not only can organize friend (follow/follower) data but also consolidate the access control of personal data, including the profile data in each social media service and in various players (users). The

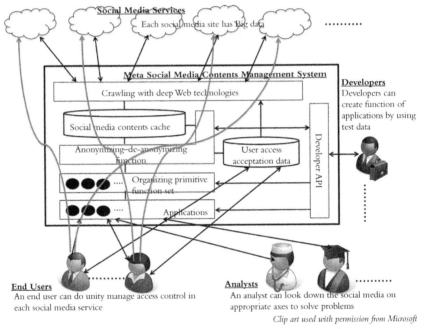

FIGURE 4.8 Our entire concept of next-generation system: meta social media contents management system.

system can discover necessary data and appropriate axes and map the data into the axes. In this process, the heterogeneity of all of the data is solved, and the system compares them and prepares primitive functions and applications for analysts. Since some developers can create functions or applications using appropriate test data, our system enhances the functions from developers.

12. Social Impact

Our meta social media contents management system will globally solve some problems of the Big data era, including end users who cannot remember so many IDs and passwords for communicating to others to bridge various social media. This system will control Big data from various sites, such as end users, social media sites, blogs, consumer-generated media (CGM), traditional websites, etc.

In addition, our meta social media contents management system will cause a paradigm shift. In the current system flow, an assumption was formulated, a system was constructed and the data were aggregated; finally, a system analyzed the aggregated data to verify the assumption. However, our meta social media contents management system first aggregates the data without making any assumptions. It discovers appropriate axes, which are the candidates of the assumptions to represent the aggregated data, and provides assumptions of the required field with the aggregated data that are verified by an expert. The roles of computers and humans are reversed.

This reversal will have many effects. By greater data exploitation, much more interdisciplinary field progress will be made about assumption discoveries in computations. By verifying assumptions by calculating in the cyber and real worlds, mutual cooperation will increase. The integration values of data will become more important.

Actually, data–centric science, which is an example that shows these things, provides clues for new discovery by high-performance computing and existing data. This is completely different from the current simulation science, where assumptions are formulated, a system is constructed based on them and experts simulate them using real-world data and high-performance computing techniques. On the other hand, data–centric science finds assumptions from existing data. The roles of computers and humans are again reversed.

The assumptions extracted from the system's computation are assumption candidates or clues for deriving facts. Experiments or experts must verify this system's outputs. Although clues for computer systems to support decision making can be given, the individuals themselves have to make the decisions.

Our system provides a centralized control system for such personal data for end users as user profiles, locations, comments, image data, sound data, etc. It also provides an environment for a new social media function for developers and clues that solve problems by various social media contents sets for analysts.

13. Research Issues and Critical Fields for Realizing Social Media Contents Management Systems

Next, we focus on the main required techniques or researches for realizing our next-generation system: a social media contents management system.

Single sign-on and a secure deep Web

Currently, the Web provides many social media services, each of which has Big personal data. We want to organize all such data from each social media service by gaining access control to various kinds of user data. To aggregate such dispersed data, we have to continue to research single sign-on and secure deep Web technologies.

Statistical correlation computing on data heterogeneity

Aggregated data include heterogeneous data types, contents, etc. We have to discover appropriate axes for organizing our data. For realizing this, we need appropriate sampling, extracting, fitting, comparing, etc. These processes include statistics and correlation analysis techniques. A new field must be established: statistical correlation computing.

Anonymizing and de-anonymizing

For user access control and organizing all data, the system has to guarantee privacy. This step is critical to anonymize and de-anonymize the aggregated data.

Secure broadband networks, etc.

14. Conclusions

We represented our state-of-the-art social media contents analysis method and our next-generation meta social media contents management system. First, we introduced our research about next-generation systems and represented our research scopes, the entire concept of our next-generation system, its social impact and the technologies and research required to realize it.

With our proposed next-generation system, many fields and lifestyles will be changed. Searches or retrieval concepts will become an operation that provides clues to user problems. In science, the system will give researchers important assumptions or clues, and the integration of social communities might occur in the real world. Social media will contribute to the real world by acting as a catalyst for social change.

15. References

Berman, J. (2013). *Principles of Big Data*, USA, Morgan Kaufmann.

Berners-Lee, T. (2006, July). *Linked Data, W3C Design Issues*. Retrieved from http://www.w3.org/DesignIssues/LinkedData.html

Big Data Planet. (2013). Retrieved from http://www.bigdataplanet.info/p/what-is-big-data.html

Bizer, C., Heath, T., & Berners-Lee, T. (2009). Linked data—The story so far. *International Journal on Semantic Web and Information Systems, 5*(3), 1–22.

Gonzales, E., Nakanishi, T., & Zettsu, K. (2011). Large-scale association rule discovery from heterogeneous databases with missing values using genetic network programming. In *Proceedings of the 1st International Conference on Advances in Information Mining and Management* (pp. 113–120).

Greaves, M., & Mika, P. (2008). Semantic web and web 2.0. *Journal of Web Semantics, 6*(1), 1–3.

Nakagawa, T., Inui, K., & Kurohashi, S. (2010). Dependency tree-based sentiment classification using CRFs with hidden variables. In *Proceedings of Human Language Technologies: The 2010 Annual Conference of the North American Chapter of the Association for Computational Linguistics* (pp. 786–794).

Nakanishi, T., Uchimoto, K., & Kiadawara, Y. (2013). Inconsistencies of connection for heterogeneity and a new relation discovery method that solved them. In *Proceedings of 12th IEEE/ACIS International Conference on Computer and Information Science (ICIS 2013)* (pp. 521–528).

Nakanishi, T., Uchimoto, K., & Kiadawara, Y. (2013). Topic-based browsing of tendencies in twitter conversations by using social global information extraction. In *Proceedings of IADIS International Conference e-Society 2013* (pp. 316–325).

5

SOCIAL MEDIA FOR, WITH, AND BY PROFESSIONALS—PARTICIPATORY DESIGN THROUGH REFLEXIVE ENGAGEMENT

Suvi Pihkala & Helena Karasti

WOMEN'S AND GENDER STUDIES, UNIVERSITY OF OULU, FINLAND AND INFORMATION PROCESSING SCIENCE, UNIVERSITY OF OULU, FINLAND; COMPUTER AND SYSTEMS SCIENCE, LULEÅ UNIVERSITY OF TECHNOLOGY, SWEDEN

1. Introduction

This chapter discusses reflexivity and participation as much needed approaches in the design and research of social media-supported practices for professionals. We begin with our study of a participatory design of a social media-supported collaboration model for, with, and by professionals working against workplace harassment. Our study encourages participation-oriented and user-centric fields of information and communication technologies (ICT) to embrace an orientation of "reflexive engagement" that addresses the dynamics of the design and research process (Pihkala & Karasti, 2013).

We continue by discussing social media for professional uses as an underexplored territory. As social media affords participation in a very central manner, designing social media for professional purposes and uses with and by professionals requires an approach that accounts for their different interests, involvements and expectations, and which fosters a reflexive approach by all those involved in research and design. Here, we extend our reflexive engagement focused on research to exploring ways to embrace reflexivity and the various arenas of participation in the design of sustainable social media-supported practices for professionals.

2. Reflexivity and Participation in and for Participatory Design

2.1. The Aim of Our Study

Our study was initially inspired by recent calls for more reflexivity in the field of participatory design (PD) (Balka, 2010; Blomberg & Karasti, 2012; Finken, 2003; Karasti, 2010; Stuedahl, Morrison, Mörtberg, & Bratteteig, 2010). Although PD is commonly regarded as one of the most reflexive approaches in ICT design due to the guiding principle of users and designers collaborating in design, a literature review showed that there is room for more discussion on the topic. In fields like PD, some researchers draw from feminist-inspired and ethnographic traditions to discuss reflexivity and extend it beyond reflection on practice (e.g., Schön, 1983) to address the positionality and the values, biases and assumptions underlying research and design (Karasti, 2010; Stuedahl et al., 2010). Similarly, we emphasize reflexivity and continue to view reflexivity as an orientation that makes visible the dynamics of the research and design processes and challenges us to pay critical attention to the relationships involved, make inquiries into our own subjectivity, and negotiate the process of participation.

In our study, a social media-supported collaboration model was designed in a PD manner for, with, and by professionals working against workplace harassment. We draw from discussions on reflection and reflexivity in PD and unearth reflexivity from the experiences in our study. Based on our empirical encounters and interdisciplinary dialogue, we introduce "reflexive engagement," which we describe as a new orientation to design and research (Pihkala & Karasti, 2013, p. 90). Our study encourages all those involved with user-centric and participatory design of and research on ICT to embrace reflexivity as a way of addressing current practical and disciplinary challenges, particularly those involving multiple stakeholders and new users, uses, contexts and technologies.

3. Methodology

Our research was one of four pilot studies in a large two-year research project on the use of social media in workplace safety and well-being in Finland (Heikkilä, Näkki, Ruuhilehto, Bäck, Pihkala, Huhtamäki, & Tervakari, 2011). Our pilot was organized as a university and trade union study center partnership with the aim of developing a social media-supported collaboration model for professionals in their work against workplace harassment. From the university, the first author, with a background in anthropology and feminist research, engaged in the research and design as a field working researcher. The second author, a senior researcher with a background in information systems, PD, and feminist technosciences, as well as her own fieldwork experience in learning to relate ethnography and PD, participated in interdisciplinary discussions with the fieldworker throughout and after the project.

The field working researcher carried out participatory design in collaboration with the study center. As an educational service provider for two of the Finnish trade union confederations and their members, the study center had previously developed a manual for workplace harassment interventions. In the beginning, the study center invited a group of professionals from their network to form an expert group. These professionals were representatives of the target groups and future users of the collaboration model: occupational safety representatives, shop stewards, and union professionals who deal with cases of harassment. Later on in the pilot, an extended network was formed as the members of the expert group, based on mutual decisions, used their networks to invite their colleagues, also future users of the collaboration model, to join the collaboration.

During the course of the participatory design, meetings were held with the two key members from the study center to outline the pilot process. The expert group planned and experimented with the collaboration model and the social media platforms in workshops. Between the workshops, collaboration was maintained online using the chosen social media platform. Through exploration and evaluations, a mutually agreed-upon social media–supported work model was created and adopted. The extended network of professionals (numbering hundreds) continued to work using the new model and tools.

Data were collected in ethnographic notes and in audiovisual format. Google Analytics data were collected concerning the use of and visits to the pilot social media platforms and used with the professionals to discuss the collaboration. Qualitative analysis was integrated into the research as a cyclical, reflexive process. This combined the collected data with the observations, creating a dialogical relationship between them. The analysis incorporated the fieldworker's reading of the materials and continued in the interdisciplinary discussions with the senior researcher.

4. Key Findings

The field working researcher collaborated in the research and design with a reflexive orientation toward the dynamics of participation. This orientation called to attention the ways in which the different understandings of social media affected the collaboration and how all participants positioned themselves within the frames of given roles. To negotiate participation, different experiences of the participants were foregrounded, and social media technology was collaboratively redefined. The design was turned into a process of discovery—instead of "making them learn" to use social media—and we planned for new ways of working together to meet the needs, expectations, competencies and cultures of the participants. This "discovering" afforded new insight for developing collaborative practices in social media, for the development of ownership of the process on the part of the participating professionals, and for design outcomes that extended beyond the pre-visioned results. The reflexive orientation in the field was interlaced with reflexive dialogue between the two researchers, which contrasted the empirical encounters with conceptual questions, thereby feeding back to the field and supporting the reflexive stance.

5. Reflexive Engagement for, with and by Professionals

5.1. Social Media for Professionals

As the uses of social media have expanded, social media has also become the target of interest in professional settings. Social media has had a clear, and more studied, role for marketing and communications, that is, for external uses. However, enterprise social media offers professionals other possibilities as well, including encouraging dialogue and supporting collaborations within organizations (Leonardi, Huysman, & Steinfield, 2013) as well as between them. Additionally, social media includes networking activities for individual professionals. For social media enthusiasts and ICT professionals, there is something inevitable in the ways social media affects work practices, but for many organizations and employees, the use of social media as part of their everyday work practices is still in the early stages (Heikkilä et al., 2012).

Despite the trends and push toward the use of social media for professional purposes, some organizations may be wary of adopting it (e.g., Abeysinghe & Alsobhi, 2013). Integrating social media with existing work practices or designing new ones is not always easy. Organizations may encounter challenges regarding the introduction of social media for new users, working in an organizational context, facilitating a network or negotiating work-related professional topics for social media (Heikkilä et al., 2011). With professional use in particular, social media seems to be in the crosswind between informal and formal, official and unofficial, work and pleasure. Many of the characteristics considered central to social media—for example, openness or self-organization—may not seem to fit well with the existing work practices and structures in many professional organizations. As social media has permeated everyday lives, it has also evoked emotions and interpretations (Talsi, 2013). In our study, we discovered that social media as a professional tool was set against the larger frameworks of ICT at work, where social media was seen as one more new thing among many technical tools to learn at work. In addition, social media was perceived as risky and unsecure in relation to the sensitive topic of workplace harassment but was also seen as enticing and up to date. What social media meant in and for work was also framed by public discussions. At the time of our study, social media was discussed quite often in the newspapers and not always viewed in the best light. From the participants' professional points of view, social media was situated somewhere between needs, desires and risks.

Organizations' and professionals' participation in social media is encouraged through guides and recommendations (Hämäläinen & Heikkilä, 2011). For example, in Finland, the broader field of professionals in organizations such as municipalities and government is supported by developing guidelines, which sometimes include commenting, feedback and content production through social media (e.g., Aalto, 2010). The guides provided to organizations include advice on, for example, how to negotiate publicity, plan social media strategies and teach employees about social media uses. The guides also address issues such as how to negotiate overlaps between private and professional uses and how to adjust to the more informal and "open" culture of social media (Hämäläinen & Heikkilä, 2011).

We believe the relevance of social media will increase for professionals in various fields and in various forms. Public debate and discussion on the potential and risks of social media will continue to have a place in the future in supporting social media use. However, there is a need for discussion of examples and lessons learned that represent the many possibilities of social media and encourage explorations of the possibilities of social media from different perspectives. Furthermore, to explore social media for professional uses with and by participants from various fields and to achieve sustainable design outcomes, those involved in the design and research need to address the needs, hopes and expectations of different users and non-users in a more sensitive manner.

6. Participation, Reflexivity and the Professional Uses of Social Media

Based on our empirical encounters and in response to the expanding uses and unexplored potential of social media for professional use, we first recommend an emphasis on reflexivity for addressing the challenges of engaging in more sustainable and participatory design for the professional uses of social media. As discussed above, in our study, reflexivity arose as a central orientation that afforded engagement in design, research and various participatory processes that took place during the pilot. Our approach to reflexivity and participation led to our notion of "reflexive engagement."

Looking back, we discovered several manifestations of reflexivity in our study. The most essential one was performed through the fieldworker's self-reflexive stance as reflexive interrogation of herself and her participation and through her observations on reflexivity during the pilot. The fieldworker's reflexive stance depicted a turn inwards as a form of introspection although acknowledging reflexivity as interdependent with other participants and the evolving situations. The fieldworker's reflexivity was accompanied by a reflexive, interdisciplinary dialogue between the two authors. This dialogue contrasted the experiences in the field with conceptual and theoretical discussion and informed the processes of research and design. With reflexivity as a central orientation, the study provided insights into the processes of locating oneself, negotiating participation, and making discoveries in research and design and into addressing the engagement and interdependencies of relationships in and beyond the design/research. However, our focus in the project and the explorations of reflexivity were centrally focused on research. When looking at the expansion of social media for professional uses, what emerged as a future perspective was the need for a more nuanced understanding of reflexivity and the various arenas of participation taking place and influencing the research and design of new social media-supported practices and work models.

Second, we recommend engaging in participatory design when planning and designing social media for professional contexts. The need to address participation comes from the fact that social media by its nature is based on the centrality of content creation, sharing, networking and co-production (Lietsala & Sirkkunen, 2008)—in other words, on participation. In contrast to many traditional technologies, at least by definition, social media is user driven. It embraces users as the ones with the ability to define and design what social media, its content and its networks essentially are. Social media technologies provide low-threshold access to tools and practices online with less need for technological expertise. Moreover, organizations or groups of employees can take on new tools more easily than before, participate in design processes and engage in design "in the wild" (Hagen & Robertson, 2010), also independent of professional designers. This occurs due to the low threshold, easy-to-apply solutions and free or affordable social media tools.

The inherently participatory nature of social media must be accompanied by participatory design processes, which bring together stakeholders from research, design and different groups of professionals—that is, people with different involvement interests. However, the many backgrounds, knowledge and interests involved are not always easily combined. In our study, the arenas of participation included discussions with professionals during co-design, the two authors' discussions throughout the project and the collaboration in the larger framework of the project, which included three other pilots and the researchers. Reflexive engagement allowed us to embrace the nuances of participation, also giving us the ability to review our approaches, implicit understandings and taken-for-granted assumptions. To make the most of the broad participation called for by social media, our third recommendation is to reflexively revisit accustomed roles, relationships and participatory practices, and to take a critical look at how different participants have the opportunity to become and belong as participants. As participation is encouraged, attending to the dynamics of power and support for equal agency will be paramount.

Acknowledging the different arenas of participation requires a more inclusive view of reflexivity that expands the scope of our prior discoveries with reflexive engagement. This means studying what kinds of reflexive processes are taking place individually by and collaboratively between the participants in different arenas and how the different reflexive processes influence one another. Based on this, our final recommendation is to view design processes from the perspective of reflexivity, which includes individual, collective and interdependent reflexivity as its components (e.g., Finlay, 2002; Phillips, Kristiansen, Vehviläinen, & Gunnarsson, 2012). Working with participatory technologies, such as social media, and working in a collaborative manner in design processes opens up a need to look at what reflexive engagement means in terms of the professionals involved and how to address and make the most out of different arenas of participation. Participatory design through reflexive engagement for, with and by all those involved will support the learning, ownership and continuity of the process and outcomes and the sustainability of the results.

7. Conclusions

In this chapter, we have presented our experience of reflexivity in the participatory design of a social media-supported collaboration model and highlighted the possibilities of this reflexive orientation—reflexive engagement—in design for, with and by professionals for professional uses of social media. Social media may be participatory by definition, but without a participatory approach in the design processes, it can be subjugated to a mere technological tool introduced to users. We conclude with the following recommendations:

- Emphasize reflexivity when engaging in design for the professional uses of social media.
- Involve different stakeholders in order to embrace the participatory nature of social media.
- Reflexively view the roles and relationships and what participation means and how it is played out.
- Explore a more inclusive view of reflexivity.

We maintain that designing social media for professional uses "beyond projects," that is, for sustainable, long-lasting practices in work settings, requires processes that are participatory and reflexive. To make the most of the broad participation, we propose the need for all those involved—professionals, designers and researchers—to have an orientation toward reflexive engagement that accounts for the dynamics of the participatory processes and involvement.

8. References

Aalto, T. (2010). Sosiaalisen median mahdollisuudet hallinnolle (The Possibilities of Social Media for Administration). Oikeusministeriö.

Abeysinghe, G., & Alsobhi, A.Y. (2013, March 13–15). Social media readiness in small businesses. In N. M. Baptista, P. Isaías, & P. Powell (Eds.), *International Conference Information Systems* (pp. 267–272). Lisbon, Portugal: IADIS Press.

Balka, E. (2010). Broadening discussion about participatory design: A response to kyng. *Scandinavian Journal of Information Systems, 22*(1), 77–84.

Blomberg, J., & Karasti, H. (2012). Positioning ethnography within participatory design. In J. Simonsen & T. Robertson (Eds.), *Routledge international handbook of participatory design* (pp. 86–116). London, New York: Routledge.

Finken, S. (2003). Discursive conditions of knowledge production within cooperative design. *Scandinavian Journal of Information Systems, 15*(1), 57–72.

Finlay, L. (2002). Negotiating the swamp: The opportunity and challenge of reflexivity in research practice. *Qualitative Research, 2*(2), 209–230.

Hagen, P., & Robertson, T. (2010). Social technologies: Challenges and opportunities for participation. *Proceedings of the 11th Biennial Participatory Design Conference (PDC '10)* (pp. 31–40). New York, NY, USA: ACM. doi:10.1145/1900441.1900447.

Hämäläinen, P., & Heikkilä, J. (2011). Sosiaalisen median käytön ohjeistus. Katsaus internetissä julkaistuihin turvallisuus- tai työhyvinvointialan toimijoiden ohjeisiin (Guidelines to social media. The review of guidelines published in Internet by safety and well-being related organisations) (VTT Working Paper 186). VTT Technical Research Center of Finland. Retrieved from http://www.vtt.fi/publications/index.jsp

Heikkilä, J., Bäck, A., Heikkilä, A. M., Hämäläinen, P., Näkki, P., Ruuhilehto, K., Pihkala, S., et al. (2012). Sosiaalinen media turvallisuutta ja työhyvinvointia edistävien yhteisöjen tukena. Openrisk-hankkeen loppuraportti (Social media as a support to communities promoting safety and well-being at work. Openrisk. Final report). Espoo: VTT Technical Research Centre of Finland. Retrieved from http://www.vtt.fi/publications/index.jsp

Heikkilä, J., Näkki, P., Ruuhilehto, K., Bäck, A., Pihkala, S., Huhtamäki, J., & Tervakari, A. (2011, November 5–8). Social media in expert networks handling safety—Experiences from three cases. In B. White, P. Isaías, & F. Santoro (Eds.), *Proceedings of the IADIS International Conference on WWW/Internet* (pp. 437–442). Rio de Janeiro, Brazil: IADIS Press.

Karasti, H. (2010). Taking PD to multiple contexts: A response to kyng. *Scandinavian Journal of Information Systems, 22*(1), 85–92.

Leonardi, P. M., Huysman, M., & Steinfield, C. (2013). Enterprise social media: Definition, history, and prospects for the study of social technologies in organizations. *Journal of Computer-Mediated Communication, 19*(1), 1–19. doi:10.1111/jcc4.12029.

Lietsala, K., & Sirkkunen, E. (2008). *Social media. Introduction to the tools and processes of participatory economy.* Tampere: University of Tampere.

Phillips, L., Kristiansen, M., Vehviläinen, M., & Gunnarsson, E. (2012). Tackling the tensions of dialogue and participation: Reflexive strategies for collaborative research. In L. J. Phillips, M. Kristiansen, E. Gunnarsson, & M. Vehvilainen (Eds.), *Knowledge and power in collaborative research: A reflexive approach* (pp. 1–20). New York: Routledge.

Pihkala, S., & Karasti, H. (2013, July 22–26). Reflexive engagement—Reflexive orientation for participatory design. In P. Kommers & C. Gauzente (Eds.), *Proceedings of the IADIS International Conference ICT, Society and Human Beings* (pp. 85–92). Prague, Czech Republic: IADIS Press.

Schön, D. A. (1983). *The reflective practitioner. How professionals think in action.* Basic Books.

Stuedahl, D., Morrison, A., Mörtberg, C., & Bratteteig, T. (2010). Researching digital design. In I. Wagner, T. Bratteteig, & D. Stuedahl (Eds.), *Exploring digital design. Multi-disciplinary design practices* (pp. 3–16). London: Springer-Verlag. doi:10.1007/978-1-84996-223-0.

Talsi, N. (2013, July 22–26). Voices from the margins—User's perspectives on technology and technologically mediated society. In P. Kommers & C. Gauzente (Eds.), *Proceedings of the IADIS International Conference ICT, Society and Human Beings* (pp. 77–84). Prague, Czech Republic:. IADIS Press.

6

CYBERPSYCHOLOGY AND SOCIAL MEDIA

Online Social Support in Mental Health

Kyriaki G. Giota & George Kleftaras

DEPARTMENT OF SPECIAL EDUCATION, UNIVERSITY OF THESSALY, GREECE

1. Introduction

Information and communication technology (ICT) is profoundly changing the way society operates (Floridi, 2007). Research on human computer-based inter-action shows that computer technology's effects on the human psyche signifi-cantly shape both our interactions with each other and our perceptions of the world. Everyone has their own special little corner in cyberspace that allows them to share information, collaborate, discuss common interests and build relation-ships. Extracting meaning from the way people interact on the Web and trying to make sense of a world unimaginable a few years ago is the focus of the developing field of cyberpsychology (Barak & Suler, 2008).

As the general public becomes more comfortable using computer-mediated communication (CMC) technology, even more people turn to the Internet in search of support (i.e., information, advice, shared experiences) (White & Dorman, 2001). Research on online support groups and communities shows that the more time people spend in an online group, the larger their online social network and the higher their satisfaction with the received support (Wright, 1999).

Research evidence shows that computer-mediated environments could become alternative settings for obtaining support (Tichon & Shapiro, 2003), even though the question on whether online relationships provide meaningful social support still remains controversial (Eastin & LaRose, 2004). Social interactivity, even in a virtual environment, can lead to emotional and physical benefits, sug-gesting that social engagement of any kind—even virtual—is better than isolation (Richards & Viganó, 2012).

Social support could be described as an interactive process that includes verbal and non-verbal communication provided by ties or links (social networks), that individuals have (friends/family, other contacts in the real world, as well as on the Internet) and that aims to improve an individual's feelings of coping, competence, belonging and/or self-esteem. There are two basic dimensions: actual support (the support that an individual actually receives) and perceived social support (the perception of the availability and adequacy of social support) that is measurable and sometimes more important (Cohen, Gottlieb, & Underwood, 2000). Social support is beneficial to and an important predictor of physical health, psychological health and overall well-being (Burleson & MacGeorge, 2002). Psychological adjustment, improved efficacy, better coping with upsetting events, resistance and recovery from disease and reduced mortality are only few of the health outcomes that are linked with the existence of adequate social support (Griffiths et al., 2012).

2. Proposal

The social power of networks like Facebook and Twitter to connect, entertain, and enrich our lives is undeniable (DeLambo et al., 2011). Understanding how these networks impact on social support and overall well-being is vitally important research, especially in a generation that has grown up with media and technology. The social benefits of social networking sites (SNS) are yet to be investigated, even though they are believed to have drastically changed the psychosocial evolution of current young adults (Manago et al., 2012).

2.1. Aims

Our study aims to investigate how the use of social networking sites in Greece affects online social interactions and interpersonal relationships. Emphasis is given to how socio-demographic factors (gender, age, place of residence and unemployment), individual characteristics (personality traits and user motivations) and psychopathology indicators (depressive symptomatology and problematic SNS usage) are related to seeking social support online. Furthermore, the perceived quality of the participants' online relationships, the degree of online self-disclosure and the existence of online assistance that peers provide (perceived social support) are examined.

2.2. Methodology

A sample group of 500 young adults from the extended area of Thessaly in central Greece, varying from 18–34 years of age, participate on a voluntary basis and complete a short demographic survey, providing information on their SNS habits as well. Furthermore, they complete a series of measures that are translated, adapted into Greek and revised through back-translations. The questionnaires consist of multiple-choice questions, 5- and 7-point Likert scales, as well as "Right/Wrong" answers that take approximately 40 minutes to fill.

2.3. Key Findings

Preliminary findings of the study emerging through statistical analysis show that the participants' personality traits and motives affect the use of SNS for social purposes, as well as the perceived quality of the online relationships they create ($R = .59$, $F(4,273) = 35.68$, $p < .0001$). Depressive symptomatology and problematic use of social networking sites are good predictors of seeking online social support ($R = .55$, $F(2,416) = 90.04$, $p < .0001$). Seeking social support online can lead to self-disclosure and in-depth communication, which enhances the quality of the participants' online relationships ($r = .30$, $p < .01$). Men, in contrast to women, are significantly more attracted to online social support ($M = 87.8$, $SD = 19.76$ for men whereas $M = 80.2$, $SD = 20.2$ for women, $t(276) = 3.17$, $p < .01$).

An interesting and unexpected finding concerns the lack of gender differences on depressive symptomatology, since studies unequivocally show that the risk of depressive disorders is higher in females than males (e.g., Piccinelly & Wilkinson, 2000). Recent epidemiological studies in Greece show that depression has risen among men due to the economic crisis (Economou, Madianos, Theleritis, Peppou, Patelakis, & Stefanis, 2013), a fact that could be responsible for this result. Additionally, the factor of residence, in relation to the use of SNS, constitutes an interesting issue that has not yet been investigated sufficiently in international literature. Our results show that participants living in rural areas (up to 1,500 residents) exhibited higher scores in problematic SNS usage ($M = 71.04$, $SD = 17.8$) than those who lived in cities with more than 100,000 residents ($M = 57.1$, $SD = 16.73$, $t(141) = -3.53$, $p < .001$). These different usage patterns could indicate that social media are used as compensation for a possibly restricted in quantity, if not quality, social environment, which is the case for small villages in Greece that do not usually offer young people the variety in opportunities for socializing, recreation and entertainment that larger cities do. The aforementioned results will be refined by the end of the data processing, a work still in progress.

3. Predictive Scenario

Future aims of the proposal involve the use of experimental methods to further explore the motivations behind postings, as well as how various Facebook activities (status posts, participation in online groups and social networking site-enabled applications and games) influence the perceived online social support of the users. Furthermore, the actual effectiveness of the social supportive messages that participants receive when they self-disclose negative emotions and/or comments should be explored.

The way young people use social media technology needs to be further investigated so that the many different mediums they use can be adapted to psychological interventions, particularly in important areas of mental health, such as anxiety and depression research, as well as suicide prevention (Moreno et al., 2011). Psychological research online can be made simpler by (a) easily recruiting subjects without specific geographic, time and/or mobility constraints, (b) easily extracting data and (c) facilitating through confidentiality protocols and anonymity features healthcare surveys, reducing the stigma that is often associated with completing such questionnaires (Griffiths et al., 2006).

Social networking sites, in particular, hold promise for improving the ability to screen depressive symptomatology (Youn et al., 2013), as well as the creation of intervention initiatives in adolescents and young adults. Behavioural intervention technologies, for example, deliver care for depression and other disorders via the Internet or mobile phones as well as via computer programs. They typically teach principles of cognitive–behavioural therapy or some other evidence-based treatment and could be especially attractive to adolescents and young adults who are immersed in the world of technology (Griffiths et al., 2010).

Current research shows that technology-delivered psychotherapeutic interventions (e-therapy), through various synchronous and asynchronous means, can help people with mental health issues through many alternative ways that only social media can provide. From screening and assessment, to treatment and after care, e-therapy can assist clients to resolve life and relationship issues, unhindered by barriers related to geography, guilt, shame and stigma. It can be used as an alternative for face-to-face therapy, or in combination with other treatment modalities (Postel, de Haan, & De Jong, 2008).

Additionally, the growing body of knowledge concerning the therapeutic process and outcome, the counselor–counselee relationship, the characteristic features of online counseling, and ethical considerations for delivering therapeutic interventions online, help increase awareness among professionals. However, there are difficulties associated with access and technology usage skills, confidentiality issues, lack of nonverbal cues, possible client disinhibition and lack of emergency services to consider. The potential effectiveness of online counseling, the establishment of a therapeutic relationship in cyberspace, as well as the potential benefits and challenges of working online with clients are still the topics of major debates (Richards & Viganó, 2013).

Social media have already become a major part of the world's healthcare work and their use as possible sources of health information is rapidly growing (Vance, Howe, & Dellavalle, 2009). Young adults in particular are increasingly turning to social networking sites such as Facebook and Twitter to seek health information (Muise, Chistofides, & Desmarais, 2009). The Healthcare Hashtag Project is an example of connecting people and devices for the possibility of better health outcomes. It is a method to categorize keywords in Twitter that identifies them by the symbol "#" in the front, creating a huge database on various healthcare fields (i.e., #depression), organized and easily accessible by users who filter their home-feed to just see tweets about a particular subject (Lee, 2010).

Social media seem to change the patterns of health and treatment of illness in communities and alter access to health interventions (Griffiths, 2012). The health-care industry, seeking out ways to improve "customer" satisfaction and increase engagement, began to reach out to consumers in the same way that has proven successful for communication and marketing companies. Mayo Clinic is a fine example of a healthcare industry with a strong presence in social media. The most popular medical provider channel on YouTube has hundreds of thousands of followers on Twitter, multiple pages on Facebook and three blogs that share their expertise with the masses through resources, webinars and extensive training programs (Hackworth & Kunz, 2011).

Knowing what e-patients are seeking from social media websites can provide insight to health professionals designing intervention programs, but also increase customization of the interventions delivered through these technologies, making them more relevant to the target population (European Directory of Health Apps, 2012–2013). The most difficult goal in mental healthcare is improving the youth-friendliness of mental health resources and increasing participation among indi-viduals who might not otherwise seek care (Clough & Casey, 2011). Young people are big users of technology, which is reflected in how mental health resources are being accessed. As smartphones and social media are also now widely used, there has been a sharp rise in texting helplines rather than using the traditional 1-800 hotline numbers. To make information even more youth friendly and widely available to young people seeking support and advice, improvement must be made in existing channels through smartphone technology, Facebook, text alerts and other mobile and Internet tools (Italie, 2013).

Social media applications are becoming more embedded into our everyday lives, both professionally and personally. Wireless devices help gather health data and online behavioural tools for smartphones help improve not only access to thera-peutic interventions, but also the therapeutic experience (Susick, 2011). Examples include smartphone applications such as MindShift (teaches relaxation skills and new ways of thinking and suggests health-related activities), Positive Activity Jack-pot (combination of professional behavioural health therapy for depression called pleasant event scheduling with activities available in the user's location, mapped with GPS) and T2 Mood Tracker (tracks symptoms of depression, anxiety, PTSD, traumatic brain injury, stress and general well-being) (Kiume, 2013).

4. Conclusions

Are social media the future of psychology?

The advent of Web 3.0 poses even more new challenges for the cyberpsy-chologist. A technology that catalogues user behaviour, provides personalized and intelligent search capabablities, as well as behavioural advertising according to the users' subscriptions and for the users' instant gratification, and that uses search engines that can capture indications that may lead to the creation of a profile close to who the user is, what they've been doing and where they would like to go next might seem to be science fiction, but it is coming in the near future.

Cyberspace is, psychologically, a new realm of human experience that has the potential to transform psychology and psychotherapy. Cross-disciplinary research collaborations, with scientists that work in the fields of social sciences as well as the technical fields of human-computer interactions, will play an integral role in researching and developing online social media that can become tools to increase our understanding of health behaviour and to enhance the impact of behavioural interventions regarding social support, mental health and overall well-being.

5. Acknowledgement

The research has been co-financed by the European Union (European Social Fund—ESF) and Greek national funds through the Operational Program "Education and Lifelong Learning" of the National Strategic Reference Framework (NSRF)—Research Funding Program: Heracleitus II. Investing in knowledge society through the European Social Fund.

6. References

Barak, A., & Suler, J. (2008). Reflections on the psychology and social science of cyberspace. Retrieved from http://construct.haifa.ac.il/~azy/01-Barak%26Suler.pdf

Burleson, B. R., & MacGeorge, E. L. (2002). Supportive communication. In M. L Knapp & J. A. Daly (Eds.), *Handbook of interpersonal communication* (2nd) (pp. 374–420). Thousand Oaks, CA: Sage.

Chuang, K., & Yang, C. C. (2010). Social support in online healthcare social networking. Retrieved from https://www.ideals.illinois.edu/bitstream/handle/2142/14927/chuang.pdf

Clough, B. A., & Casey, L. M. (2011). Technological adjuncts to increase adherence to therapy: A review. *Clinical Psychology Review*. doi: 10.1016/j.cpr.2011.03.006.

Cohen, S., Gottlieb, B., & Underwood, L. (2000). Social relationships and health. In S. Cohen, L. Underwood, & B. Gottlieb (Eds.), *Social support measurement and intervention: A guide for health and social scientists* (pp. 3–25). New York: Oxford University Press.

DeLambo, D. A., Homa, D., Peters, R. H., DeLambo, A. M., & Chandras, K.V. (2011). Facebook and Social media: Implications for counseling college students. Retrieved from http://counselingoutfitters.com/ vistas/vistas11/Article_68.pdf

Eastin, M. S., & LaRose, R. (2004). Alt.support: Modeling social support online. *Computers in Human Behavior*, Elsevier, Article in press.

Economou, M., Madianos, M., Theleritis, C., Peppou, L. E., Patelakis, A., & Stefanis, C. N. (2013). Major depression in the era of economic crisis: A replication or a cross-sectional study across Greece. *Journal of Affective Disorders, 145*(3), 308–314.

European Directory of Health Apps. (2012–2013). A review by patient groups and empowered consumers. PatientView, 2012–2011. Retrieved on October 14, 2013, from http://www.patient-view.com/uploads/6/5/7/9/6579846/pv_appdirectory_final_web_300812.pdf

Floridi, L. (2007) A look into the future impact of ICT on our lives. *The Information Society, 23*(1), 59–64.

Griffiths, F. E. et al. (2012). Social networks—the future for health care delivery. *Social Science & Medicine*, Article in press.

Griffiths, F. E., Lindenmeyer, A., Powell, J., Lowe, P., & Thorogood, M. (2006). Why are health care interventions delivered over the Internet? A systematic review of the published literature. *Journal of Medical Internet Research, 8*(2). Retrieved from http://www.jmir.org/2006/2/e10/

Griffiths, K. M., Farrer, L., & Christensen, H. (2010). The efficacy of Internet interventions for depression and anxiety disorders: A review of randomised controlled trials. *Medical Journal of Australia, 192*(11), S4–S11.

Hackworth, B. A., & Kunz, M. B. (2011). Health care and social media: Building relationships via social networks. *Academy of Health Care Management Journal.* Retrieved October 20, 2013, from http://www.thefreelibrary.com/Health care and social media: building relationships via social...-a0263157551

Italie, L. (2013). Crisis hotlines turning to text to reach teens. Retrieved October 14, 2013, from http://bigstory.ap.org/article/crisis-hotlines-turning-text-reach-teens

Kiume, S. (2013). Top 10 mental health apps. Psych Central. [On-line]. Retrieved October 14, 2013, from http://psychcentral.com/blog/archives/2013/09/20/top-10-free-mental-health-apps/

Lee, T. M. (2010). Healthcare hashtags—A social project. Retrieved October 14, 2013, from http://www.symplur.com/blog/healthcare-hashtags-social-project/

Luciano, F. (2007). A look into the future impact of ICT on our lives. The Information Society. Retrieved from http://uhra.herts.ac.uk/xmlui/bitstream/handle/2299/2068/901125.pdf?sequence=1

Manago, A. M., Taylor, T., & Greenfield, P. M. (2012). Me and my 400 friends: The anatomy of college students' Facebook networks, their communication patterns, and well-being. *Developmental Psychology, 48*(2), 369–380. doi:10.1037/a0026338.

Moreno, A. M. et al. (2011). Feeling bad on Facebook: Depression disclosures by college students on a social networking site. *Depression and Anxiety, 28*, 447–455.

Muise, A., Christofides, E., & Desmarais, S. (2009). More information than you ever wanted: Does Facebook bring out the green-eyed monster of jealousy? *CyberPsychology & Behavior, 12*, 441–444.

Piccinelly, M., & Wilkinson, G. (2000). Gender differences in depression: Critical review. *The British Journal of Psychiatry, 177*, 486–492. doi:10.1192/bjp.177.6.486.

Postel, M. G., de Haan, H. A., & De Jong, C. A. J. (2008). E-therapy for mental health problems: A systematic review. *Journal of Telemedicine and E-Health, 14*(7), 707–714. doi: 10.1089/tmj.2007.0111.

Richards, D., & Viganó, N. (2012). Online counseling. In Y. Zheng (Ed.), *Encyclopedia of cyber behavior* (Vol. 1, pp. 699–713). New York, NY: IGI Global.

Richards, D., & Viganó, N. (2013). Online counseling: A narrative and critical review of the literature. *Journal of Clinical Psychology, 69*(9), 994–1011.

Sadat Nurullah, A. (2012). Received and provided social support: A review of current evidence and future directions. *American Journal of Health Studies.* Retrieved October 20, 2013, from http://www.thefreelibrary.com/_/print/PrintArticle.aspx?id=308741526

Susick Jr., M. (2011). Application of smartphone technology in the management and treatment of mental illnesses. Unpublished Thesis. University of Pittsburgh.

Tichon, J. G., & Shapiro, M. (2003). The process of sharing social support in cyberspace. *CyberPsychology & Behavior, 6,* 161–170.

Vance, K., Howe, W., & Dellavalle, R. P. (2009). Social Internet sites as a source of public health information. *Clinics in Dermatology Journal, 27*(2), 133–136. doi: 10.1016/j.det.2008.11.010.

White, M., & Dorman, S. M. (2001). Receiving social support online: Implications for health education. *Health Education Research: Theory & Practice, 16*(2), 693–707.

Wright, K. B. (1999). Computer-mediated support groups: An examination of relationships among social support, perceived stress, and coping strategies. *Communication Quarterly, 47*(4), 402–414.

Youn, S. J. et al. (2013). Using online social media, Facebook, in screening for major depressive disorder among college students. *International Journal of Clinical and Health Psychology, 13,* 74–80.

SECTION III
ICT Communities

7

CHALLENGES IN PROMOTING DIGITAL COMMUNITIES IN RURAL COOPETITIVE SETTINGS

Federico Cabitza & Carla Simone

UNIVERSITÀ DEGLI STUDI DI MILANO-BICOCCA, ITALY

1. Introduction

We were involved in a project aimed at the development of rural organizations in Northern Italy and led by a Growers' Organizations Association (GOA, or Association of Growers' Organizations, GO). This GOA was established in 2006 by local growers as a way to challenge the "monopoly" prices imposed by large retailers, especially within the progressively larger market of fresh-cut, ready-to-eat vegetable products. The paper reports on the outcomes of this project that aimed to study a network of farmers and promote the adoption of social computing technologies addressing their needs. This aim proved to be highly challenging since the network was heterogeneous, characterized by tiers of different nature and composed of competing/cooperating (coopetitive) actors. The paper illustrates the challenges we faced, the strategy we conceived that led to the introduction of a community-oriented ICT, and further steps to perform in this complex process of ICT adoption.

2. Our Proposal

2.1. Proposal Aims

The project addressed a general question: Can ICT, and more specifically social computing, help the involved growers build and maintain a tighter and more efficient community, strengthen their sense of belonging to this community (Andriessen, 2005) and support and enhance their mutual cooperation without downplaying the constraints imposed by competition, what is called coopetition (Brandenburger & Nalebuff, 2011)? As far as we know, the projects that can be related to our research (Arnold, Smith, & Trayner, 2010) and cooperative-based systems development (Heeb & Roux, 2002) have not so far addressed the phenomenon of coopetition, which has been recently recognized as a challenging requirement of global economies. Cooperation among competitors produces tensions and criticalities in the information flow among the network's nodes (Devi, Gnyawali, & Ravindranath, 2006) that any ICT design in this domain must address. The paper presents the challenges we faced in this particular scenario and the strategy we identified for their management, which led to the development of a survey and a preliminary system.

2.2. The Methodology and Related Issues

Since the huge number and heterogeneity of the GOA members made the true structure of the network obscure even to the GOA staff, the steering committee (SC) of the project promoted a survey aimed at shedding some light on complementary aspects, like socio-economic indicators at the grassroots level and the degree of adoption and actual use of ICT by the growers.

Even in the design of this survey, it was very soon evident that we had to deal with two main methodological challenges. First, the SC decided to take on all the strategic aspects of the project and to supply a "proper" representation of the main groups of stakeholders involved in such a distributed domain; this led to a sort of "imposition" of a top-down view of the structure of the GOA network and of how communication and information were currently flowing between its nodes (see Figure 7.1). According to this hierarchical structure, the communication involved in the GOA's activities was described as a flow following strictly hierarchical connections: interactions that traverse the hierarchical levels were considered sporadic, solely related to specific and institutional events (e.g., meetings, exhibitions, projects) and in any case marginal. With this (simplistic) model in mind, investigations based on an ethno-methodological approach (Dourish, 2001), that is encompassing direct interactions with the network stakeholders, were firmly contrasted, especially with the farmers working at the "bottom" tier of the architecture depicted in Figure 7.1.

The second methodological challenge concerned the complexity of data collection and the seasonal constraints of the farming domain. These latter ones forced us to start the technology design before the survey and the data analysis had been completed. On the other hand, the committee filtered our interviews with the stakeholders and in the initial phase of the project allowed us to interact with the CEOs and CIOs of the GOs only. In order to deal with this constraint, the survey was supported by a series of meetings with these executives who allowed us to grasp the main economic structure to the network and the related communication flows from their perspective.

In this not so canonical process, the interviews and the results incrementally emerging from the survey highlighted the heterogeneity of the network and most notably the relevant role of the agricultural consultants in the GOA. This was because these consultants had strong relations not only with the GOs and their growers, but also with the GOA's staff. We agreed with the SC to investigate this latter kind of relations as this was the only way to interact with at least one operational role acting in the field in a direct, unmediated way.

The survey contained a set of closed questions organized to address three specific concerns: (1) relationships and communication media used between the grower and, respectively, the Growers Organization (GO) it belongs to, peer growers and customers; (2) knowledge management, which was articulated in terms of (a) enabling factors and obstacles to effective communication and problem solving, (b) recurring problems that involve collaborative efforts, and (c) storing and retrieval of business contacts to support expertise finding; and lastly, (3) sense of belonging to the network itself and to other communities grounded in the same domain and region.

2.3. Key Findings and Their Implications

In regard to the communication flow between growers and the other actors, the survey showed that growers rely on mobile phones more often than on regular mail and land lines. E-mails were used more often than facsimiles but less frequently than phone calls; both SMS and social networks (like Facebook and Twitter) were used very seldom. Moreover, growers declared that in their meetings and conversations with the GO employees and consultants, they discussed production planning, production in itself (i.e., sowing, harvesting) and the supply of produce, in this order of importance. The same macro-topics were also discussed between growers and their GO; yet, this happened more often and through different technologies with respect to the grower–GO relationship. Growers spoke with each other using mobile phones more frequently than facsimiles (i.e., a textual technology) and used SMS (another textual technology) much more often than e-mails. Most notably, electronic means were allegedly used more often than traditional mail for inter-grower interaction.

As we suspected, the problem that growers mentioned most often regarded weather conditions and forecast, then problems related to treatment and preventions of plant diseases and then problems related to red tape with the Public Administration. The main sources of expertise and problem solving capabilities were acknowledged first in the growers' personal experience, then in assistance provided by GO personnel and agricultural consultants and, third, in consulting technical policies, which are documents issued by an authority and institutional body to regulate various aspects of agricultural practice.

Figure 7.1 illustrates these help seeking/providing flows in a schema-like representation of the GOA network.

Internet-based resources (e.g., results from search engines, forums, articles) were consulted as much as paper-based manuals. The majority of growers declared that they would be willing to share their "knowledge" with their peers, specifically how "not to repeat mistakes made by others or leverage good practices developed by others that coped with similar situations." A quite close number of

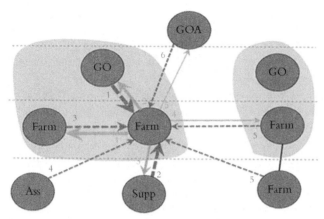

FIGURE 7.1 A schematic representation of the GOA network. Oriented arcs represent how help interventions flow among the nodes. Numbers (and thickness) indicate the ranking of the in/out-bound flows of help.

respondents chose "to make collective purchasing." This point illustrates the need to create mutual awareness of growers' common needs and to help them share personal experiences to prevent avoidable mistakes or waste of resources. The majority of the respondents thought that ICT can either greatly or moderately simplify the smooth flow of information and knowledge between the nodes of the GOA network. Respondents felt themselves moderately belonging to both the GO network and their district, but very little to the GOA wider network and just a little more to their professional category or other local representative bodies. Asking the same question to GO employees yielded the same results. Lastly, "feeling of being on the same boat" and "being part of the same community" were considered among the most important factors that make communication better and knowledge sharing easier and smoother.

All in all, the interviews with the GOs, CEOs and agricultural consultants, integrated with the survey results, highlighted five outcomes: (a) the ties among the network's nodes are heterogeneous and generally weak; (b) the growers would like to reach a stronger sense of belonging/participation; (c) in the sub-networks composed of a GO and its growers, ties are stronger but could be improved; (d) the agricultural consultants play the role of bridges (Wenger, 1998) between the sub-networks and, finally, (e) growers show an acceptable readiness to adopt communication technology and perceive it as a means to improve relationships within the network.

These outcomes led to the identification of a mixed strategy that combines technologies of different natures. On one hand, the instantiation of a Web 2.0 platform (Drupal 6) with the concept of a working group (WG) became the leading one: this tool was developed to combine top-down and bottom-up approaches to team work and tasks thanks to a careful and flexible definition of the involved roles with different capabilities and rights. On the other hand, the pivotal role of the agricultural consultants suggested the definition of two modules characterizing two initial WGs to support two main collaborative activities: the drafting of documents that contain indications and specifications useful for growing vegetables and fruits in a more effective way and the amendment of a policy document specifying regional/national directives, respectively.

3. Future Research

Within almost two years from the delivery of the collaborative platform mentioned above, the main tools that now support the two WGs have been tested in the field with positive reactions, which led the SC to (successfully) apply for a new funding program that should allow for the further evolution of this experience. This is a clear sign that the project had some influence on the network and that a greater commitment by the GOA and the GOs in sustaining the network and reaching a tighter involvement of its members in collaborative activities is part of this evolutive picture. Meanwhile, the GOA has scaled up to become a district, i.e., a more comprehensive network including a wider set of actors (e.g., suppliers, financial and insurance institutions). The platform has been recently put to work in this new context, after a "restyling" of the user interface on the basis of the outcomes of the previous experience. We are currently monitoring the use of this platform to support the collaboration within the district as well as designing a new survey by which to check its members' needs in terms of more complex services that the district should offer (Ravarini, Pacicco, & Strada, 2013). The experience gained in the project (and discussed in more detail in Cabitza, Simone, & Colombo, 2013c) has proved to be useful in avoiding some of the difficulties we met earlier at both the relational and organizational levels. The new situation is more favorable since the members of the district are more familiar with ICT and some progress in this sense occurred also at the growers' level. This conceptual and organizational effort is the starting point to fulfill a second important goal of the district: to become a recognized institution for the continuous monitoring of the economic, organizational and technological trends in the agricultural domain of the region. In this scenario, the district would play an increasing role of moderator/mediator of the communications that occur among its members. More specifically, the district should start some initiatives to trigger the active participation of the associated organizations in order to let them appreciate the value of well-defined collaborations beyond abstract and formal agreements. As an example, months ago the district discussed a joint program to promote the Italian expertise in producing high-quality vegetable outside Europe. The discussion was very lively at the beginning, but the contextual situation (including the complex laws, the norms and the supportive programs of the central government) made its progression toward a concrete result difficult. Such initiatives require continuous care by the district's staff that should be more equipped in terms of human resources and their training to collect the needed competencies. Besides offering the services that the currently on-going survey will help detect, the commitment and involvement of the top management is probably the most important point to guarantee a true change in the current practices, that is to enable the transformation of a set of relationships that were initially motivated by the need to have a unique (and stronger) identity towards the institutions, the competitors and other "powerful" market actors (notably, the mass retailers) into a solid platform for actual collaboration.

From a technological perspective, the evolution toward more friendly interfaces and the growing familiarity with Web 2.0 functionalities are increasing the importance of ICT in supporting the interactions that involve different kinds of actors with different views on how coopetition can be dealt with: management, employees and external consultants. The tension among these actors can hinder the success of the overall process, irrespective of the ICT solution that is under consideration.

In any case, the different levels of technological maturity of the district's organizations, which often are a symptom of different attitudes toward innovation (not only in terms of technology adoption but also in terms of change management in the broadest sense), must be taken seriously when selecting the initiatives and designing the supportive technology according to actual local needs and capabilities. Coopetition is not managed by abstract entities; indeed, it is dealt with by people in their daily and situated practices. The strategies for managing coopetition can be defined at the local and district levels, but their implementation is performed at any level of the organizational structure, with different responsibilities, in a flexible cooperative way to be successful. These considerations, also corroborated by our field work in healthcare (Cabitza & Simone, 2013; Cabitza et al., 2013a, 2013c, 2009), led us to engage in the definition of a software architecture that should act as carrier of a different way to conceive and construct ICT applications: the approach we propose (in Cabitza & Simone, 2014; Cabitza et al., 2013b) and that we called (in an evocative way) "Logic of Bricolage" allows communities of frontline users to be in control of the construction of their tools, from elementary components up to more complex aggregates, and of the ways these communities exchange information to fulfill the mission of the target organization. This approach, we submit, can be applied not only to shadow, informal office applications (Cabitza & Simone, 2013; Handel & Poltrock, 2011), which flank the "big" information systems, but also to these latter systems. This is proposed as a novel way to improve the resilience of information systems and office applications to many kinds of unexpected (and ultimately unpreventable) forms of coopetition in distributed settings, like the district discussed above, by breaking unnecessary barriers and by creating a negotiated sense of trust in the stakeholders involved.

4. References

Andriessen, J. H. E. (2005). Archetypes of knowledge communities. *C&T 2005*, 191–213. Springer, Netherlands,

Arnold, P., Smith, J.D., & Trayner, B. (2010). One more tool—or exploring the practice of introducing new technologies in dispersed communities. *Networked Learning*, 18–25.

Brandenburger, A. M., & Nalebuff, B. J. (2011). *Co-opetition, Currency/Doubleday*. ed. New York, USA: Crown Business.

Cabitza, F., Colombo, G., & Simone, C. (2013a). Leveraging underspecification in knowledge artifacts to foster collaborative activities in professional communities. *International Journal of Human—Computer Studies*, 71, 24–45.

Cabitza, F., & Simone, C. (2013). Drops hollowing the stone. Workarounds as resources for better task-artifact fit. In L. Ciolfi, M. A. Grasso, & O. W. Bertelsen (Eds.), *ECSCW 2013*. Springer Berlin, D.

Cabitza, F., & Simone, C. (2014). *Building socially embedded technologies: Implications on design, designing socially embedded technologies: A European challenge* (p. forthcoming). Springer Berlin, D.

Cabitza, F., Simone, C., & Colombo, G. (2013c). Challenges in promoting communities with ICT in a widely scattered and heterogeneous setting. In *WBCSM 2013* (pp. 22–29). IADIS Press,.

Cabitza, F., Simone, C., & Gesso, I. (2013b). Back to the future of EUD: The logic of bricolage for the paving of EUD roadmaps. In Y. Dittrich, M. Burnett, A. I. Mørch, & D. Redmiles (Eds.), *IS-EUD 2013* (pp. 254–259). LNCS. Springer, Heidelberg, D,.

Cabitza, F., Simone, C., & Sarini, M. (2009). Leveraging coordinative conventions to promote collaboration awareness. *CSCW* 18, 301–330.

Devi, R., Gnyawali, Jinyu He, & Ravindranath ("Ravi") Madhavan. (2006). Impact of co-opetition on firm competitive behavior: An empirical examination. *Journal of Management* 32, 507–530.

Dourish, P. (2001). *Where the action is: The foundations of embodied interaction*. Cambridge, USA: MIT Press.

Gnyawali, D. R., & He, J. (2006). Impact of co-opetition on firm competitive behavior: An empirical examination. *Journal of Management, 32*(4), 507–530.

Handel, M. J., & Poltrock, S. (2011). Working around official applications: Experiences from a large engineering project. In *CSCW'11* (pp. 309–312). ACM,

Heeb, J., & Roux, M. (2002). *Platforms and innovation co-operations for sustainable development of landscapes and regions. Local environmental management in a north-south perspective. Issues of participation and knowledge management*.

Ravarini, A., Pacicco, L., & Strada, E. (2013). Industrial clusters evolution enabled by digital platforms: A framework. In *ItAIS, Proceeding of the 10th Conference of the Italian Chapter of AIS, Milano, December 14–15, 2013*.

Wenger, E. (1998). *Communities of practice: Learning, meaning, and identity*. Cambridge, UK: Cambridge University Press.

Zineldin, M. (2004). Co-opetition: The organisation of the future. *Marketing Intelligence & Planning*, 22, 780–790.

8

NON-USERS OF ICT AND SOCIAL MEDIA—MARGINAL VOICES

Noora Talsi

UNIVERSITY OF EASTERN FINLAND, FINLAND

1. Introduction

When viewing Finland and Finnish people through statistics, it is obvious that Finland is a highly digitalized country. According to statistics from the World Economic Forum, Finland is now in first place in the Global Information Technology Report (World Economic Forum, 2013). Finland scores at the top on overall readiness of ICT with subindexes on environment, readiness, usage and impacts. Finnish society provides a fertile ground for Finns to adopt new technologies and domesticate novelties as an important and integral part of their everyday lives. In the Programme for the International Assessment of Adult Competencies (PIAAC) study conducted during 2013 in OECD countries, Finland also scores high. Within the comparison of 24 countries, Finland was second best in adult literacy, numeracy and problem solving in the context of a technology-rich environment. Still, one-fifth of Finland's working-age population (ages 16–65) has major difficulties when using IT in problem solving. The ones who have problems are mostly between 40–65 years old. For the population already retired, no numbers are available (OECD, 2014).

Behind the statistics, however, a lot of people are not using any information technologies, not to mention social media. Who are these Finns who restrict or oppose the use of the latest ICT? Why do they not use the Internet, computers or other ICT devices? How do they feel the pressure of the Finnish technologically mediated society? This group is hard to reach through Internet surveys and questionnaires, which aim to discover how people are using ICT. Some Finns actively oppose the use of ICT, but for many it is not the question of choice but the lack of technical and economical (and more often also cultural and social) competence. Elderly people, especially, are dropping out of the digitalized society. Only 20% of elderly people over 75 years old are using the Internet; in addition, twenty percent of those over 85 years old do not own any information or communication technologies (Wessman et al., 2013). Within this population are many disabled and lonely elderly people. They do not have the skills or opportunities to use ICT, and they do not have equal access to basic services like healthcare or banking. The problems with elderly people and ICT use are not minor since the Finnish population is aging more rapidly than people of any other country apart from Japan.

2. Non-Users of ICT

2.1. Facing the Technological Pressure

In current societies, many practices are technologically mediated and technologies have a meaningful part in people's everyday lives. Different social and cultural structures, practices and discourses guide people's use of technologies. I have used the term "technological imperative" to refer to these social and cultural pressures that force people to use culturally crucial technologies (Talsi, 2013; Talsi & Tuuva-Hongisto, 2009). I base the idea of technological imperative on the social and cultural studies of technology, which approach technology as a culturally constructed phenomenon. Technology can be seen as a socio-material product—a seamless web or network that combines artefacts, people, organizations, cultural meanings and knowledge (Wajcman, 2004). Technologies both shape, and are shaped by, their social, political, economic and cultural contexts (Grint & Woolgar, 1997; Lievrouw & Livingstone, 2002).

In a society where using information technologies is a norm and the whole society is more or less mediated by information technologies, not using them is interpreted as abnormal activity. Not using ICT affects the lives of non-users, but it also affects technology policy and development. The pressure of using ICT also has effects, which are often felt more strongly by those who are not using them. I have concentrated my research on questioning how non-users of ICT interpret the pressure of using technologies and why, in spite of this pressure, they are not using ICT.

2.2. Multisited Qualitative Research

The research data have been gathered and analyzed with the methods of multisited qualitative research. I have applied ethnography and oral history, which are both methodologies of qualitative research used widely in social sciences and cultural studies. With ethnography and oral history, it is possible to collect mundane experiences with technologies and the effects that technologization has had on informants' lives. The strengths of multisited qualitative research are its ability to understand everyday life experiences and to question self-evident facts.

The data are based on (1) ethnographic longitudinal interviews of women living in remote areas in eastern Finland who participated in ICT education, (2) interviews of local level technology policy-makers in eastern Finland and

(3) a nationwide collection of technobiographies of elderly people. By technobiographies, I mean autobiographical writings where people describe their relation to technologies (cf. Henwood et al., 2001). These sets of data were gathered in Finland from 1998 to 2007. With these extensive qualitative data, it is possible to understand the long processes of technologization in Finnish society and everyday life and how technology relations of the users have developed and changed over time.

The (non-)users of ICT that I have studied are far from mainstream users. The focus is on user groups that are marginalized from the technologically mediated society based on their age, gender and/or place of living. I have given voice to those user groups that are hardly heard when developing a technologically mediated society or creating technology policy. Usually, technology relations and needs of elderly people or people living in remote areas are defined by others—by technology policy-makers or developers of technologies. In my research, they can speak with their own voice and tell about their relation to technology and a technologically mediated society and why they are not using ICT.

2.3. Opponents and Bystanders

In my research data, a technologically mediated society, where using culturally center technologies feels mandatory, was interpreted through everyday life practices. The pressure towards using technologies was a fuzzy feeling that "everyone knows how to use these things." Users have different ways of reacting to the demands and pressures caused by technological imperative in a technologically mediated society. The elderly users' ways of reacting were more or less opposing or left aside from the development. The dynamics between actively opposing new ICT or passively being left aside from the development of new technologies and more or less from the whole technologically mediated society are interesting.

Opposing technologies requires quite a lot of skills and knowledge about that technology. Actively opposing ICT is a way of reacting for elite users. It is not an option for marginalized groups. They do not have knowledge about the technological artefacts, knowledge of how to use it or knowledge enough to make decisions (cf. Grint & Woolgar, 1997). It is important to differentiate between being left aside and opposing the use of technologies (Wyatt, 2003). Freedom of choice between using or not using technologies is essential when looking at the ways of reacting to technological imperative and adopting new technologies. Opposing technological imperative and latest technologies requires abilities, motivations and resources, and without those, the risk of being left aside from technological development increases. On the other hand, opposing the latest technological development can also be seen as a criticism for consumerism. If marginalized groups of users are not able to oppose certain technological devices, they certainly can oppose society that they feel is run by consumerism and techno-optimism.

Being left aside from the development of the latest technology is mostly happening to elderly citizens. It is giving up when, as some of my informants said, "we are in the margins anyway." Left aside from the latest technological development more often also means left aside from the whole technologically mediated society. When all the vital practices are mediated by technologies, living without them can marginalize people not only from technologies but also from society itself. Non-use of the Internet means also being very restricted in the use of bank, tax, healthcare, travel or education services in Finland. The situation is new and especially shocking for elderly informants: use or non-use of technologies used to be a private thing and no one was excluded from society if they were not using, for example, a washing machine or a chain saw. Non-use of social media can also exclude people from a social environment and social relationships.

Technologies become meaningful when they are connected to everyday life (Lie & Sørensen, 1996). Likewise, technologies that do not find a place in users' everyday lives remain meaningless. They are not domesticated, which means they are not adopted and settled in users' lives (Talsi, 2012). Opposition against new technologies seems to happen because the rhythms of everyday life and technologically mediated society are not interacting. Everyday life is already settled and routines are fixed but changing society is pushing new demands to which especially elderly people are not willing to respond. I considered everyday life practices and their problematic encounters with the demands of the technologically mediated society through practice theory (Shove et al., 2012). The use of technologies is seen as a practice. All the functions of society are mediated through technologies, and citizens are assumed to use especially the Internet. This development is seen as deterministic, mandatory and necessary, and no space for alternative thinking can be found. This puts pressure on people to use the latest technologies. The pressure caused by technological imperative is felt worse and worse when the demands of the technological imperative are far away from everyday life practices and responding to these demands would require reshaping and renegotiating these practices (Talsi, 2014).

Great changes in technologies have happened over the lifetime of my informants. For decades, homes were filled with technologies that have only one function like vacuum cleaners, washing machines, transistor radios and electric saws. Now technologies have become more complex. Changes in technologies require changes in practices. Elderly users are often unwilling to change their practices. According to my data, it seems that technology relations are quite stabile. For example, the elderly men in my research enjoyed technologies when they were young and when technologies were simpler to modify and build. Their technology relations were based on taking apart and putting back together technologies like cars. They felt joy when they could fix a broken washing machine or typewriter. Now that technologies have become more complex, it is harder and almost impossible for the elderly to build these technologies anymore. These elderly men are not ready to change how they work with technologies: they are not ready to just be mere end-users so they easily oppose or are left aside from the whole development of technologies (Talsi, 2014).

In short, the reasons elderly people do not use technologies lie deeply embedded in lifelong technology relations and everyday life practices. Technologies are not settled into these practices, and elderly people are not willing to change their practices and domesticate new technologies into their lives.

2.4. Just Wait—Soon Everyone Will Use Social Media

Values like competitiveness and effectiveness are extensively guiding the development of Finnish technologically mediated society. In this development, marginalized groups of users such as elderly people and people living in remote areas are seen as ever more problematic. The development based on market logic does not encounter the needs of these users groups, and they are easily left aside from technologically mediated society. There is no place for technological dropouts in a society where all the practices are mediated through technologies and assumption of technologically savvy users is prevailing.

More and more people worldwide are using social media. However, this does not mean that digital divide, the divide between those who have competence, ability and devices to use social media and those who have not, is shrinking even within the same country. The gap between savvy users of social media and non-users is large, multifaceted, and in some ways, it is not shrinking. Moreover, the divide is socially patterned, so that there are systematic variations in the kinds of people who are on and off social media. It varies within and between countries (Chen & Wellman, 2005, 467). In Finland, the gap between information technology haves and have-nots is strongly related to age.

Chen & Wellman wrote (2005, 468) about Internet use: "Within countries, the uneven diffusion of the Internet appears along familiar lines of social inequality such as socioeconomic status, gender, age, geographic location, and ethnicity. Moreover, having access to computers and the Internet and possessing the ability to use them effectively are two different issues. While markets, media, and governments often report only the number of people who have access to the Internet, the digital divide is not the binary yes/no question of having access to the Internet. The question is not whether people have ever glanced at a monitor or put their hands on a keyboard but the extent to which they regularly use a computer and the Internet for meaningful purposes." The same setting that Chen & Wellman used to describe use of the Internet is now accurate in the contemporary use of social media. First of all, being able to use social media requires technological and language skills that elderly people often lack. It also requires the ability to buy and use multiple software and hardware. Third, being able to use social media and actually using it are two different things.

The use of social media increases year by year in Finland. The biggest growth of social media usage, especially Facebook, is in the 45–64 age group. The potential for growth also lies in this age group: more than 50% of those under the age of 45 are using Facebook, compared to over 45 years old, where less than 50% use Facebook (Social Media Review, 2013). The divide between young and middle age users of social media is narrowing in the sense that middle age Finns have started to use social media. However, their use is relatively occasional and conservative. Only among the group under 45 years old can active and creative users of social media and Web 2.0 be found; they are blogging, vlogging, using Twitter, Facebook, Pinterest, Instagram and other social media to keep in touch and creating new networks (YLE & 15/30 Research, 2011). There are no statistics concerning the use of social media in the age group over 65. We can predict that working age people, who are now using social media, will continue using it after they retire. The problem is the constant change and development of social media—the social media we use now may not exist in 20 years.

According to Finnish technology and innovation strategies and the interviews I have conducted with local level technology policy-makers, it appears that it is only a matter of time before everyone will know how to use the latest ICT technologies. It is believed that when elderly non-users of technologies pass away, the new generations of elderly people will naturally use the latest technologies. However, it is not recognized that when technologies are constantly developing, both devices and skills for using them must also be updated. Also required are a readiness and ability to buy, adapt and use new technologies. When elderly people do not have the financial or technical support from their employers, the motivation and resources are even harder to achieve.

Technology and innovation policy are more or less based on the assumption that active citizens are lifelong learners and techno-optimistic. In my data, it is quite obvious that technological skills are considered as part of working life. After their retirement, my informants may use the already existing technologies but not buy or learn to use new ones anymore. It seems that a new generation of pensioners will face the same problems when new technologies are introduced to Finnish society and its vital practices. Technologies are developing so fast that even after a couple of years of retirement, not to mention a couple of decades, technological solutions that this elderly population are able to use will seem outdated. The stabile nature of technology relation will make it quite hard to adapt fundamentally different new technologies that would demand changes in these practices.

Keeping in mind that Finland has the fastest aging population in Europe, it is quite obvious that solving the problem requires social and political actions—not just waiting until everyone knows how to use the latest ICT and social media. More research is needed about elderly users and non-users of ICT, and statistics for the age group over 65 years old are especially crucial. Also, both political and technical innovations are needed to make ICT more available for elderly citizens. The technologies should be designed for elderly and disabled people: they should be easy to use and affordable. The greatest fears for ICT and social media are related to privacy and security risks (Wessman et al., 2013). When marginalized user groups do not have an understanding of technology or the skills to use it, especially social media will remain a scary and unknown entity—a black box that can spread your personal and financial information to the whole world. Not using ICT and social media can on the other hand strengthen social relations when especially younger family members must be consulted constantly by elderly citizens who need services available only online. Third sector organizations also play a meaningful role when organizing services for non-users. This social support should be better acknowledged in political decision making.

3. Conclusions

In this article, I have shown how elderly people are dropping out of digitalized society. These non-users of ICT feel pressure to use the latest technologies caused by technological imperative. They often oppose or are left aside from use of the latest technologies, including social media. New technologies, software and applications are developing so fast and becoming more complex that adapting and using them would require changes in practices. Marginalized user groups, especially elderly people, are unwilling and sometimes unable to change their practices. Development of a technologically mediated society seems inevitable and deterministic for those people who are non-users or limited users of technologies. When all vital practices are mediated through technologies, not using them makes everyday life harder. Not using ICT does not mean exclusion of certain technologies but rather exclusion of the whole society and lifestyle mediated through technologies.

4. References

Chen, W., & Wellman, B. (2005). Charting digital divides: Comparing socioeconomic, gender, life stage, and rural–urban Internet access and use in five countries. In W. Dutton et al. (Eds.), *Transforming enterprise. The economic and social implications of information technology* (pp. 467–497). Cambridge, Massachusetts, London: The MIT Press.

Grint, K., & Woolgar, S. (1997). *The machine at work. Technology, work and organization* (p. 19). Cambridge: Polity Press.

Henwood, F. et al. (2001). Cyborg lives in context: Writing women's technobiographies. In F. Henwood et al. (Eds.), *Cyborg lives? Women's technobiographies* (pp. 11–34). York: Raw Nerve Books.

Lie, M., & Sørensen, K. H. (1996). Making technology our own? Domesticating technology into everyday life. In M. Lie & K. H. Sørensen (Eds.). *Making technology our own? Domesticating technology into everyday life.* Oslo: Scandinavian University Press.

Lievrouw, L. A., & Livingstone, S. (2002). The social shaping and consequences of ICTs. In L. A. Lievrow & S. Livingstone (Eds.), *Handbook of new media* (pp. 1–15). London, Thousand Oaks, New Delhi: Sage.

OECD—Programme for the International Assessment of Adult Competencies. (2014). Forthcoming. Retrieved from http://www.oecd.org/site/piaac

Shove, E. et al. (2012). *The dynamics of social practice*. London, Thousand Oaks, New Delhi: Sage.

Social Media Review. (2013). Retrieved from http://www.slideshare.net/hponka/sosiaalisen-median-katsaus-092013

Talsi, N. (2012). *Technologies entering the home—The domestication of mundane technologies*. IADIS International Conference ICT, Society and Human Beings (pp. 3–10). IADIS Press.

Talsi, N. (2013). *Voices from the margins—Users' perspectives on technology and technologically mediated society*. Proceedings of the IADIS International Conference ICT, Society and Human Beings. IADIS Press.

Talsi, N. (2014). *Kodin koneet—Teknologioiden kotouttaminen, käyttö ja vastustus. [Mundane Machines—Domesticating, Using and Resisting Technologies at Home]*. Publications of the University of Eastern Finland. Dissertations in Social Sciences and Business Studies. Forthcoming.

Talsi, N., & Tuuva-Hongisto, S. (2009). Ei vietetty sinä jouluna tekniikan riemujuhlaa. Teknologinen imperatiivi teknologiaelämäkerroissa. [The Technological Imperative in Technobiographies]. *Kulttuurintutkimus*, 26, 2–3, 71–82.

Wajcman, J. (2004). *Technofeminism* (p. 106). Cambridge: Polity Press.

Wessman, J. et al. (2013, February 2). *Ikääntynyt ja teknologia* [Elderly People and Technology]. Käkäte-tutkimuksia. The Union for Senior Services & The Central Union for the Welfare of the Aged. User Centered Technology for the Elderly People and Caregivers. Retrieved from http://www.ikateknologia.fi

World Economic Forum: Bilbao-Osorio, B. et al. (2013). The Global Information Technology Report 2013. Retrieved from http://www.weforum.org

Wyatt, S. (2003). Non-users also matter: The construction of users and non-users of the Internet. In N. Oudshoorn & T. Pinch (Eds.), *How users matter? The co-construction of users and technologies* (pp. 67–79). Cambridge, MA: MIT Press.

YLE & 15/30 Research. (2011). *Suomalaiset verkossa* [Finns at the Internet]. Retrieved from http://www.slideshare.net/ylefi/yle-esitys-ppt

9

THE USE OF A SOCIAL MEDIA COMMUNITY BY MULTICULTURAL INFORMATION SYSTEMS DEVELOPMENT TEAMS TO IMPROVE COMMUNICATION

Roelien Goede & Moleboge Emma Nhlapo

NORTH-WEST UNIVERSITY, SOUTH AFRICA

1. Introduction

The use of a social media community by multicultural information systems development teams to improve communication

Communication is one of the success factors in developing new information systems. Experts agree that failure to communicate is the greatest threat to project success, especially information technology projects (Schwalbe, 2011). According to Avison & Fitzgerald (2006), people and organizational factors, rather than technical factors, have led to many information systems failures.

The South African government laws and statutes in the last 20 years have given rise to multiculturalism in the workplace. South African society is categorized by many groups classified by themselves or others using specific identities (Grosberg, Struwig, & Pillay, 2006). These categorizing identities have resulted in tensions in the South African society founded on "racial, ethnic, religious, gender, and linguistic groupings" (Grosberg et al., 2006).

The purpose of this chapter is to propose the use of a social network community for a multicultural information systems development (ISD) team in order to enhance the quality of the team's communication.

The first part of the chapter reports on a completed study that highlights the fact that it is more challenging to work in a multicultural team than it is to work in a homogeneous team from a communication perspective. This study is reported on in terms of aims, methodology and findings. The second part of the chapter discusses a proposal for a future study to investigate and implement a social media community (SMC) in an ISD team. The proposal is structured according to the phases of an action research (AR) project as it is a suitable methodology for this problem situation.

Before presenting the case study report, it is necessary to clarify the stance of the researchers on some key terms of which different scholars use different definitions. In this study, culture is viewed as learned way of life passed on to group members (similar to Martin & Nakayama, 2011). All the cultural elements are learned through interaction with others in the culture (Jandt, 2004; Lui, Volčič, & Gallois, 2011). The use of the word "culture" by interculturalists means different culture contexts, namely national culture, corporate culture, professional culture, gender, age, religious culture, regional culture and class culture (Gibson, 2002; Oetzel, 2005). The different cultural contexts complicate the interpretation of the nonverbal aspects of communication (Beamer & Varner, 2008). Hofstede & Hofstede (2005) refer to these cultural contexts as layers of culture. They outline six layers of culture as national level; regional, ethnic, religious and/or linguistic affiliation level; generation level; gender level; social class level and organizational level.

Communication involves conveying and receiving information between a sender and a recipient and this happens through words and nonverbal actions, such as gestures and facial expressions (Jandt, 2004).

2. Case Study: Intercultural Communication of Information Systems Development Team Members

2.1. Objective of Study

The aim of this study was to investigate how communication is affected by the different cultural contexts of ISD team members in order to achieve better results. The study investigated the level of difficulty of communication with ISD team members from different cultural contexts such as cultural affiliation, job class distinction, language, nonverbal communication, group size, gender, age and profession.

2.2. Methodology

An interpretive multiple-case study was conducted in the Gauteng province of South Africa where ISD team members were interviewed. The following subsections describe the collection and analysis of the qualitative data collected.

2.3. Data Collection

The participating employees are members of information systems development teams in three organizations. From each organization, five participants from diverse cultural backgrounds were interviewed. The organizations are termed

A, B and C for ethical reasons. The participants had cultural diversity in terms of race, gender, religion, age, job description and home language. Participants had experience in a multicultural ISD team context, and some had also worked in a homogeneous environment previously. Each participant was interviewed by the authors of the chapter who are representative of two different cultural groups. The interviews were semi-structured and recorded and afterwards transcribed.

2.4. Data Analysis

This study yielded a large amount of qualitative data. Interpretative content analysis was used to code and categorize the data. Table 9.1 demonstrates the categories in the data of two of the questions. Some of the questions provided such diverse answers from specific participants that the categories are not mutually exclusive. The Count column represents the number of participants and their organizations whose answers were in correspondence with a specific category. For instance, 2B means 2 participants from organization B and 1A means 1 participant from organization A.

3. Key Findings

From analyzing the data, the research team concluded that communication in general is open, but culture, personality and age may affect the level of communication difficulty. Some of the key findings were as follows:

TABLE 9.1 Example of Analysis of Interview Data

Question	Category	Count
2. What makes it easier or more difficult to talk to colleagues?	Category 2-1: Easy to communicate with friendly individuals that display openness	1A, 1B, 2C
	Category 2-2: Difficulty linked to individual's resistance to critique	1A
	Category 2-3: Difficulty linked to different opinions on everyday nonwork issues	1A
	Category 2-4: Difficult communication linked to individual personalities	1A, 1B, 1C
	Category 2-5: Other reasons for communication difficulty	1A, 2B, 1C
	Category 2-6: Question not asked or answered	1A, 1B, 1C
8. Do you prefer e-mail or direct communication?	Category 8-1: Both e-mail and direct communication	2A, 1B, 3C
	Category 8-2: E-mail communication preferred	1B
	Category 8-3: Direct communication preferred	2A, 3B, 2C
	Category 8-4: Question not asked	1A

- Eleven participants, 3 from organization A, 4 from organization B and 4 from organization C, communicate easily with colleagues while 4 participants had difficulty communicating with colleagues at times.
- Nine participants, 3 from organization A, 3 from organization B and 3 from organization C, maintain that culture influences communication with colleagues. Four participants, 1 from organization A, 1 from organization B and 2 from organization C, said that culture does not influence communication.
- Four participants, 1 from organization A, 1 from organization B and 2 from organization C, communicate easily across cultures. Individual participants maintain that communication is made easy by open people, jokes, asking questions, friendly cues and openness to others' viewpoints and ideas. A participant from organization A linked communication difficulty to individual resistance to critique. Another participant from organization A linked communication difficulty to differing opinions on everyday nonwork issues.
- Twelve participants, 4 from organization A, 5 from organization B and 3 from organization C, use English as a communication language with their colleagues. Seven participants, 3 from organization A, 2 from organization B and 2 from organization C, maintain that other languages are used in individual communications and occasionally in meetings as well. Six participants, 1 from organization A, 3 from organization B and 2 from organization C, felt that the use of a different language in their presence was unacceptable. Eight participants, 4 from organization A and 2 each from organizations B and C, maintained that they are unbothered when others use a different language in their presence.
- Six participants, 2 from organization A, 1 from organization B and 3 from organization C, prefer both e-mail and direct communication. Seven participants, 2 from organization A, 3 from organization B and 2 from organization C, prefer direct communication. One participant from organization B prefers e-mail. Direct communication is preferred because it provides instant message delivery and feedback. E-mail is preferred because it leaves the message, and it facilitates record-keeping. E-mail is disadvantageous because it is impersonal, it is open to misinterpretation and typing and message delivery take longer. Direct communication is disadvantageous because it does not provide proof of communication.

In general, the participants spoke freely about their interactions with members of other cultures. However, while demonstrating knowledge of nonwork-related aspects of colleagues of the same culture, very little knowledge of nonwork-related aspects of colleagues of a different culture was demonstrated.

4. Proposed Study: Use of a Social Media Community

From the initial study reported in Section 2, it was discovered that people do find working in multicultural ISD teams more challenging than working in homogeneous teams from a communication perspective. Informally, it was easy to observe that friendships exist across cultural boundaries and that such friendships aid communication and teamwork. From this perspective, a proposal is made to increase the use of social media platforms in the workplace to enhance informal intercultural communication. The aim of the proposed study is therefore to develop a social media community in the workplace in order to improve communication of multicultural ISD team members.

When researching matters of such individual and social nature, the authors are in favor of including the participants in as many aspects of the research process as possible. In order to facilitate this, participatory action research (AR) is proposed as research methodology (see Baskerville, 1999 for a discussion on AR). AR is performed from a critical social research perspective where the research participants should be involved in reflection and action planning to improve their environment. AR is a cyclic process consisting of five phases, namely diagnosis, action planning, implementation, evaluation and learning specification. Since the section discusses a proposal, our focus will be on the first two phases with some comments on the other phases.

Before discussing the detail of the phases, the role of theory in AR must be clarified. AR differs from consultation in that existing theory guides the intervention in the situation. The practical implication is that the researcher works together with the participants to enrich situational experiences with theoretical knowledge. Existing theories on multicultural communication can be used in this regard. The research team should be sensitive toward different theories or multiculture such as constructivism (Pinkett, 2000) and essentialism (Pfeffer, 1998).

5. Diagnosis Phase

The aim of the diagnosis phase is to improve understanding of the role of social media in the workplace. In order to achieve this objective, two studies should be conducted. First, a literature review should be conducted on studies covering informal communication using social media in the workplace. One such example is DiMicco & Millen (2007) who explore the phenomenon of people creating a second user account in social media applications for their workplace identity.

After the literature study is completed, a study should be conducted in the organisation where the implementation is planned. Multicultural ISD team members should be interviewed from an interpretive perspective, with the aim of understanding their perceptions of the use of a social media community (SMC) in the workplace. The interview questions should be enriched from the results of the literature study. Questions that may need answering include the following:

1. What would be the function of such an SMC? Would it be an extension of a project management tool, or is it an interface for social interaction?
2. Would participants use it mainly for messages to other team members, or would they make status updates to the entire group?
3. Would participants make status updates expressing their emotions?
4. Would participants use their everyday identity, or would they create a more "professional" identity? What would they prefer their colleagues do in this regard?
5. Would participants take part in polls on everyday issues?

From literature such as DiMicco & Millen (2007), it is apparent that people differ greatly on how much they want to share in the workplace.

Analysis of the interviews can be done with content analysis to identify themes in the data. These themes will most likely represent general perspectives of the use of SMC in the workplace.

6. Planning of Intervention Phase

Analysis of the data gathered in the diagnosis phase should give an indication on the openness of the participants to use an SMC to get to know their colleagues better. It might be necessary to do some more marketing of the advantages of better informal relations in ISD teams or other related issues to win more of the participants over.

It is of utmost importance to include people representing different perspectives on the SMC planning team. The result of the planning phase should be a set of guidelines coming from the participants on their use of the SMC. The guidelines should be promoted by arguing that if everyone follows them, more people will be willing to use the SMC, leading to greater success of the SMC. In order to improve the impact of the SMC, the users (ISD team members) must be made aware of the overall objective of the SMC. This overall objective should also be formulated by the research team. It could be something such as: "To create an environment where people are encouraged to share more about themselves and to learn about their colleagues."

7. Other Phases of the AR Project

Implementation is the third phase of the AR project. Although implementation of the SMC is relatively simple, acceptance might be more difficult to achieve. It might be a good idea to identify people in the group during the diagnosis phase who understand the motivation behind the SMC and ask them to actively use it. A driver for the SMC in the group is required. This should be someone that has good social skills and an outgoing personality. Such a person might create polls on the outcome of the weekend's big sporting matches. General questions such as "What is your favorite Friday night comfort food?" posted on a Friday afternoon would already have an impact.

Evaluation of success of the intervention is the fourth AR phase. It might be difficult to evaluate the success of the SMC in the short term. User activity can be used as a short-term success metric. If the SMC is used by only a small number of people, then the non-users should be the focus of the diagnosis phase of the next AR iteration. Interpretative interviews could be used to investigate changes in the ISD team's communication as a result of better social interaction of the team members and the role of the SMC regarding this.

The fifth phase of an AR project is to specify learning. Action research differs from consultation in that the process is guided by theory. Learning and, therefore, a scientific contribution can be made on different levels. The first level could be viewed as the area of application: the multicultural communication of the ISD team members. Results of the study would indicate whether the SMC improves the team's communication. On the methodology level, the study could contribute the guidelines for use of SMCs in the workplace. On a philosophical or theoretical level, this study could give insight into the applicability of mentioned theories of culture in the workplace.

8. Challenges of the Proposed Intervention

The initial case study reported in Section 2 of this chapter also investigated nonverbal communication. Thirteen participants, 5 from organization A, 5 from organization B and 3 from organization C, said that nonverbal communication is cultural. One participant argued that nonverbal communication is not cultural, and one participant did not observe nonverbal communication. According to participants, nonverbal communication expresses cultural behavior through posture, speech acts, eye movement, smiling, sitting, hand movements and head movement.

Social media communities are a form of verbal communication and will not directly improve the interpretation of nonverbal communication by people of different cultures. However, if people are motivated to socialize, their appreciation of nonverbal communication should also increase.

9. Conclusions

In South Africa, we are still more comfortable working and socializing with people of our own culture, but since we are a multicultural society, this needs changing. This chapter proposed an action research project that encourages ISD members to interact with one another informally by means of a social media community.

Action research is based on participation by the involved and affected people in the problem environment. The success of the proposed SMC is directly dependent on the ownership of the SMC in the minds of the involved people. They need to support the purpose of the SMC and understand the need for guidelines for using it.

The proposed research can make a contribution in the specific ISD team's communication, it can enhance scholarly understanding of the use of SMCs in the workplace and it can enhance scholarly understanding of the theories of multicultural communication.

10. Acknowledgement

The authors want to thank the National Research Foundation (NRF) of the RSA for funding this project and state that this work is the opinion of the authors and not of the NRF and that they are not liable in regard thereto.

11. References

Avison, D., & Fitzgerald, G. (2006). *Information system development: Methodologies, techniques and tools* (4th ed.). New York, NY: McGraw-Hill.

Baskerville, R. L. (1999). Investigating information systems with action research. *Communications of the AIS, 2*(3), Article 4.

Beamer, L., & Varner, I. (2008). *Intercultural communication in the global workplace* (4th ed.). New York: McGraw-Hill.

DiMicco, J. M., & Millen, D. R. (2007). Identity management: Multiple presentations of self in Facebook. In *Proceedings of the 2007 International ACM Conference on Supporting Group Work* (pp. 383–386). New York, NY: ACM.

Gibson, R. (2002). *Intercultural business communication.* New York, NY: Oxford University Press.

Grosberg, A., Struwig, J., & Pillay, U. (2006). Multicultural national identity and pride. In U. Pillay, B. Roberts, & S. Rule (Eds.), *South African social attitudes: Changing times, diverse voices* (pp. 54–76). Cape Town, RSA: HSRC Press.

Hofstede, G., & Hofstede, G.J. (2005). *Cultures and organizations: Software of the mind* (2nd ed.). New York, NY: McGraw-Hill.

Jandt, F. E. (2004). *Intercultural Communication: Identities in a global world* (4th ed.). London, UK: Sage Publications.

Lowe, G. (1995). *Communication science.* Pretoria, RSA: Kagiso Publishers.

Lui, S., Volčič, Z., & Gallois, C. (2011). *Introducing intercultural communication: Global cultures and contexts.* London, UK: Sage Publications.

Martin, J. N., & Nakayama, T.K. (2011). *Intercultural communication in contexts* (4th ed). Boston, MA: McGraw-Hill.

Oetzel, J. G. (2005). Effective intercultural workgroup communication theory. In W.B. Gudykunst (Ed.), *Theorizing about intercultural communication* (pp. 351–372). Thousand Oaks, CA: Sage Publications.

Pfeffer, N. (1998). Theories in healthcare and research: Theories of race, ethnicity and culture. *BMJ, 317*, 1381–1384.

Pinkett, R. D. (2000). *Constructionist learning in communities.* Unpublished doctoral dissertation, Massachusetts Institute of Technology, Cambridge, MA, USA.

Schwalbe, K. (2011). *Information technology project management* (6th ed.). Boston, MA: Cengage Learning.

10

USING SOCIAL MEDIA TO IMPROVE THE WORK-INTEGRATED LEARNING EXPERIENCE OF ICT STUDENTS

A Critical Systems Approach

Roelien Goede & Anneke Harmse

NORTH-WEST UNIVERSITY, SOUTH AFRICA AND VAAL UNIVERSITY OF TECHNOLOGY, SOUTH AFRICA

1. Introduction

Higher education programmes in information and communication technology (ICT) today are developed according to a relatively predictable standard. Organisations such as the ACM (Association of Computing Machinery, 2013) promote specific building blocks for ICT programmes. As a result, students obtain the necessary foundational knowledge of subject areas such as programming, networking, systems analysis, and database systems, but sometimes lack the practical experience to apply their knowledge in the organizational environment.

Most universities of technology (UoT) in South Africa expect ICT students to undergo a period of work-integrated learning in the ICT industry. Work-integrated learning (WIL), sometimes called experiential learning or cooperative education, facilitates the integration of theoretical and practical learning activities which are related to workplaces (Dimenäs, 2010). WIL is an umbrella term to describe curricular planning and assessment practices that integrate formal learning and industry concerns, within a purposefully designed curriculum (Council on Higher Education, 2011). Students are expected to work, preferably as paid employees, in an organization in the ICT industry. Their activities are monitored by staff members of the university by means of reporting and visits.

The aim of this chapter is to propose a research project to improve the effectiveness of WIL of ICT students from a critical systems perspective. When improvement or positive intervention is central in a research project, the critical social theory research (CSTR) paradigm provides a suitable framework for the project [refer to Myers & Klein (2011) for a description of CSTR]. Action research (AR) is a research method that provides structure to a CSTR project [refer to Baskerville (1999) for a description of AR]. The AR cycle begins with a diagnosis of the problem before improvement is planned, implemented and evaluated.

In terms of this chapter, diagnosis implies understanding of the quality of these students' experience, while improvement implies the proposal of a methodology for improving the situation. Implementation lies beyond the scope of this chapter.

The chapter is divided into two main sections. The first section aims to demonstrate an understanding of the quality of these students' experience. It uses two theoretical models, namely Maslow's hierarchy of needs and Dooyeweerd's aspectual analysis, to achieve a holistic understanding of the problem environment. The second section proposes intervention to improve the situation of these students from a critical systems perspective. Social media applications are proposed as channels of communication for mentoring students.

The chapter concludes with a focus on three methodological aspects: the applicability of chosen theoretical models for understanding the problem, the role of social media as a communication channel in this environment and problems regarding rigorous data analysis of social media.

2. Understanding Work-integrated Learning of ICT Students

The first section of this chapter serves as diagnosis of the AR project. It reports on a study done to improve understanding of the quality of these students' experience. It begins with a description of the study's purpose, describes the methodology used and concludes with findings on understanding the quality of the WIL students' experience.

2.1. Aim of the Diagnosis

This diagnostic study aims to gain a holistic understanding of the quality of experience of the students in industry from a CSTR perspective. Harvey (1990) promotes deconstruction and reconstruction of a problem situation as CSTR methodology. The aim of deconstruction is to identify oppressive structures before attempting a reconstruction of the environment without oppression. The use of constructs of scholars in the critical philosophical tradition is promoted by Myers & Klein (2011) for CSTR studies. This diagnostic study can be viewed as a deconstruction of the situation based on the work of Maslow (1943) and Dooyeweerd (1969), respectively.

2.2. Methodology

As diagnosis attempts to achieve an overall understanding of the environment, unstructured interpretative interviews were conducted with staff members of a UoT who have experience working with WIL students. In their capacity as mentors, these staff members have interviewed many WIL students. Two staff members familiar with the work of Maslow & Dooyeweerd were then asked to reflect on their experience with WIL students in terms of these two theories. Only an abbreviated summary is given here.

2.3. Understanding from a Maslow's Hierarchy of Needs Perspective

In 1943, Abraham Maslow developed a theory on satisfaction of different needs in individuals. His theory divided needs into five levels: biological, safeties, belongingness, esteem needs and self-actualization. The basic principle of the hierarchy is that individuals will not be motivated to fulfill any higher-level needs until lower-level needs have been satisfied (Brewer & Dittman, 2010).

The lowest level of individual need is biological needs. Students who enroll for ICT WIL are exposed to the world of work but have inadequate resources. Students receive a small salary while in training which makes it difficult for them to find accommodation, pay for travel expenses and buy appropriate clothing and even food. These financial constraints cause the lowest level of needs not to be met.

Safety needs follow biological needs. Very few students who are in training are employed in permanent positions. These students are unsure of future employment possibilities during their final months of training.

Belongingness, love and social needs arise as soon as humans start to feel safe. When students enter industry, they leave behind their secure environment. Most students feel that being welcomed and made part of the team are positive.

Esteem needs relate to self-esteem and self-respect, as well as respect for others. Students experience a proud feeling as they master assignments and receive responsibilities. As their WIL training continues, most students are allowed to visit users, or lead interviews, fostering in them a sense of independence and growth of their self-esteem.

Self-actualization needs focus on the realization of the individual's full potential. Students report satisfaction and progress in terms of realizing their full potential in their preferred niche area.

2.4. Understanding from a Dooyeweerd's Suite of Aspects Perspective

Herman Dooyeweerd was a Dutch philosopher (1894–1977) who focused on the meaning of different aspects of reality. His 15 aspects that can be used as a checklist to understand various aspects of reality (Basden, 2008) are used here to understand the quality of these students' experience.

- Quantitative aspect (representing quantity): The total numbers regarding students doing WIL were discussed.
- Spatial aspect (representing size): The different locations and living environments of students were discussed.
- Kinematic aspects (representing movement): Within WIL environments, students are assigned to one specific project with no movement between projects, causing little exposure to other fields of training. Basden (2008) explains that change is good and exposing students to various projects can be beneficial.
- Physical aspect: It deals with energy and mass. This aspect does not indicate either benefit or detriment within ICT WIL.

- Biotic aspect (representing life functions): The discussion was similar to that of the biological phase of Maslow.
- Sensitive aspect: Basden (2008) describes the kernel of the sensitive aspect as "feeling and responding" which focuses on a positive interactive engagement with the world. Students are satisfied in their work environment in terms of their integration in the organization.
- Analytical aspect's kernel meaning is described as conceptualizing, clarifying, categorizing and cogitating. An important aspect of a skilled ICT professional is to be an analytical thinker.
- Formative aspect (representing history, culture and technology): Students experience positive integration into companies. This causes them to voice not only their understanding of situations but also to make suggestions. Innovation and achievement are then motivated.
- Lingual aspect (representing communication): Lingual aspects are the way students are able to express themselves. A concern was raised by industry regarding communication skills of ICT students.
- Social aspect (representing relationship and community): These include social interaction, relationships and institutions. The discussion was similar to that of the belongingness need in Maslow's theory.
- Economic aspects are influenced by frugal and skilled use of limited resources. All the students experience financial problems as discussed earlier.
- Aesthetic aspect (representing interest and fun): Students experience WIL as very positive toward their personal well-being, as well as their professional development. They become excited and energized toward life and future careers.
- Juridical aspects: Rights and responsibilities are investigated. Some students work without any compensation or for just a small salary.
- Ethical aspects are recognized by self-giving, love, generosity and care. Student attitude is a stated concern by industry. Complaints vary regarding communication skills, from professionalism to poor self-management.
- The pistic aspect (representing faith, commitment and vision): ICT WIL students mature substantially within their period of training. They are committed, are motivated and believe in themselves, which also influences their vision toward their future careers.

3. Key Findings

The lowest level of Maslow's hierarchy could not be met for ICT WIL students. This corresponds with Dooyeweerd's physical, biotic and economic aspects. This opposes a major supposition of Maslow's philosophy that higher-level needs can only be addressed when lower levels are fulfilled. The students do feel safe in their workplaces, they do belong and they do believe in themselves resulting in self-actualization. Thinking about students in terms of the first aspects of Dooyeweerd led to a better understanding of the magnitude of the problems. While reflecting in terms of the aspects, many issues such as the reaction of industry entered the discussion which was not reflected upon during the discussion in terms of Maslow's theory of needs. The research team felt that the work of Dooyeweerd guided them toward a broader understanding of the life world of these students as part of the ICT industry than analysis according to the work of Maslow.

4. Proposed Intervention

From diagnosis according to Dooyeweerd's aspects, it was concluded that students will benefit from more holistic guidance and mentoring. They struggle financially and do not always make the best choices in this regard. They sign contracts of which they do not always understand the practical implications.

Action research differs from consultation in that it employs theory to guide intervention (Baskerville, 1999). Critical systems thinking (CST) and specifically critical systems heuristics (CSH) developed by Ulrich (1983) aims to give the affected parties in an oppressing situation a voice, to emancipate them by forcing the experts to reflect on the affected parties. Ulrich (1983, 257) writes: "The essential point is that the affected must be given the chance of emancipating themselves from being treated merely as means for the purpose of others." Although the WIL environment of the students is not only for the purpose of others, they do require some form of emancipation. Ulrich (1983) proposes 12 boundary questions to guide the planning of an improved situation. It is proposed here that mentors from the university, alumni, current students and industry representatives use these boundary questions to improve the situation of these students. Some of the 12 boundary questions investigate the environment of the system. The environmental factors are those factors that influence the system, but over which the system does not have control (Ulrich, 1983). Cost of living is such a factor. Remuneration of students may also be regarded as outside the control of the university at least in the near future.

5. Intended Use of Social Media from a Critical Systems Perspective

From Ulrich's quote above, it is clear that the student also has a role of self-emancipation. It is believed that better collaboration between the involved parties will improve the quality of life of the individual student. This collaboration also serves as self-reflection for the students, which is a key aspect of CST. Ulrich (1983) criticises the value society places on rational thought. He argues that the affected is sometimes ignored because of the shortcomings of their arguments in terms of requirements of rational speech. Ulrich promotes the Kantian idea of polemical reasoning where the speaker is able to voice opinions without being expected to provide rational proof of all claims. It becomes then the responsibility of the expert to consider the claims rationally.

The nature of communication within social media attracted the research team to use it as a channel to motivate students to voice their polemic claims. When we write reports, we are so careful not to write any of our perceptions without rational consideration. But when we post a social media update, we are more inclined to convey our true experiences. It is therefore proposed that the planned intervention of this AR project constitutes the development of a social media community for these students and their mentors. Students must be encouraged to post regularly on their pages. The posts should concern their whole being, everything that concerns their quality of life.

Different groups should be set up in order to manage the audience of specific posts. Students should be able to select the audience of their posts from a list that may include only their mentor at the university, all the students, their mentor at their workplace, etc.

The reaction to the posts by the mentors at the university will determine the success of the project. Reaction should be sensitive and aimed at increased understanding of the experience of the individual students.

6. Benefits from the Social Media Community

One of Ulrich's 12 boundary questions focuses on the guarantors of intervention. It guides reflection on how the proposed intervention could relieve the oppression. In this case, one cannot provide a probabilistic guarantee, but one can speculate on the benefits of the intervention. These include the following:

- Mentors from the university may be able to guide students on important nonwork-related decisions.
- Students may be able to learn from one another; they will get to know the specific circumstances of others and might be able to share resources.
- Trends in posts may guide the mentors from the university to make policy or procedural changes to the formal WIL requirements.
- Industry mentors may see opportunities for specific intervention to address shortcomings in the soft skills of the students.

7. Difficulties with the Approach

It can be very unsatisfactory when you request the guidance of someone you trust on a sensitive matter and the request goes unacknowledged. A very important post of a student might easily get lost in a sea of status updates. A mentor can easily be overwhelmed by the volume of information under their consideration. The mentor should have some kind of method to analyse the posts of the students. From our experience in interpretive data analysis using coding strategies, we suggest that posts should be divided into categories. Students and mentors can set up the categories jointly, and each post could start with a category code. Since the aspects of Dooyeweerd assisted the understanding of the situation, they might even guide the selection of categories, perhaps categories such as "work-related: social" for posts on social interaction in the work environment.

The students must be at ease with the category labels. Labels may be used in pairs and may include indication of reaction required. For example, "nonwork-related: reaction valued" could be used by a student who is contemplating the purchase of a car.

As indicated previously, a mind-set change of mentors is required and the number of students per mentor should be managed. It is not realistic to expect mentors to solve all the problems of students, but they can offer advice from their own experience or guide the students to other advisory sources.

8. Evaluation of Success

As part of the proposal, one has to determine how the success of the intervention can be measured. Action research is a cyclic approach where evaluation is followed by learning specification in order to guide further intervention for further improvement. The aim of evaluation of the intervention should be viewed as opportunity to further improvement. It is proposed that evaluation takes on the form of semi-structured interviews with students and mentors (from both industry and university). The posts can also be evaluated in terms of constructive reaction and guidance to students.

9. Conclusions

This chapter proposes a CSTR strategy to use social media to improve the WIL experience of ICT students. The aim of CSTR intervention is emancipation often guided by theory. This chapter demonstrated how Dooyeweerd's aspects may yield a more holistic understanding of a problem situation than Maslow's hierarchy of needs.

The foundation of the chosen intervention strategy is the promotion of the Kantian idea of polemical reasoning by Werner Ulrich (1983). We argued that the requirement of rational reasoning might deny mentors opportunity to give much needed advice on matters influencing quality of life since they might not be aware of problems faced by an individual student.

Social communities will become more important in the future, and while we require approaches to handle the large amount of data generated, the categorisation of posts will likely ease the burden of those responsible for responding to them.

Future work in this study can be described as appropriate intervention in reaction to continuous iterations of the AR process to improve the social media community.

10. Acknowledgement

The authors want to thank the National Research Foundation (NRF) of the RSA for funding this project and state that this work is the opinion of the authors and not of the NRF and that they are not liable in regard thereto.

11. References

Association for Computing Machinery. (2013). *Curricula recommendations*. ACM. org. Retrieved October 7, 2013, from http://www.acm.org/education/curricula-recommendations

Basden, A. (2008). *Philosophical frameworks for understanding information systems*. New York, NY: IGI Publishing.

Baskerville, R. L. (1999). Investigating information systems with action research. *Communications of the AIS, 2*(3), Article 4.

Brewer, J. L., & Dittman, K. C. (2010). *Methods of IT project management*. Upper Saddle River, NJ: Pearson.

Council on Higher Education. (2011). Work-integrated learning: Good practice guide. *HE Monitor, (12)* Pretoria, RSA: Council on Higher Education.

Dooyeweerd, H. (1969). *A new critique of theoretical thought* (2nd vol.) (Freeman, D. H., & Young, W.S. transl.) Philadelphia, PA: The Presbyterian and Reformed Publishing Company.

Dimenäs, J. (2010). Beyond dichotomization: A different way of understanding work integrated learning. *Journal of Cooperative Education & Internships*, 43–49.

Harvey, L. (1990). *Critical social research*. London, UK: Unwin Hyman.

Maslow, A. H. (1943). A theory of human motivation. *Psychological Review, 50*(4), 370–396.

Myers, M. D., & Klein, H. K. (2011). A set of principles for conducting critical research in information systems. *MIS Quarterly, 35*(1), 17–36.

Ulrich, W. (1983). *Critical heuristics of social planning*. Chichester, UK: Wiley.

SECTION IV

Social Media Technologies in Higher Education

11

HIGHER EDUCATION

The Incorporation of Web 2.0

Paula Miranda (1), Pedro Isaías (2), & Sara Pífano (3)

(1) ESCOLA SUPERIOR DE TECNOLOGIA DE SETÚBAL, IPS, PORTUGAL, (2) UNIVERSIDADE ABERTA, PORTUGAL AND ADVANCE RESEARCH CENTER - ISEG - TECHNICAL UNIVERSITY OF LISBON, PORTUGAL, AND (3) ISRLAB - INFORMATION SOCIETY RESEARCH LABORATORY, PORTUGAL

1. Introduction

As Web 2.0 asserts its influence in the daily lives of students, teachers and educators in general are exploring the possibility of its application in formal education. Educators have both a fascination with the reasons why it has become so popular and a curiosity about the education potential it offers. Strawbridge (2010) argues that the challenges associated with Web 2.0, similar to the issues raised by other types of technology used in an educational context, can be surmounted and those who pioneer its use will demonstrate how. The more researchers and practitioners document their findings, the easier it will be for educators to know how to best implement Web 2.0 in educational settings. This will maximise their chances of success and will help substantiate Web 2.0's role in education. This chapter underlines the importance of empirical research in assessing Web 2.0's didactic value. Additionally, it argues that the deployment of the social Web in education must be adapted to the specificities of each setting.

2. Pros and Cons of Higher Education 2.0

It is important to understand the contribution made by social technologies at all levels of students' development, on the institutions and on other contexts not traditionally recognized as educational.

2.1. Research Aims and Methodology

The central part that education plays in society conduces educators to constantly search for inventive pedagogical approaches to enhance teaching–learning practices. This search has been progressively giving emphasis to social technology

(Wheeler, 2009). The decision of adopting Web 2.0 resources should derive from an informed view of its rewards and limitations. There is a need to rethink educational structures in light of new employability demands and the need for institutional sustainability. This chapter intends to explore the role that Web 2.0 has been playing in higher education, by examining both its potential and its challenges. Moreover, it advocates the necessity of considering the peculiarities of each educational context and the vital role of empirical research. For this purpose, it provides a brief review of relevant literature and presents two case studies, which portray both a successful and an unproductive scenario of Web 2.0 application.

2.2. Key Findings

The perceived benefits of implementing Web 2.0 applications in the higher education arena are leading a rising number of lecturers to approve their development in educational settings. Web 2.0 allows interdepartmental and interinstitutional cooperation involving both students and teachers in information exchange practices and the possibility of producing scholarly content (Conole & Alevizou, 2010; Johnson et al., 2011). The Web 2.0 applications that are most commonly used by the higher education community include blogs, wikis, media sharing, social networks and social bookmarking (Grosseck, 2009).

The knowledge of social technologies, obtained via the students' private and social usage, facilitates their use in education. If they understand how they work it will be probably easier to accept and master them in an academic context. Nonetheless their will to do so is a matter of debate in the research community (Kennedy et al., 2006). The peculiarities of social technologies lead students to a path of community building and networking. They potentiate the feeling of belonging to a group or a network with similar interests (Melville, 2009).

A significant source of tension deriving from Web 2.0's facilitation in terms of student authoring lies in the complexity of assuring the assessment of the content produced by the students. Some researchers consider this challenge a considerable impediment for the progress of the deployment of Web 2.0 in higher education settings (Gray, Thompson, Sheard, Clerehan, & Hamilton, 2010). At the same time, this opportunity can lead to the increase of shallow content. The real experts can be outspoken, because anyone can voice their wisdom and be seen as a specialist (Conole & Alevizou, 2010). Content itself can pose a challenge, not only for reasons connected with quality and substance, but also due to copyright, security and trustworthiness issues (Strawbridge, 2010). Culturally and structurally speaking, there are noteworthy differences between the values of Web 2.0 and the precepts that guide higher education institutions. Web 2.0 is democratic, it focuses on a bottom-up perspective and it is socially motivated. Higher education is structured hierarchically from the top down; the course content is scrupulously selected for its quality (whereas Web 2.0 is not concerned with editorial aspects) and higher education is academically oriented, not socially focused (Weller & Dalziel, 2007).

As with any technology, Web 2.0's success in the educational arena depends substantially on how its features are employed and on how it will be introduced in the conventional routines of education. As one of higher education's favorite tools, blogs have been widely described and documented as didactic assets. The empirical research that is presented below illustrates the need to avoid a depiction of Web 2.0 as a valuable educational resource per se.

Kang, Bonk, & Kim (2011) conducted a study in two graduate education classes, during a semester in a Korean university. The students were asked to participate in a learning process that was based on blogging. The data collected from the case study conducted by the authors reflect a multiplicity of manners in which blogs can be used. The two classes of students not only contributed with their own posts and viewpoints on their learning path but were also active reviewers of their peers' work, which provided a sense of community among them. "It is the combination of reflection, interaction, and personal expression which makes blogs extremely exciting and unique as a learning tool" (Kang et al., 2011). The positive outcomes of their experience mean that the use of blogging is effective under the specific conditions that the authors created, which is not the same as arguing the value of blogging in all educational circumstances.

Xie, Ke, & Sharma (2008), for example, reported a different result from their research. These authors intended to assess if students could develop their reflective thinking and thus improve their learning proficiency, by using blogging combined with feedback from their colleagues. Hence, some students were directed to blog in an isolated manner, with no feedback, and the others were to receive and provide feedback. While all the students showed, over time, an improvement in their reflective thinking competencies and consequently received higher grades, those not involved in the process of giving and receiving feedback had a notably superior and consistent degree of reflection skills throughout the study. The authors highlighted some possible reasons for this outcome: (1) being a self-reflective act, journaling might have led students to become too aware of the examining eyes of their peers and instead of writing what they really felt and thought, they tended to be more reserved and circumvented subjects that could have raised less positive feedback and (2) the comments from other students were very limited in terms of constructive content and were basically restricted to feedback of a more social nature, for example, "good job" or "I agree" (Xie et al., 2008).

3. Future Research

The analysis of Web 2.0 pros and cons in terms of its application in higher education settings is fundamental, as it provides the necessary knowledge to assist teachers and students to become more familiar with this type of technology. Nonetheless, this analysis is solely the stepping stone of a long process of implementation. The actual impact of Web 2.0 in higher education can only be defined by empirical evidence of its employment. Additionally, for that evidence to become comprehensible and valuable, it is paramount to create a methodology that assists its assessment. Further research should place a meticulous emphasis on the development of measurement methods that evaluate just how effective these technologies are when applied in practice. Future research will inevitably have to encourage people on the front lines of implementation to keep detailed records of their experiments with Web 2.0 in order to substantiate its value.

This chapter contributes to the evolution of the debate of Web 2.0's implementation in higher education. Since the higher education sector has to compete with new ways of delivering knowledge and the traditional classroom setting is progressively being questioned by Web-based educational environments, it becomes paramount to continue harnessing the value of social technology. In order to do so, this debate has to move forward not solely in terms of the questions it tries to answer, but also in terms of the questions it poses. Future research should gravitate around the core challenges of Web 2.0 and strategies to address them. The more researchers and practitioners understand Web 2.0's impact, the more they will be capable of developing the necessary conditions for its successful deployment.

The relation that has arisen between higher education and Web 2.0 is the subject of many research studies, but there is still a lack of literature focused on measurement and empirical experience. An examination of Web 2.0's repercussions in higher education will highlight institutions' responsibility to develop infrastructures that will harbour social technologies in an academic context. The creation of more adequate conditions for Web 2.0's implementation deserves the attention of prospective research ventures.

According to Bennett et al. (2012), "the emergence of Web 2.0 technologies has provided new opportunities for creating and sharing content and interacting with others." The scenarios that have emerged from the social Web are being harnessed by several arenas of society, namely business, health, politics and education. Some Web 2.0 tools have the potential to be used as efficient educational instruments (Strawbridge, 2010). Hence, the deliberation of Web 2.0's value is transversal to several areas of society. Progress in one sector usually means progress in the remaining sectors. Overall, numerous arenas in society can profit from an open discussion and a growing body of empirical research. Implementation, measurement and assessment are key elements in the deployment of social technology in educational environments.

Young generations have now, at least in most cases, easy access to computer technology. Over the years this technology has been making its way into higher education. The growing importance and evolution of the Internet and its applications have allowed a user-friendly access to information. During what is called the Web 1.0 period, users were sheer spectators: the information that was available was searchable but not editable by regular users. The second stage of the Web, Web 2.0, represented a technological shift that granted users the power to manipulate content. Users became producers and distributors of information. Access to Web 2.0 tools is in most cases assumed to not be a problem, but when discussing the incorporation of these tools in higher education it becomes necessary to remember that the fear of a digital divide is pertinent and timely. It cannot be assumed that all students have equal access to them, because that is not reality (Selwyn, 2011). The minimisation of the digital divide is of interest to educators, but also to leaders in the business sector and the economy. A more digitally prepared population produces engaged citizens. When technology is viewed as a solution to some of education's pressing issues, the spotlight is equally focused on the intensification of technology access and technological skill, which benefits the entire society.

Web 2.0 has earned its recognition at a European institutional level, and its knowledge and usage have become important skills in the 21st century. Regardless of this fact, higher education entities have not yet significantly incorporated Web 2.0 in their curricula (Buchem & Hamelmann, 2011; Crook et al., 2008). Future trends in this area will include the approximation of social technology to academic institutions and vice versa. Education is one of the primordial assets of any society, holding the important mission of organising superior academic programmes and of propagating knowledge. Information societies are breeding a new generation of students, with increasing proficiency in IT and skills born from "the rapid and huge expansion of information accessible through the web coupled with tools that can be used to repurpose and create new knowledge on-line [which] have created a very different information and a communication environment" (Armstrong & Franklin, 2008).

The volatile nature of Web 2.0 services constitutes an important challenge for teachers: what they know and teach about a platform may become outdated sooner than they expect and the pedagogical benefits that were originally clear become blurry or even nonexistent. Web 2.0 evolves faster than the universities' IT departments can introduce new technology. Their policy of caution hinders the adoption of newly developed technology (Strawbridge, 2010). A more selective array of Web 2.0 tools is necessary. Prospective Web 2.0 advocates are to embrace innovation in a more balanced manner. As pure enthusiasm is converted into reliable and consistent data, the number of Web 2.0 tools that are deemed as central becomes smaller and more pertinent. Another common problem deriving from the growing panoply of social technologies is the abusive employment of Web 2.0 which can transform the technology into a distraction, rather than an educational aid, thus reducing the quality of the learning process (Walker, 2008). A better knowledge of applications, tools and features will minimise this issue in the future.

The social Web conduces to a great increase in and creation of knowledge. Besides contributing directly to easier access to data, it also facilitates research and provides a growing number of features for the manipulation of information. Users' contributions increase the flow of knowledge that is available (Conole & Alevizou, 2010). Regardless of the debate around the validity and quality of user-generated content, the fact that users have the power to contribute their own content not only stimulates creativity, but it also allows them to contest the power of mainstream information (Wheeler, 2009).This phenomenon has been increasing and will likely to continue to grow as more people participate in social websites.

A significant present and prospective concern is the transference, to a Web-based setting, of the problems that trouble the traditional educational context, such as bullying. Cyberbullying, for instance, appears as a form of intimidation that can exerted over other users in many ways. Some students find that social networks are an extension of the pressures that they already feel outside the Internet. This and other challenges of an open social Internet with almost no editorial triage will certainly remain as central sources of disquiet for students and educators.

As Isaías, Miranda, & Pífano (2009) argued in their framework of Web 2.0's critical success factors, it is necessary to gather a series of conditions in order to successfully develop, implement and maintain a Web 2.0 platform. Given Web 2.0's social, interactive and collaborative nature, it is paramount to create proper conditions for the participation of users, to capture as many users as possible into the application, to enrich the application with pertinent content and to ensure that the application is user-friendly (Isaías et al., 2009). Besides these general considerations, for Web 2.0 to be effective in an educational setting, apprehension with and preparation for its implementation need to be adjusted to each educational setting and learning environment. The evolution of research will prospectively illustrate and validate the argument that each learning scenario has its own particularities and that cookie-cutter solutions should not be implemented. Instead, it is the teaching professional's responsibility to assess their students' needs and characteristics and each course's specific traits and demands.

4. Conclusions

Implementing Web 2.0 in higher education requires essential changes when it comes to learning and teaching. Both processes must adjust to the features of this social technology as it promises to introduce innovative practices inside higher education (Buchem & Hamelmann, 2011). The broadly announced impact that Web 2.0 tools have and will have in the future is part of the reason why it is so important to prepare institutions for their execution. The more students and staff are using them, the more they have a continuous presence, reminding all higher education entities that their incorporation in academic curricula may be a valuable resource.

5. Acnowledgement

This work was financed by National Funds through FCT—Fundação para a Ciência e a Tecnologia within the project Pest-OE/EGE/UI4027/2011.

6. References

Armstrong, J., & Franklin, T. (2008). *A review of current and developing international practice in the use of social networking (Web 2.0) in higher education.* Other. Franklin Consulting.

Bennett, S., Bishop, A., Dalgarno, B., Kennedy, G., & Waycott, J. (2012). Implementing Web 2.0 technologies in higher education: A case study. *Computers & Education, 59*(2), 534.

Buchem, I., & Hamelmann, H. (2011). Developing 21st century skills: Web 2.0 in higher education—A case study. *Elearning Papers*, (24).

Conole, G., & Alevizou, P. (2010). *A Literature Review of the Use of Web 2.0 Tools in Higher Education.* A report commissioned by the Higher Education Academy.

Crook, C., Cummings, J., Fisher, T., Graber, R., Harrison, C., Lewin, C., ... Sharples, M. (2008). *Web 2.0 Technologies for Learning: The Current Landscape—Opportunities, Challenges and Tensions.*

Gray, K., Thompson, C., Sheard, J., Clerehan, R., & Hamilton, M. (2010). Students as Web 2.0 authors: Implications for assessment design and conduct. *Australasian Journal of Educational Technology, 26*(1), 105–122.

Grosseck, G. (2009). To use or not to use Web 2.0 in higher education? *Procedia - Social and Behavioral Sciences, 1*(1), 478–482. doi: 10.1016/j.sbspro.2009.01.087.

Isaías, P., Miranda, P., & Pífano, S. (2009). *Critical success factors for Web 2.0–A reference framework online communities and social computing* (pp. 354–363). Springer.

Johnson, L., Smith, R., Willis, H., Levine, A., & Haywood, K. (2011). *The 2011 Horizon Report.* Austin, TX: The New Media Consortium. Retrieved October 2, 2012, from http://net.educause.edu/ir/library/pdf/hr2011.pdf

Kang, I., Bonk, C. J., & Kim, M. (2011). A case study of blog-based learning in Korea: Technology becomes pedagogy. *The Internet and Higher Education, 14*(4), 227–235. doi: 10.1016/j.iheduc.2011.05.002.

Kennedy, G., Krause, K., Judd, T., Churchward, A., & Gray, K. (2006). First year students' experiences with technology: Are they really digital natives? Melbourne, Australia: University of Melbourne. Retrieved October 5, 2012, from http://www.bmu.unimelb.edu.au/research/munatives/natives_report2006.rf

Selwyn, N. (2011). Social media in higher education, in *The Europe World of Learning*–62nd edition, London, Routledge. Retrieved October 5, 2013, from http://www.education-arena.com/pdf/sample/sample-essay-selwyn.pdf

Strawbridge, F. (2010). *Is there a case for Web 2.0 in higher education? Do the benefits outweigh the risks?* Assignment for introduction to digital environments for learning. The University of Edinburgh. Retrieved from http://www.education.ed.ac.uk/e-learning/gallery/strawbridge_web_2.pdf

Walker, D. (2008). How many penguins does it take to sink an iceberg–the challenges and opportunities of web 2.0 in education. Web 2.0 in Education (UK). Retrieved October 12, 2012, from http://web2educationuk.wetpaint.com/page/Web+2.0+Research+Project

Weller, M. J., & Dalziel, J. (2007). On-line teaching: Suggestions for instructors. In L. Cameron & J. Dalziel (Eds.), *Proceedings of the 2nd International LAMS Conference 2007: Practical Benefits of Learning Design* (pp 76–82). 26th November 2007, Sydney: LAMS Foundation. Retrieved October 10, 2013 from http://lamsfoundation.org/lams2007sydney/papers.htm

Wheeler, S. (2009). Learning space mashups: Combining Web 2.0 tools to create collaborative and reflective learning spaces. *Future Internet, 1*(1), 3–13. doi: 10.3390/fi1010003.

Xie, Y., Ke, F., & Sharma, P. (2008). The effect of peer feedback for blogging on college students' reflective learning processes. *The Internet and Higher Education, 11*(1), 18–25. doi: 10.1016/j.iheduc.2007.11.001.

12

FACTORS THAT INFLUENCE ACCEPTANCE OF SOCIAL WEB TECHNOLOGIES FOR LEARNING

Razep Echeng (1), Abel Usoro (2), & Grzegorz Majewski (3)

(1) UNIVERSITY OF THE WEST OF SCOTLAND, UNITED KINGDOM, (2) UNIVERSITY OF THE WEST OF SCOTLAND, UNITED KINGDOM, AND (3) FACULTY OF INFORMATION STUDIES, NOVO MESTO, SLOVENI

1. Acceptance of Technologies

Acceptance of technology has long been a challenging issue in information systems research (Davies, 1989; Swanson, 1994) and rightly so because understanding the reason why people accept or reject technology can be a very essential guide for investors, manufacturers and institutions and for managerial intervention to reduce lack of use.

Over the years, information system researchers have suggested models from social psychology as a good theoretical foundation to predict human behaviour (Christie, 1982 in Swanson, 1994; Swanson, 1994). Thus, one of the first theories on technology acceptance, called the "theory of reasoned action" (Ajzen & Fishbein, 1980), is based on social psychology. This theory, which has been widely used by various researchers, posits that the three major factors that affect behaviour are belief, attitude and social norms. Other theories that have gained popularity in information systems research and are seen as models that contain constructs that could predict technology acceptance are the unified theory of acceptance and use of technology (UTAUT) (Venkatesh, Morris, Davis, & Davis, 2003), the technology acceptance model (TAM) (Davis & Warshaw, 1989) and TAM2 (Davis & Warshaw, 1989). However, researchers have at the same time criticised these models. One major criticism is their inability to exhibit validity across cultures (Straub, Keil, & Brenner, 1997; Teo, Su Luan, & Sing, 2008). These criticisms call for researching on their core constructs to be sustained in a framework that will be used to predict acceptance and use of technologies for learning.

2. Social Media Technologies in Learning in Higher Education

The use of Web 2.0 technologies for learning is gradually gaining popularity in educational sectors. Web 2.0 has generally been acknowledged in literature as a potentially effective means of engaging students in their learning. At the same time, there are issues with effective utilization of these tools. These issues include how to integrate them with existing systems and the full acceptance of new technologies in learning.

Web 2.0 is an interface that allows the Internet user to interact with the content of Web pages and with any person online. Examples of Web 2.0 tools are blogs, wikis, podcasts, Flicker and Twitter. There is also a need to enhance the use of Web-based learning to produce more effective learning and cognition with social networks for a better learning experience.

The impact of social computing tools in teaching and learning is currently being investigated by a lot of researchers because the frequent use of these tools in an educational context is known to enhance effective learning (Franklin & Van Harmelen, 2007; Redecker, Ala-Mutka, Bacigalupo, Ferrari, & Punie, 2009). Web 2.0 technologies are now the most effective ways of acquiring, creating and managing knowledge and information in a modern educational system. Unlike the more traditional lecture style of teaching, e-learning with Web 2.0 social computing tools, such as wikis, blogs, tweets, podcasts and YouTube, has been increasingly researched and used in recent years (Franklin & Harmelen, 2007; Redecker et al., 2009). We are also aware that the use of these technologies alone is not enough: the style of teaching and the presentation of materials for teaching and learning are very important as programs need to be organized in a way that will allow learners to have a good understanding of what is being taught. However, following the fact that effective teaching is a function of both student motivation and the content of the material presented, there is a need to stimulate students and to encourage engagement in an interactive and participatory way with the use of social networking tools for effectiveness and quality learning outcomes.

3. Empirical Evidence of the Usefulness of Social Computing Tools in Education

The number of empirical studies done in Europe on the use of social networking tools (e.g., blogs, wikis, podcasts and Twitter) in education has increased significantly in the last few years. For example, Xie & Shama (2010) had first- and second-year undergraduates use blogs for interaction and peer feedback in one semester. They found that the use of blogs promotes development of metacognitive knowledge and skills. The reflective thinking levels of students were increased significantly as they updated their blogs every week.

Parker & Chao (2007) carried out an empirical research on students using wikis for projects in software engineering. Their research showed that the students found it easy to use wikis as a good collaboration tool. Mayer & Rauber (2009) researched whether wikis support collaborative learning on language modules. They reported that students found wikis beneficial, but their enthusiasm was dampened because they were not familiar with the tool due to lack of training in wiki technology. Nevertheless, students commented positively on accessibility of information and were satisfied. The students also felt a sense of ownership from the editing properties of wiki comments.

Another tool that has been used recently in educational discipline is the podcast. Podcasting has been used in nursing education (McKinney, Dych, & Luber, 2009) and for various educational purposes such as enhancing distant learners' personal study, assisting reading-impaired students, supplementing traditional lecture materials and supporting language learners. Vogt, Schaffner, Ribar, & Chavez (2010) studied two groups of nursing students: one was given lectures in the traditional method and the other group was given lectures using a podcast. The study found no significant difference in their learning outcome as measured by their test scores. Wallis (2010) researched students' readiness to adopt podcasting for dissemination of educational content. However, they were concerned that students may not be ready for this technology, but the students reported that podcasting was valuable to their learning. The mixed outcomes of such studies mirror the fact that the educational use of podcasting is still new and therefore calls for additional research as to its acceptance and effectiveness in learning.

4. Acceptance of Technology for Learning

Students' and academics' perception on the use of technologies for learning must be assessed because the users' views will help to identify how these tools can be used effectively. Fry, Ketteridge, & Marshall (2009) report that adoption of technology should start with inducting students on the platform; hence, students also need to be assisted or supported to participate effectively. This induction will enable students to use these technologies in their learning activities and to express themselves or explore critically to understand the subject better. However, students need to be stimulated and encouraged to engage in interactive and participatory learning activities such as using Web 2.0 technologies (Bell & Davis, 2000).

At this point, we want to present an empirical study that was done to address the issue of technology acceptance on learning by developing a model with the following variables: motivation to use, perceived usefulness, social factors, perceived ease of use, performance expectancy, facilitating condition and prior knowledge. These variables which were used to examine behaviour intension to use Web 2.0 technologies for learning were developed by combining constructs from three technology acceptance models: technology acceptance model (TAM), unified theory of the use and acceptance of technology (UTAUT) and theory of reasoned action (TRA). These constructs were operationalised in order to develop a questionnaire. This questionnaire was distributed (in an online form) to students and lecturers in a university in Scotland. Data from 270 respondents (78 lecturers and 192 students) show that these variables influence the acceptance of Web 2.0 in learning with 0.01 and 0.05 significance levels. The correlation values were high enough to indicate that the model should be a useful tool for investigating Web 2.0 acceptance in higher education.

5. Instrument Development

A pilot study was first conducted to collect students' and academics' views in order to understand the problem of collaboration and their perception and attitude toward the use of Web 2.0 social media tools in learning for enhanced collaboration. This pilot study was helpful in the selection of variables in these three models used to underpin the research.

Variables from three models have been combined to form a theoretical model which is meant to explain and predict the acceptance to adopt Web 2.0 tools in learning in higher education in developed and developing countries. A combination of variables from the UTAUT, TAM1, TAM2 and TRA models with one additional variable were operationalised into a questionnaire (see Table 12.1). Table 12.2 shows how the variables were selected and sources of the variables used. Some demographics of the respondents (gender and age) were used in the questionnaire. A few questions were added to investigate the motivation, level of satisfaction, and present facilities used in teaching and learning especially in the area of feedback. The rest of the questions assess how the adoption of social networking tools in teaching and learning is viewed and the pedagogical role social networking tools could play in improving learning outcomes.

TABLE 12.1 Selection of Variables from Similar Theories and Pilot Study

Constructs	UTAUT	TAM	TRA	Pilot Study
Perceived usefulness (PU)		Perceived usefulness		Usefulness
Prior knowledge (PK)	Experience			Prior knowledge
Social factors (SF)	Social influence	External factors		Social interaction, communication and collaborative environment
Performance expectancy (PE)	Performance expectancy			Performance expectancy
Actual use	Use behaviour	Actual use	Actual use	Usage
Motivation to use (M)			Motivation	Motivation to use, emotional support, encouragement, interest and power
Perceived ease of use (PEoU)	Perceived ease of use			Ease of use
Facilitating condition (FC)	Facilitating condition			Computers, Internet facilities, awareness seminars and trainings, signal availability and cost
Behavioural intention (BI)	Behavioural intention	Behavioural intention	Behavioural intention	Future use

TABLE 12.2 Summarised Sources of Variables

Variables	Source
Attitude	TAM1, UTAUT
Behavioural intention	TAM1, UTAUT
Social factors	TAM1, UTAUT
Perceived usefulness	TAM1
Performance expectancy	UTAUT
Motivation	TAM2
Ease of use	TAM1
Facilitating condition	UTAUT
Actual use	TAM2
Prior knowledge	New

6. Hypothesis Development

6.1. Perceived Usefulness (PU)

Perceived usefulness is the belief that an individual or organization places importance on an object. This belief of usefulness makes an individual pay better attention to that object. Frequent use of social network tools in education for collaboration has been reported to improve the learning experience (Redecker et al., 2009). In this context, the perceived usefulness of social networking tools is a determinant of the use of these tools. Thus, the hypothesis:

H₁: Perceived usefulness influences the use of social networking tools in learning.

6.2. Social Factors (SF)

A social factor is an interpersonal agreement that binds individuals or people within a particular social environment (Davis et al., 1989). The people we relate to at our workplaces and educational organizations also affect our use of social network tools. This is because some activities may require teamwork or collaboration in order to do the work well. To achieve this goal, there is a tendency that social factors will affect actual use of network tools.

H₂: Social factors affect the use of social networking tools in learning.

6.3. Prior Knowledge (PK)

From cognitivists' point of view, people's prior knowledge constitutes a large part of their future attitudes (Ajzen & Fishbein, 1980). In the context of this research, the students' and lecturers' attitude toward using Web 2.0 technologies for other purpose may influence their future intentions to use them for educational purposes. Their present knowledge of such tools is considered an important factor to determine their use in learning.

H₃: Prior knowledge influences behaviour in the use of social networking tools in learning.

6.4. Facilitating Condition (FC)

Access to Internet facilities, availability of good Internet signals and cost of broadband can be regarded as facilitating conditions for the use Web 2.0 technologies for learning. Therefore, they may influence the use of Web 2.0 technologies in the Nigerian higher education. Thus, it can be hypothesized that:

H₄: There is positive relationship between *facilitating conditions* and *behavioural intention* for acceptance of Web 2.0 tools in learning in Nigeria universities.

6.5. Perceived Ease of Use (PEoU)

The easier an application is to use, the more people will use it (Davis et al., 1989). Ease of use is the degree to which an individual agrees that using an application is free from effort. In this context, the easier it is to use social network tools, the more people will use them.

H₅: Perceived ease of use influences the use of social networking tools in learning.

6.6. Motivation to Use (M)

Motivation is what moves individuals to act in certain ways. There are different approaches to motivate people. In educational systems, the major ways to get students to act are setting penalties (failure, repeat and withdraw) on assignments, course work and examinations; giving timely and contractive feedback and taking attendance. Motivating students increases their interest in using social network tools for collaboration. For instance, motivation can be in the form of support from lecturers through their teaching and feedback. Other forms of motivation include university policies, course content, student-to-student interaction and student-to-lecturer interaction. Motivating students to use these social network tools would change their attitude and also influence the use of social networking for educational collaboration and feedback. Thus:

H₆: Motivation affects intention to use social networking tools in learning.

6.7. Performance Expectancy (PE)

Performance expectancy is the degree to which an individual or group of people expects to be proficient in the work or education in which they are engaged (Venkatesh et al., 2003). In the context of this article, performance expectancy can also be an expectation of students or lecturers that their performance will improve through the use of social network tools. The expectation should affect the use of these tools.

H₇: Performance expectancy influences the use of social networking tools in learning.

6.8. Behavioural Intention (BI)

Ajzen & Fishbein (1980) also emphasized that attitude can be used to determine behaviour. For the purpose of this study, behaviour intention to use Web 2.0 technologies is likely to influence users' attitude and actual use of these tools or their intention to use them in the future, hence these hypotheses:

H₈: Behavioural intention influences the use of social networking tools in learning.

6.9. Actual Use

H₉: Behavioural intention affects the use of Web 2.0 technologies for learning. The research developed the conceptual model shown in Figure 12.1.

The new model has been operationalised into a questionnaire and administered to students and lecturers from one Scottish university. This yielded 270 responses. This research reports the perception attitude and acceptance of Web 2.0 tools in teaching and learning in a developed economy.

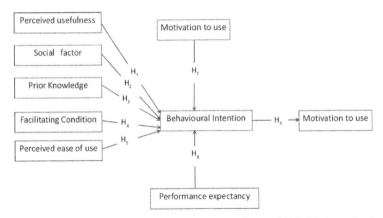

FIGURE 12.1 Conceptual model: Acceptance and use of Web 2.0 in an institution of higher learning.

7. Data Analysis

The construct in the model was operationalised in a questionnaire (see Table 12.4) and administered to students and lecturers in one Scottish university via e-mail. The data were analysed to check the difference between the lecturers' and students' views of the usefulness of Web 2.0 for learning (see Figure 12.2). A composite reliability of the constructs in the model was also analysed (see Table 12.4) and discussed.

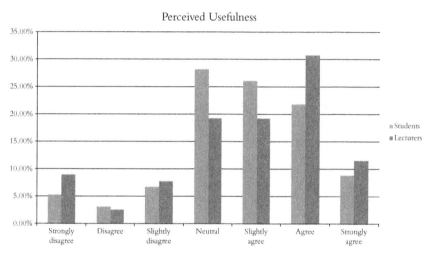

FIGURE 12.2 Perceived usefulness.

TABLE 12.3 Summary of Correlations Between Variables

Dependent Variable	Independent Variable	Correlation Coefficients	Significance	Hypothesis
BI	TAM(PU)	.616**	Yes 0.01	H_1
BI	TAM,UTAUT(SF)	.674**	Yes 0.01	H_2
BI	PK(Mine)	.625**	Yes 0.01	H_3
BI	UTAUT(FC)	.130*	Yes 0.05	H_4
BI	TAM(PEoU)	.221**	Yes 0.01	H_5
BI	UTAUT(PE)	.620**	Yes 0.01	H_6
BI	MtU (TRA)	.290**	Yes 0.01	H_7
AU	TAM,UTAUT(BI)	.155*	Yes 0.01	H_8

TABLE 12.4 Link to the Full Questionnaire: https://www.surveymonkey.com/s/QGWTPGK

Constructs		Questions	Question No.
Perceived ease of use		How easy do you find using these Web 2.0 tools (listed in question No. 6) to obtain the resources you need for your studies?	7
Perceived usefulness		To what extent do you agree that Web 2.0 tools would speed up acquisition of knowledge?	12
		To what extent do you agree that Web 2.0 tools will encourage active participation in learning?	13
Actual use		How often do you use Web 2.0 tools for academic purposes per week?	8
Social factors		To what extent do you agree that the social part of e-learning platforms (e.g., Module and Blackboard) motivate learner to a great extent to achieve learning objectives?	10b
Motivation		E-learning platforms enable you to send e-mails, download course materials, upload assignments, read announcements, access the library material and discuss with other students, professionals and your lecturers. To what extent do you think such a system would motivate you to achieve your learning objectives?	10a
Facilitating condition		Regarding facilities available for learning and teaching in the university, how satisfied are you? Add any comments regarding conditions necessary to facilitate Web 2.0 in learning.	4
Performance expectancy		To what extent do you agree that the use of Web 2.0 technologies for learning will help to improve performance?	14
Prior knowledge		How often do you use Web 2.0 tools (e.g., blogs, wikis, Twitter) for social purposes per week?	6
Behavioural intention		To what extent do you agree that social computing should be adopted in higher education and training for sharing of knowledge and information?	11
Demographics	Gender	What is your gender?	16
	Status	Are you a student or lecturer?	1
	Field	What is your field?	19
	Age bracket	What is your age bracket?	17

8. Discussion on Analysis

The graph in Figure 12.2 shows that more lecturers than students intend to adopt Web 2.0 technologies for learning. The relationship between *behavioural intention* and *performance expectancy* (see Table 12.3) is highly significant and is in agreement with other research (Alrawashdeh et al., 2012; Oshiyanki et al., 2007; Terzis & Economides, 2011; Venkatesh et al., 2000; Venkatesh et al., 2003), meaning that there is a relationship between acceptance to use Web 2.0 technologies for learning and performance expectancy. The correlation between *behavioural intention* and *social factors* is highly significant and this also agrees with previous research (Alrawashdeh et al., 2012; Oshiyanki et al., 2007; Terzis & Economides, 2011; Venkatesh et al., 2003). This means that there is a relationship between social factors and intention to use Web 2.0 technologies for learning. In the same vein, the correlation between *behavioural intention* and *actual use* in Table 12.3 is significant. This is in line with Davis et al. (1989), Venkatesh et al. (2003), Oshiyanki et al. (2007), Terzis & Economides (2011), and Alrawashdeh et al. (2012). Table 12.3 also displays the correlation between *behavioural intention* and *motivation* (M) and this correlation is significant. This is in agreement with the research by Ajzen & Fishbein (1980) meaning that there is a relationship between behavioural intention and motivation. The relationship between *behavioural intention* and *perceived ease of use* is significant and agrees with other research (Davis et al., 1989; Straub et al., 1997). This means that there is a relationship between behavioural intention and perceived ease of use. There is a significant correlation between *behavioural intention* and *facilitating condition,* meaning that there is a relationship between acceptance and facilitation condition which agrees with other research (Alrawashdeh et al., 2012; Oshiyanki et al., 2007; Terzis & Economides, 2011; Venkatesh et al., 2003).

The result initiates a research that tries to determine the level of use, acceptance and level of motivation in the academic environment of developed and developing economies toward technology-based learning. The findings show that the use of social network tools for non-academic purposes is really high compared to the use of these tools for academic purposes. From the analysis, the usefulness and impact in education will promote better learning experience. There are indications of positive attitude and behaviour for future use. This research indicates that the use of social networking tools in learning can be achieved by using motivational measures in order to enhance students' and academics' attitude, having seen that the relationships examined in the model were all significant. The research agrees with existing research (Alrawashdeh et al., 2012; Davis et al., 1989; Oshiyanki et al., 2007; Terzis & Economides, 2011; Venkatesh et al., 2003) that the combination of these variables (perceived usefulness, performance expectancy, perceived ease of use, prior knowledge, motivation, facilitating conditions, and social factors) is a better predictor of intention to use Web 2.0 technologies for learning. The factors of this research influence behavioural intention, which could then be a predicting factor of actual use of Web 2.0 technology for learning.

9. Recommendations

The implications of this research indicate that the use of social networking tools in teaching and learning can be achieved. However, students need to receive good support to enhance their frequent use of these technology platforms. This could be done by the lecturer giving them information on its usefulness, making it necessary for students to have face-to-face communication in a group project and via these social media platforms in their learning activities. Finally, social media platforms for learning should be simple, easily accessible, easy to use and available offline or online anytime, anywhere with any device (mobile or otherwise) for better student satisfaction and learning experience.

The key findings in this research include students' needs, motivation, prior knowledge, facilitating conditions (e.g., readily available Internet facilities, getting students to work in teams, regular student interaction), easy access, social features, and support features such as performance expectancy to enhance effective use of these technologies for learning. Thus, implementation plans and design of social media platforms for learning need to bear these factors in mind and provide features that attract users to use it frequently.

10. References

Ajzen, I., & Fishbein, M. (1980). *Understanding attitudes and predicting social behavior.* Englewood Cliffs, NJ: Prentice-Hall.

Alrawashdeh, T., Muhairat, M., & Alqatawnah, S. (2012). Factors affecting acceptance of web-based training system: Using extended UTAUT and structural equation modeling. *International Journal of Computer Science, Engineering and Information Technology (IJCSEIT), 2*(2).

Bell, P., & Davis E. (2000). In B. Fishman & S. O'Connor-Divelbliss (Eds.), *Fourth International Conference of the Learning Sciences* (pp. 142–149). Mahwah, NJ: Erlbaum.

Bell, P., & Davis, E. A. (2000). Designing mildred: Scaffolding students' reflection and argumentation using a cognitive software guide. In B. Fishman & S. O'Connor-Divelbiss (Eds.), *Fourth International Conference of the Learning Sciences* (pp. 142–149). Mahwah, NJ: Lawrence Erlbaum.

Davis, F., Bagozzi, R., & Warshaw, P. (1989). User acceptance of computer technology: A comparison of two theoretical models. *Management Science, 35*, 982–2003.

Field, A. (2009). *Discovering Statistics Using SPSS.* London EC1Y 1SP: Sage Publications Ltd.

Franklin, T., & Van Harmelen, M. (2007). *Web 2.0 for content for learning and teaching in higher education.* London: Joint Information Systems Committee.

Fry, H., Ketteridge, S., & Marshall, S. (Eds). (2009). *A handbook for teaching and learning in higher education; Enhancing academic practices,* (3rd ed.). Routledge.

Lee, A., & McLoughlin, C. (2006). Students as producers: Second year students' experiences as podcasters of content for first year undergraduates. In *Proceedings of the 7th Conference on Information Technology Based Higher Education and Training (ITHET).* University of Technology, Sydney.

Lee, M., Cheung, C., & Chen, Z. (2003). Acceptance of Internet based learning. *Information & Management, 42*, 1095–1104.

Mayer, R., & Andreas, R. (2009). Establishing context of digital objects' creation, content and usage. *Proc. Int. Workshop on Innovation in Digital Preservation*. Retrieved from http://publik.tuwien.ac.at/files/PubDat_177735.pdf

McCoy, S., Galletta, D., & King, W. (2007). Applying TAM across cultures. *European Journal of Information Systems, 16*, 81–90.

McKinney, D., Dych, J. L., & Luber, E. S. (2009). I-tunes university and the classroom: Can podcasts replace professor? *Computer & Education Journal, 52*, 617–623.

Oshiyanki, L., Cairns, P., & Thimbleby, H. (2007). Validating unified theory of acceptance and use of technology (UTAUT) tool cross-culturally. British Computer Society, Volume 2 Proceeding of the 21st Century BCS Group Conference.

Parker, K., & Chao, J. (2007). Wiki as a teaching tool. *Interdisciplinary Journal of Knowledge and Learning Objects, 3*, 57–72.

Redecker, C. (2009). *Review of Learning 2.0 Practices: Study on the Impact of Web 2.0 Innovations on Education and Training in Europe*. Retrieved from http://ipts.jrc.ec.europa.eu/publications/pub.cfm?id=2059

Redecker, C., Ala-Mutka, K., Bacigalupo, M., Ferrari, A., & Punie, Y. (2009). Learning 2.0: The Impact of Web 2.0 Innovations on Education and Training in Europe. Final Report. JRC Scientific and Technical Report, EUR 24103 EN. Retrieved from http://ipts.jrc.ec.europa.eu/publications/pub.cfm?id=2899

Straub, D., Keil, M., & Brenner, W. (1997). Testing the technology acceptance model across cultures: A three country study. *Information and Management, 33*(1), 1–11.

Swanson, E. (1994). Information systems innovation among organizations. *Management Science, 40*(9), 1069–1092.

Teo, T., Su Luan, W., & Sing, C. (2008). A cross-cultural examination of the intention to use technology between Singaporean and Malaysian pre-service teachers: An application of the technology acceptance model (TAM). *Educational Technology & Society, 11*(4), 265–280.

Terzis, V., & Economides, A. (2011). The acceptance and use of computer based assessment. *Computers & Education, 56*, 1032–1044.

Venkatesh, V., & Davis, F. D. (2000). A theoretical extension of the technology acceptance model: Four longitudinal field studies. *Management Science, 46*(2), 186–204.

Venkatesh, V., Morris, M. G., Davis, G. B., & Davis, F. D. (2003). User acceptance of information technology: Toward a unified view, *MIS Quarterly, 27*(3), 425–478.

Vogt, M., Schaffner, B., Ribar, A., & Chavez, R. (2010). The impact of podcasting on the learning and satisfaction of undergraduate nursing students. *Nurse Education in Practice, 10*(1), 38–42. Retrieved from http://www.sciencedirect.com/science/article/pii/S1471595309000584

Wallis, S., Kucsera, J., Walker, J., Acee, T., Macvaugh, N., & Robinson, D. (2010). Podcasting in education: Are students as ready and eager as we think they are? *Computers and Education Journal, 54*, 425–447.

Xie, Y., & Shama, P. (2010). The effect of peer-interaction styles in team blogging on students' cognitive thinking and blog participation. *Journal of Educational Computing, 42*(4), 459–479.

13

SMART MEDIA IN HIGHER EDUCATION—SPREAD OF SMART CAMPUS

JeongWon Choi, SangJin An, & YoungJun Le

KOREA NATIONAL UNIVERSITY OF EDUCATION, KOREA

1. Introduction

Computers and the Internet have changed the paradigm of modern society including the field of education. Represented by textbooks and pens in the past, learning has quickly changed into production of digital artefacts by computers and this trend appears more clearly in higher education. Now, the term "computer" is too general, as new media and various devices, such as the smartphone and tablet PC, have become popular. Introduction of smart media does not simply mean changes in equipment from a computer to new devices. It created new value using IT and caused a paradigm transfer to a smart society that impacts many areas of of life. Smart society has brought big changes in people's lifestyle and mindset settling as the subject of social innovation.

As the new smart media continues to change society, many changes are also being made in higher education. Colleges and universities in Korea are trying to utilize new media as a smart tool by applying them to administration and educational purposes in a smart campus project. "Smart campus" is hard to define. A smart campus can include anything from constructing infrastructure to utilize IT devices on campus to providing various campus services (Ahn, 2013). Specifically, while the early stage smart campus only focused on supplying smart devices and opening more Wi-Fi zones on campus, it has now developed into a comprehensive format that supports both administration and education of colleges. And through these changes, colleges are striving to become smarter (Lee, 2010; Park & Lim, 2012). Noh & Ju (2011) define smart campus as "to construct learner-centered campus by utilizing smart devices and information communication technology and actualizing cooperative, experimental, and open college education by making academic affairs, administration, education, research, student activity, and library service more intelligent." Figure 13.1 shows a conceptual change of smart campus

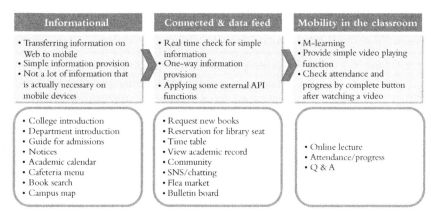

Informational	Connected & data feed	Mobility in the classroom
• Transferring information on Web to mobile • Simple information provision • Not a lot of information that is actually necessary on mobile devices	• Real time check for simple information • One-way information provision • Applying some external API functions	• M-learning • Provide simple video playing function • Check attendance and progress by complete button after watching a video
• College introduction • Department introduction • Guide for admissions • Notices • Academic calendar • Cafeteria menu • Book search • Campus map	• Request new books • Reservation for library seat • Time table • View academic record • Community • SNS/chatting • Flea market • Bulletin board	• Online lecture • Attendance/progress • Q & A

FIGURE 13.1 Conceptual and practical changes in smart campus.

in Korea. Based on previous research, this study defines smart campus as "a system that improves efficiency and effectiveness of administration and education utilizing smart devices and information communication technology." It includes factors that support convenience of college life such as academic information systems, library services, and student activities from an administrative perspective. From an education perspective, it focuses on improvement of students' learning. In addition, this study looks into the current situation and construction examples of smart campuses and estimates what kind of changes could occur. Also, it examines the power and role of social media in higher education through a smart campus environment.

2. Smart Campus

2.1. Factors of Smart Campus

Noh & Ju (2011) classified the factors to implement a smart campus into educational factors, technical factors and environmental factors and suggested that a smart campus be established based on these factors. Table 13.1 details these factors necessary for a smart campus. Each factor was derived from analyses of many preceding research projects related to construction of a smart campus.

2.2. Methodology

This study looks into some cases of smart campuses that are currently being implemented in Korea and considers implications that occurred during the process to verify what kind of impact a smart campus has on higher education. In Korea, various types of smart campuses have been developed since 2009, and some results of their actual operation are available. Using the results from one of these examples, this study analysed what kind of impact a smart campus can have on college administration services and the educational environment. And it also examined how social media can change the various aspects of education.

TABLE 13.1 Factors for Smart Campus System

Factors	Characteristics
Educational	• Providing learner-centered learning space • Securing accessibility to learning resources without limitations • Maximizing interaction and cooperation • Supporting experimental learning to maximize learning effect (pursues realistic and problem-focused learning, game learning and simulation learning) • Technical support for intellectualization (enormous knowledge DB, contents DB)
Technical	• Infra technology: RFID, wireless LAN, MANET, sensor network • Device technology: smartphone, smart TV, tablet PC, flexible display, voice-activated computer • Service platform: cloud computing, app store • Social computing technology: social software, cooperative LMS technology • Brain cognitive technology: cognitive ability measuring device, neuro-tool (cognitive ability improvement tool), individual ability improvement matter • Experimental technology: simulation technology, game base technology, augmented reality, virtual reality
Environmental	• Infrastructure factor: Smart U-campus • Administration service factor: administration service and open service system provided for learning subject • Political support factor: comprehensive plan and budget for education model development

Adapted from Noh & Ju (2011)

2.3. Example of Smart Campus

The following is about the latest smart campus implementation case in a Korean university (called K University), and it is divided into an administrative perspective and an educational perspective.

2.3.1. Background and System Building

Korea's IT infrastructure is very developed, especially in colleges and universities for research and education. Korea's most developed university has its own high-speed network and holds the fastest wireless network, and most of the members

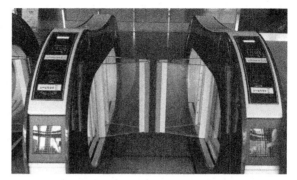

FIGURE 13.2 Electronic attendance check system and authentication system in the library.

of the university own more than one smart device. Most of the administrative work involving student life is accomplished through a computer system, and they are accustomed to this environment. In this case, K University holds a high-speed wired network, a wireless network and its own management system, and students and campus members own portable smart devices.

Under these circumstances, it takes about a year to establish a smart campus at K University. In buildings that require authentication (e.g., library, cafeteria, dormitory), the access system that includes authentication function has been installed and the electronic attendance system has been set up in front of large lecture rooms. Smart cards and mobile authentication with apps are used for authentication. Smart cards, which replace previous forms of student ID, are designed to perform various functions such as student ID, ATM card and electronic wallet (e-wallet). Radio-frequency identification (RFID) and near field communication (NFC) technology built into smart cards provide students with various types of authentication methods. The mobile authentication process proceeds through the mobile app made available by the school. This app was designed for convenience in using administrative and educational functions as well as certification methods. Figure 13.2 shows the electronic attendance check system (left) and smart library gates (right).

2.3.2. Administrative Perspective

K University's smart campus includes various forms of administrative support to provide learners with convenience in their school life. Figure 13.3 shows the smart campus app of K University running on the Android operating system. It provides smart card student ID and mobile QR student ID so that they can be used for an electronic attendance check, library card, dormitory use, and cafeteria use. The existing mobile QR student ID could be easily copied which created a potential for expropriation. By using a one-time password (OTP), the created QR code now can be used only once. This student ID allows for an attendance

FIGURE 13.3 Mobile app for smart campus.

check at the classroom door by scanning it at the electronic attendance check device. When using the cafeteria, students can pay for meals electronically using a mobile ID or smart card. This allows for convenient use of the cafeteria as members do not have to use meal tickets and eliminates the inconvenience of meal ticket managing for cafeteria management. In the campus library, public PCs can be easily operated as the smart authentication system allows easy reservation. It also interlocks reading room seat allocation and library gate allowing automatic termination of the seat when a user leaves the library. Therefore, it can solve problems like reading room seat privatization and long use of public PCs. In dormitories, students can use laundry machines, access drinking water, gain entrance, and record special activity attendance using a smart student ID. This technology makes students' school life more convenient in general and also helps automate school management.

2.3.3 Educational Perspective

A smart campus provides a learning experience that is quite opposite the traditional learning situation. Instructors post contents of their lectures online in advance of offline lectures so that learners can preview class contents and participate in class. This is called an inverted learning model (ILM) (Kim, 2012). It allows learners and instructors to discuss class contents and solve problems in an offline classroom, which makes the actual class more creative and enriched. This type of learning model surpasses the existing process where learners acquire one-sided knowledge, and it allows creative and actual learning (Kim, 2011).

Another method is to learn using digital data that are provided online before an offline lecture and to proceed with Q&A and assignment submission. Even though this is similar to the previous ILM method, it is a bit different as teaching-learning activities are online-focused. During an offline lecture, instructors and students can have a more enriched class through discussions and experiments.

3. New Media for Education

3.1. Administrative Utilization

New media changes the existing concept of college administrative services at a fast speed. The existing labour-intensive activities can be processed with much less effort from individuals and administrative tasks that previously required a long involved process can be accomplished with a quicker simplified process. The following administrative changes can be expected through a smart campus.

First, expansion of short-range wireless technology, such as RFID and NFC, is expected to provide new administrative services. For example, the existing electronic attendance check that is done at the classroom entrance by scanning a smart card or mobile QR code at an electronic attendance device can be changed to check attendance directly at each seat in the classroom. An NFC electronic attendance check system is very economic as it only costs 1/100 of existing device authorizing systems. It simplifies the attendance check process for instructors, which allows them more time for education. These techniques can be mounted easily on mobile devices so they can be used in various ways.

Second, Web services can be simplified. Colleges and universities operate multiple websites and an authentication process is required for each website. Smart campus applications operated on smart devices reduce the effort required for website access and allow for fast acquisition of necessary information. Adopting a single sign on (SSO) method will create a student portal system through which students can use all services conveniently with one authorization process.

Third, it allows estimation of various school administrative demands. Estimation of administrative demands can contribute to allocating limited college resources. On a smart campus system, school operators can receive a lot of data on various issues around the college and allocate enough resources at the right time to allow efficient college operation.

Administrative changes by a smart campus system can provide students with campus convenience through campus life related application distribution. Also, as communities provided on the Web transfer to smart devices, it is expected that there can be more proactive communication space (Si et al., 2011).

3.2. Educational Utilization

Higher education utilizes various media and adopts new media relatively actively. Smart devices contain many useful functions, and they are highly utilizable for educational purposes due to their characteristics. As new media changes education in general, smart devices used on smart campuses can change education as follows.

First, smart devices can improve accessibility to education. Various long-distance education programs such as e-learning and m-learning are currently available. Utilization of smart devices can greatly improve accessibility to these long-distance education programs (Jeong, 2012). Although face-to-face classes between instructors and students are meaningful, these regular lectures in classrooms will gradually become less available.

Second, development of smart campuses will continuously bring changes in education methodology. In addition to an instructor's lecture on a subject, learners can acquire a variety of knowledge with smart devices and reproduce that information. Changes in acquisition and production of knowledge will cause instructors to use various smart devices for teaching while changing the existing learning paradigm for learners. For example, it is possible to have real-time online cooperation for group work that is currently happening mainly offline. Moreover, learners can utilize smart devices for remote functions rather than for simple replay of text or videos. Remote function allows instructors to write material they want to deliver to students on smart devices which reflect the information on a classroom board. It allows instructors to be able to move freely among students and generates more interaction between instructors and learners.

Third, they can change utilization of educational data. Learners' results in colleges are usually calculated by GPA. Even though this shows a learner's ability the most compressed way, it is too abstract and difficult to check what kind of abilities learners have. On a smart campus, learners can transport their learning results, organize them in portfolio forms and track their learning process in a more concrete way.

If we look into current online education programs which will be more readily available in the future, it is necessary to distinguish clearly how a learner will participate in assignments and cooperative work. In other words, a learner's effort, devotion and degree of learning can be evaluated. That is to say, it is very important to be able to filter submitted assignments to determine if they are truly done by the student or were completed by other persons.

3.3. Social Media in Education

Traditional education has shifted dramatically due to the use of personal computers. They affect the overall education environment, such as teaching-learning methods, and they have been successfully introduced in recent decades. Smart devices and various equipped technology make this computing environment more convenient and private. A smart campus environment is a good example of using smart technology in higher education. Though it needs various infrastructures, the key is software apps which can take advantage of those infrastructures. There will be more discussion about how to utilize contents provided by a smart campus environment.

The apps used in the smart campus environment can be scale-down social media. Various existing social media are being operated in an open form and produce a variety of topics, but smart campus apps are only for people who are part of the campus community. The information that is produced and shared with that app can be even more useful for community members so it can be used for administrative and educational purposes. Though openness and sharing are characteristics of social media, those apps used in educational fields may have some exclusive features for educational purposes.

4. Conclusions

This article defines a smart campus as "a system that improves efficiency and effectiveness of administration and education utilizing smart devices and information communication technology" and looks into examples of changed higher education due to the introduction of smart devices and smart campuses to estimate future development direction. To do so, this study divided the smart campus system into administrative support and educational perspective. From the administrative perspective, this study looked into student convenience services such as the academic information system, library system, and student activities. From an educational perspective, it looked into the improvement of learners' effective and efficiency learning.

A smart campus is a paradigm that goes down in higher education and it improves efficiency and effectiveness of school life from administrative support and educational perspectives using smart devices. As adaptation of a smart campus enriches learners' college life by allowing more convenience and easy use of many facilities, it will be dispersed to more specific areas. From an administrative point of view, however, many colleges lack the economic foundation to fund the establishment of a smart campus environment. As an alternative, colleges may construct a smart campus through agreement with various corporations (Kang, 2012). However, corporations basically exist to pursue profit so college members could be used for the corporation's advertisement. Colleges need financial strength of their own or stable financial support from the government to be able to independently operate a smart campus. Financial support will allow colleges and universities to provide a greater variety of services for school members than if they must rely on supporting corporations' strategic purposes. It also will result in a more satisfying college life for students, a sense of pride about their college, and improved learning efficiency.

From an educational point of view, we need to continuously monitor whether online education using smart devices is effective. In the case of traditional education, we have various teaching-learning processes and evaluation methods that can check the level of knowledge accumulation. Even though instructors can generate new teaching-learning methods and evaluation materials utilizing various media, our focus should not be on utilizing new media but on checking their effectiveness and reliability to confirm if they have a positive impact on the learning process. This is the essential process for securing the quality of higher education and a process that we should go through repeatedly when applying new media to education.

As an institution that leads a paradigm of education, changes in the college education environment will affect the lower level school education environment. Strengths and weaknesses in constructing a smart campus system for a college or university will be referenced by other educational institutions attempting to construct a smart education environment. In addition, examples of smart campus operation will be transferred to various educational institutions. School management and learning processes of this new era will be absolutely different from previous periods in eduation. This change will continue as new media appear. A smart campus is the beginning of this change, and this change in education administration and education method will quickly disperse to various education environments.

5. References

Ahn, B. T. (2013). A study of smart campus education service based on ubiquitous. *Journal of Advanced Information Technology and Convergence*, *11*(5), 137–146.

Jeong, H. J. (2012). The development of operational guidelines for smart media-based distance education institute. Korea Education & Research Information Service Research Report CR 2012-19.

Kang, J. H. (2011). A study on utilizing SNS to vitalize smart learning. *The Journal of Digital Policy & Management*, *9*(5), 265–274.

Kang, S. O. (2012, March 30). The implement of smart campus through future-oriented infrastructure and services. *Network Times*, 159–161.

Kim, Y. A. (2011). The current status and future direction of smart education. Korea Education & Research Information Service Issue Paper, OR 2011-02-7.

Kim, Y. W. (2012). An exploratory study of the relationship between smart learning and smart work: The use of personal laptops by graduate students in a smart campus environment. *The Journal of Digital Policy & Management*, *10*(5), 27–35.

Lee, J. M. (2010). M-learning as a challenge for cyber universities: The present and the future. *Journal of Cyber Society & Culture*, *1*(1), 91–119.

Noh, G. S., & Ju, S. H. (2011). An exploratory study on smart campus model. *The Journal of Digital Policy & Management*, *9*(3), 181–190.

Park, M. C. (2013). The approach model of adolescent's Internet addiction. 2013 Proceedings on Korea Society of Computer and Information, AnSeong, Korea.

Park, S. Y., & Lim, G. (2012). Suggestions for building 'smart campus' based on case studies on the effectiveness of instructions with smart-pads. *The Journal of Digital Policy & Management*, *10*(3), 1–12.

Si, J. H., Park, D. G, Choi, A., & Kim, D. S. (2011). Discussion-based interface design research on the smart phone at cyber universities. *Journal of Korean Association of Computer Education*, *14*(5), 81–96.

SECTION V

Security and Privacy in ICT or Social Media

14

AN INVESTIGATION INTO JAPANESE UNIVERSITY STUDENTS' ONLINE PRIVACY CONCERNS

Yukiko Maruyama

TOKAI UNIVERSITY, HIRATSUKA, KANAGAWA, JAPAN

1. Introduction

Social media sites, including social networking sites (SNSs), Twitter, blogs, video-sharing sites and buzz marketing sites, are vehicles for the sharing of various types of user-created content on the Internet and have permeated our daily lives. The diffusion of SNSs in particular has been remarkable. The assimilation of social media sites into our daily lives has attracted the attention of many researchers, as it provides new research opportunities in areas such as the motivation to use SNSs and impression management and friendship performance.

One important research topic is the relationship between online privacy and information disclosure behaviour. As social media sites further permeate our lives, the amount of user-created content (blog posts, photos, videos, etc.) on the Internet is increasing. This content often includes information related to users' daily lives. Often, SNS users are willing to share their personal information with others on their profile pages to attract more online friends. However, this personal information can be accessed by both friends and strangers. Exposing one's personal information on the Internet leads to an increased risk of involvement in various kinds of trouble, both online and offline. It is important for Internet users to acquire the knowledge and skills necessary to protect their online privacy. However, their efforts are often insufficient, and many users unknowingly disclose their information online. Therefore, it is important to learn about the relationship between online privacy and information disclosure behaviour, as well as factors that influence this relationship. This study aims both to examine this relationship and the factors that influence it and to construct a model of interrelationship between factors that can apply to various areas of social media research.

2. Investigation into Online Privacy Concerns

2.1. Aim

One of the factors that influence the relationship between online privacy and information disclosure behaviour is online privacy concerns. Some behaviours related to online privacy are influenced by privacy concerns. As a first step, this study focuses on those privacy concerns.

Stutzman (2006) mentioned that compared with traditional methods of personal information disclosure, such as a campus directory, a social network community fosters more subjective, holistic disclosure of identity information. Through comparative analysis of students' use of SNSs and their feelings about the disclosure of identity information, Stutzman showed that a need exists for further analysing the value and jeopardy of identity information in a social network community. Fogel & Nehmad (2009) studied risk-taking, trust, and privacy concerns regarding SNSs among 205 university students in the United States. Their results showed that general privacy concerns and identity information disclosure concerns were of greater concern to women than to men.

The two studies mentioned above focused on SNS usage. As previously mentioned, an SNS is one kind of social media site, but others exist that should be considered as well. Moreover, user concerns about privacy and information disclosure probably vary according to their online activities. This study focuses on Japanese university students' usage of social media sites and on their online privacy concerns.

2.2. Methodology

In the present study, 343 university students in Japan answered a questionnaire; all were enrolled in a computer class for beginners. The students ranged in age from 18 to 26, with the average age being 20.1 years (age data were missing for seven students). There were 261 male students (77.2% of the total) and 77 female students (22.8% of the total) (gender data were missing for five). In October 2012, students were invited to participate in the study, provided with information about the aim of the study and informed that participation was voluntary and confidential. They were then given a URL through which the survey was conducted as an online questionnaire.

The questionnaire had four parts: (1) demographics, (2) social media site use, (3) online privacy concerns and (4) experiences with and perceptions of social media sites. This study analyses the answers concerned with social media site use (Part 2) and online privacy concerns (Part 3). Part 2 was composed of 25 items asking about the frequency with which the respondents used functions (post, read, etc.) on social media sites (SNSs, Twitter, blogs, video-sharing sites and buzz marketing sites), as indicated on a five-point Likert-type scale where 1 was "not at all," 2 was "once in a while," 3 was "sometimes," 4 was "often" and 5 was "very often."

Part 3 was composed of 22 items asking about respondents' concerns regarding the various aspects of their online privacy, as indicated on a five-point scale where 1 was "not concerned at all," 2 was "not concerned," 3 was "neutral," 4 was "concerned" and 5 was "very concerned."

2.3. Key Findings

Questionnaires that were missing data in Parts 2 or 3 were eliminated from the dataset; then, Parts 2 and 3 of the 265 remaining questionnaires were analysed. These students ranged in age from 18 to 25, with the average age being 20.1 years (data were missing for six). There were 199 male students (76.0% of the total) and 63 female students (24.0% of the total) (data were missing for three).

First, we used principal component analysis (PCA) to analyse the students' answers about their social media site use, and we derived five principal components. In order to interpret PCA information, the component loadings must be studied. The five components include the following: PC1, "overall measure of social media use;" PC2, "measure of public or private orientation;" PC3, "measure of Twitter use;" PC4, "measure of communication with friends on blog" and PC5, "measure of strangers' blogs reading."

Next, we calculated the principal component scores for each student, and the scores were subjected to a cluster analysis to identify different types of social media users. Six clusters were found, and average principal component scores were calculated for each cluster in order to name each cluster. C1 (N = 17, or 6.4% of the total) represents "people who are private blog users," C2 (N = 61, or 23.0% of the total) comprises "less frequent users of social media," C3 (N = 84, or 31.7% of the total) represents "private SNS users," C4 (N = 49, or 18.5% of the total) comprises "Twitter users," C5 (N = 41, or 15.5% of the total) is called "blog users" and C6 (N = 13, or 4.9% of the total) represents "people who communicate with strangers on SNSs and blogs."

The students' answers about their online privacy concerns were analysed by factor analysis with promax rotation; three factors were determined. The first factor (F1) was "concern about their content being accessed on the Internet by strangers," the second factor (F2) was "concern about their personal information on the Internet being abused by others" and the third factor (F3) was "concern that their information would be revealed by others." One-way analysis of variance (ANOVA) was performed to test whether there were differences in online privacy concerns between each cluster. Mean scores of items included in each factor were calculated and used as dependent variables. The results show that the mean scores according to clusters in F3 were significant [$F(5, 259) = 3.187$, $p < 0.01$]. The Tukey test was applied as a post hoc test. The results showed significant differences between C1 and C2 and between C2 and C3.

As a result, the largest cluster is "SNS user for private" who performs activities on SNSs such as post comments, read friends' comments and use the "like" function. About one-third of students (84 of 265) were categorised into this group. On the other hand, few students were categorised in the groups "Twitter user," "blog user" and "communicate with strangers on SNS and blog." Japanese university students' usage of social media sites is seemingly privacy-oriented. Moreover, about one-fourth of students (61 of 256) were categorised into the group "less frequent users of social media." This indicates that social media sites are still not very popular among Japanese students.

Regarding concerns about online privacy, students who mainly communicate with friends on social media sites mostly worry about "their personal information on the Internet being abused by others." The next main worry is "concern that their information would be revealed by others." The results of ANOVA indicate that those students worry more about their personal information being revealed by others than students who were categorised into "less frequent users of social media." On the other hand, "concerns about their content being accessed on the Internet by strangers" is not high. This suggests that these students should be taught about the knowledge and skills required to protect their online privacy.

3. Future Research

This study has made a good start in gaining insight into university students' usage of social media sites and their online privacy concerns. However, as mentioned above, some other factors affect the relationship between online privacy and online information disclosure behaviour. I need to determine those other factors and construct a model for online privacy and information disclosure that is based on social media research. In the next stage of this study, we will examine the inter-relationship between factors and integrate them into the model. We believe the model will be useful in various research areas.

3.1. Construct the Model

A number of studies focusing on online privacy have been performed since before the massive growth of social media sites. Buchanan, Paine, Joinson, & Reips (2007) developed Internet-administered scales that measure privacy-related attitudes and behaviours. They developed a Web-based questionnaire that contained 82 items related to privacy; from this, three scales that measure privacy-related attitudes ("Privacy Concerns," with 16 items) and behaviours ("General Caution" and "Technical Protection," each with six items) were derived. Kurt (2010) conducted an investigation by questionnaire to determine the Internet privacy behaviours of university students in Turkey in order to develop precautions to address privacy concerns. The questionnaire included three subdimensions to assess the privacy behaviour of students: general caution (six items), technical protection behaviours (12 items), and privacy concerns (24 items). Li (2012) reviewed 15 established theories in online information privacy research on e-commerce and developed an integration framework based on his review. In this study, Li indicated that the theory of reasoned action (TRA) and the theory of planned behaviour (TPB) were used in order to investigate people's volitional behaviour (such as protect online privacy and information disclosure). These theories suggest that people's volitional behaviour is determined by attitude, subjective norm, motivation and ability. These factors are influenced by past experience and the anticipated abilities to perform the behaviour. Although these studies focused on general usage of the Internet rather than usage of social media sites, these factors (general caution, technical protection, subjective norm, motivation, ability, past experience, and the anticipated abilities to perform the behaviour) should be investigated in the area of social media sites. It is necessary to determine items included in each factor in the area of social media sites and to reveal their relationship.

Moreover, Fogel & Nehmad (2009) studied risk taking, trust and privacy concerns regarding SNSs. They suggest that in order to investigate the relationship between contradictory behaviours (i.e., protect privacy and disclose information), risk and benefit factors should be considered. Risk and benefit beliefs of social media users vary according to the aim of usage of social media sites. For example, people who use social media sites to connect with friends might worry more about their personal information being accessed by strangers than people who use social media sites to find new friends. Determining the risks and benefits in various situations of usage is necessary.

Hereafter, I will determine items included in each factor and examine the interrelationship between these factors. And I will integrate them into the model. The model will be useful in various research areas. In the next subsection, some potential areas to which the model would contribute are mentioned.

3.2. Potential Contribution of the Model

3.2.1. Contribution to Education

As mentioned earlier, Internet users still do not have sufficient knowledge and skills to protect their online privacy. This situation can be improved by education. In order to design educational programming, the model is useful.

Researchers and teachers try to use social media sites in the educational setting. Some of them suggest that students' skill in using social media sites is not enough to use them effectively in education. The results of this study suggest that social media sites are still not popular among some students. However, the number of young people experiencing trouble from their disclosure of personal information on social media sites is increasing. It is conceivable that these students' behaviours derive from various factors. In cases where social media sites are unpopular, it is possible that one of the reasons some students do not use social media sites is their extreme protection of their online privacy. Their worries about online privacy are possibly such that they prevent use of social media sites, or their protections for online privacy are such that they can use social media sites effectively and then they stop using the sites. On the other hand, although it is evident that students' misbehaviours on information disclosure come from their knowledge and skills, there are some potential factors that affect their behaviours (e.g., having protection skills or low risk-taking behaviour). By knowing the causes of their behaviour, it is conceivable that teachers can design educational programing appropriately.

3.2.2. Contribution to the Design of Social Media Site

Although it is important for Internet users to protect their online privacy by themselves, it is necessary to try to design social media sites that are trustworthy in protecting users' online privacy. The model aims to contribute to the design of trustful sites.

Some social media sites clearly tell users that their information collected will be offered to some companies. If users think that sites' policies for using their information are inappropriate, they worry about their online privacy and distrust and finally leave the sites. To design trustful sites, designers must consider what kind of personal information to require during user registration to their social media sites and to collect on social media. Consideration should also be given to the sites' functions of setting up and guarding users' online privacy on the basis of both users' online concerns and skills as well as users' aim of usage of the social media sites. Thus, for social media site designers, the model is useful because it provides knowledge about users' online privacy behaviours.

3.2.3. Contribution to Foster an Online Community on Social Media Sites

Most users currently use SNSs to connect with their friends and to make new friends. Henceforth, various ways to use social media sites are proposed and researched (e.g., for information sharing during a disaster and in an educational situation). Under those situations, users will connect with both their friends and various people who have different cultural backgrounds (e.g., different ages and different nationalities) and make online communities. Different cultural backgrounds drive different online privacy and information disclosure behaviours, which cause some conflict in communities. To reduce conflict and foster online communities, designers need to know the characteristics of users' behaviour. The model can be used to reveal differences in the characteristics of their behaviour.

4. Conclusions

As social media sites further permeate our lives, Internet users have to acquire the knowledge and skills to protect their online privacy. Therefore, it is important to learn about the relationship between online privacy and information disclosure behaviour, as well as factors that influence that relationship. This study aims both to examine the relationship and the factors that influence the relationship and to construct a model of interrelationship between factors that can apply to various areas of social media research.

As a first step, this study focused on Japanese university students' usage of social media sites and on their online privacy concerns and gained some insights on relationships between students' usage and online privacy concerns. However, other factors affect the relationship between online privacy and online information disclosure behaviour. I need to determine those other factors and construct a model for online privacy and information disclosure that is based on social media research. This model will be useful in various research areas.

5. References

Buchanan, T., Paine, C., Joinson, N., & Reips, U. (2007). Development of measures of online privacy concern and protection for use on the Internet. *Journal of the American Society for Information Science and Technology, 58*(2), 157–165.

Fogel, J., & Nehmad, E. (2009). Internet social network communities: Risk taking, trust, and privacy concerns. *Computers in Human Behavior, 25*(1), 153–160.

Kurt, M. (2010). Determination of Internet privacy behaviors of students. *Procedia—Social and Behavioral Sciences, 9*, 1244–1250.

Li, Y. (2012). Theories in online information privacy research: A critical review and an integrated framework. *Decision Support System, 54*(1), 471–481.

Stutzman, F. (2006). An evaluation of identity-sharing behavior in social network communities. *iDMAa Journal, 3*(1), 10–18.

SECTION VI

Social Media and Smart Technologies

15

CONNECTING AND COMMUNICATING WITH THE NEAR FIELD

How NFC Services for Smartphones May Benefit Consumers/Citizens Through Social Media Integration and Augmentation

Dag Slettemeås, Bente Evjemo, & Sigmund Akselsen

NATIONAL INSTITUTE FOR CONSUMER RESEARCH (SIFO), NORWAY, TELENOR, RESEARCH AND FUTURE STUDIES, NORWAY, AND TELENOR, RESEARCH AND FUTURE STUDIES, NORWAY

1. Introduction

Today's information society is increasingly being shaped and experienced through mutual engagement between people, institutions and technology. The expansion of a "digital logic" as well as technological infrastructures blur the lines between what is being considered real and virtual, or near and distant in modern society. Simultaneously, diffusion of ubiquitous mobile devices tends to increase flexibility and mobility and reinforces this development. This calls for holistic approaches and critical engagement to understand the "life" of these large socio-technological systems (Slettemeås, 2009).

Our research contribution is positioned amidst these challenges as we seek to explore how a large socio-technological system—a piloted near field communication (NFC) ecosystem developed for smartphone usage—is experienced, consumed and communicated among its users. The promise of NFC technology is to simplify service interaction and reconnect people with place through localized service interaction. It is literally offering place-based services at the "tap of your hand." In this chapter, we build on research presented in Evjemo, Slettemeås, Akselsen, Jørgensen, & Wolf (2013), which critically assesses the salience of the "simplicity" notion often prevalent in complex technological systems. Then we look into future prospects of integrating NFC services with social media. In this way, consumers can augment their personal experiences and their social gratification of NFC services through tighter integration with social media.

2. NFC—Enabling Local Contactless Service Interaction

2.1. Research Aim

The study referred to in Evjemo et al. (2013) is part of an ongoing comprehensive research effort—NFC City—which is a large Norwegian-based open innovation project. Programming "empty" tags was set up as one of several tasks in order to generate a sense of ownership and familiarity among users to the "unfamiliar" NFC technology. However, a range of other services has been developed and tested by the same users. The key feature of the project is therefore a multi-service trial where all the NFC services are piloted simultaneously in the city of Tromsø, northern Norway.

The main aim of the NFC City project is to develop and test an "NFC eco-system" and as a result produce consolidated knowledge on technical, business and consumer issues related to this ecosystem. NFC is a short range wireless technology that has been embedded in several of the latest advanced smartphone models. This new technological feature enables immediacy and proximity to a wide range of arenas and services. Users "tap" their handheld devices at specific tag points in the local environment to seamlessly activate informational or transactional services. The aim of the "contactless" feature of NFC is to bypass several, often laborious, steps on the way to reaching the core service. This feature provides for instant gratification and may augment consumer experience of localized services, in particular if these can be shared with other users in the network or community.

2.2. Methods Used

Acknowledging the criticality of meaningful services the project has designed a field trial in order to test and evaluate all the NFC services developed through the project (Slettemeås, Evjemo, Akselsen, Munch-Ellingsen, Wolf, & Jørgensen, 2013). A tremendous complexity is involved in generating ecosystems that enable such diversity of services. These systems involve multiple actors, technologies and business models. However, it is argued that the actual complexity should be "hidden" from the consumer experience in order to simplify interactions and operations (Deuffic, 2011; Guaus, 2011). This is also the promise held by NFC—that complexity can be met by smart tools and devices that minimize effort, reduce complexity and improve efficiency.

The NFC City trial has been devised in a way that allows for a plethora of data to be gathered, either continuously or at specific intervals. The trial involves a selection of 50 users (students) experiencing services over a period of 12 months. The idea behind this design has been to "cluster" services locally in order to generate a sense of omnipresence of NFC. This design choice aims at spurring active and continuous engagement with services, and at the same time creating a "semi-realistic" scenario to which people naturally relate. In this way, researchers can tap into already established use practices, and identify new ones, while avoiding the hypothetical experimental setup free of contextual realism.

The services to be tested in the trial show great diversity: a prepaid coffee card; a bus card; a house key; a fitness poster and tags on exercise equipment; a range of check-in tags; tags containing information about cantina menus, campus events, timetables and recent news from the student paper; pairing of devices to exchange photos, business cards and social media friend requests and programmable tags for users to develop their own personalized services. We applied a multi-method approach which allowed us to "juggle" data according to specific research needs (Tashakkori & Teddlie, 2010). The data gathered include surveys, interviews, participant observations, focus groups, design workshops, social media entries, log data, video/photo documentation and self-reporting.

2.3. Key Findings

The field trial is still ongoing and has generated some preliminary findings. In Evjemo et al. (2013), we studied users' engagement with self-programmable tags. We questioned the taken-for-granted espousal of the "simplicity notion" as success criteria for technology adoption. Some users were hesitant to use NFC services, so we set out to evaluate the reactions of users as they took part in workshops and engaged in co-producing personalised services by programming their own NFC tags. We wanted to assess whether "active" engagement could fuel a sense of relevance, familiarity and trust in technologies, tailoring them to the users' own needs and priorities (Barkhuus & Polichar, 2011).

Self-programming enabled users to explore new and creative functions, such as controlling phone applications, sending messages and accessing websites or social networks. The users were fascinated by the smartphone, its multi-functionality and the NFC features, but had limited understanding of its potential. The fact that the smartphone stores the "entire life" of people activated anxiety and privacy/security concerns (Eze, Gan, Ademu, & Tella, 2008; Shin, 2009). However, hands-on experience and the problem-solving setting made users more confident, proving the importance of engagement and learning. Familiarity and trust also seemed to be essential elements (i.e., the ability to "tame" and make technology "one's own") (Silverstone & Hirsch, 1992; Hynes & Richardson, 2009). Furthermore, the aspect of active and co-producing users resonates well with the prosumer perspective (Toffler, 1980), where users participate in the value chain to improve design and services. In this way, our research challenged the notion that too much focus on simplicity may be at odds with utilizing the full potential of multifunctional technologies such as smartphones.

Regarding the other services, only preliminary analyses have been performed. The bus ticket has been well received and appears to be a key driver of NFC services. Loyalty services, such as prepaid coffee cards, are promising, but their success depends on availability (more cafés) and an easy-to-handle system for salespeople. Key/access services also need to fit in with the daily activities of its users. The ability to share digital keys with others was considered a vital future function. In the gym, the NFC poster and tags on exercise equipment were immediately appealing and exciting, but users articulated that more dynamic and personalised content would inspire future use. Information tags were considered simple, accessible, practical and future oriented. At the same time, strategic placement and more context information and personalised content were addressed as key drivers to sustain interest. The check-in tags were rarely used as few students had Foursquare profiles. Rather, users hoped to see other familiar social media platforms such as Facebook.

3. Future Research

Based on our research so far, more effort should be put into exploring the entanglement of spaces that smartphones enable, affecting communication and consumption patterns in unprecedented ways. NFC services may increase users' active involvement with locality (information and services), while social media may further intensify these experiences. Coskun, Ozdenizci, & Ok. (2013) point out that although NFC technology has great potential for applications like payment and ticketing, applying NFC technology in entertainment and social media applications is receiving more and more attention. Hence, we should study the social and communicative aspect of service engagement when communicated to relevant receivers via social media.

In their survey of NFC technology, Coskun et al. (2013) claim that NFC technology is an enabler for social networking tools and can be integrated with the existing social network applications (Hardy, Rukzio, Holleis, Broll, & Wagner, 2010; Köbler, Koene, Krcmar, Altmann, & Leimeister, 2010). Generally, these applications enable users to interact with tagged objects in the environment and to publish information online, while some trials have also used peer-to-peer mode to allow users to share and access their personal information and to create friendships in a more tangible and user-friendly way (Haikio, Tuikka, Siira, & Tormanen, 2010; Siira & Törmänen, 2010).

Returning to our research investigation, the NFC City project has only partially addressed the social media dimension. The Foursquare check-in tags placed in many different spots around the campus area were set up to generate locational transparency among those using NFC services (and immediate others in their social network). Users could automatically signal (by tapping their phones at tap points) when they were in the café for a coffee break, in the cantina for lunch, in the lecture hall for lectures, in the library for studying or in the gym for exercising. However, most students did not have a Foursquare profile required for using the check-in tags. Some pointed out that an alternative Facebook check-in would have worked better. Second, students had other means of communicating their whereabouts on campus, often using direct communication with those they wanted to meet up with. Third, they felt no need to constantly signal their location to everybody as they moved around the campus area. These aspects are tied to students' subtle "communicative cultures" and must be addressed when setting up future social media facilitators. Last, the tags did not generate any added value other than indicating students' locations.

One way of exploring the salience of social media integration with NFC capabilities is through connecting check-ins with augmented experiences or value-added promotions. The first concept could relate to café experiences. By connecting a check-in function to a variably discounted coffee card, more frequent attendance or higher volume of purchase could induce price reductions. This rewarding of loyalty could be further enhanced through customer relationship management (CRM) activity in social media outlets such as Facebook. An NFC tag could also connect to Tripadvisor, generating a marketing effect. Hence, a person in the café could automatically post attendance, purchases and overall experience in social media via the Tripadvisor function. This could trigger rewards to the user if people in the social network respond (by comments) or meet up at the café in person.

Another opportunity can be realised with the gym experience. Most students bring their smartphones to the gym. Hence, if the NFC-based exercise tags were developed to include dynamic logging of activity and progress, this could be shared in the social network, in particular with training companions. This function could also be integrated with check-in tags at the gym. In this way, socially communicated training competition could be enhanced as well as inspire other people in the social network to join the gym. The studio could then reward and reinforce this active engagement through promotions (from beverages to personal gym assistance), consolidating and enhancing the gym experience.

The student organization partaking in the project stressed the need for meeting places and leisure activities to support social networking. The first steps of making friends for new students might be supported by touching phones and utilizing the NFC peer-to-peer mode to exchange contact information (Haikio et al., 2010) or to add a humoristic dating test to the "handshaking" act (Andersen & Karlsen, 2012). Having met and been introduced to each other, the students may be ready for sharing activities and joining games. NFC can ease the game initiation by touching one another's phone (Huang, Tsai, Lin, & Hsu, 2010), but also turn traditional artefact-collecting games (e.g., treasure hunting) into social sharing activities.

Moreover, social media can be integrated with NFC-based marketing. Various services other than bus/transport information may be offered to people at bus stops or other public places where there is a natural need to kill time. This could include a wide range of advertisements, such as movie posters. NFC tags on posters could be tapped to activate movie trailers that can be viewed on smartphones. This can be developed further with features that immediately allow for

16
BIASOMIC FUTURE

Esad Širbegović

INSTITUTE OF SOFTWARE TECHNOLOGY & INTERACTIVE SYSTEMS, AUSTRIA

1. Introduction

The fact that it is impossible to report all news events or to even determine the newsworthiness of an event forces media to be selective and consequentially biased. Media bias has characterised mass media since its birth with the invention of the printing press, as the prohibitive costs of new technology forced publishers to accommodate the ideological perspectives of their financial backers (Heinrichs, 2005).

The argument that all media outlets are biased is valid because a variety of biases can be easily identified. A geographical bias exists: local media cover local issues. A simple count of topics in *The New York Times* proves its positive bias toward North America. Cultural bias is another prominent form (e.g., Australian media are inclined to cover the United Kingdom more than they cover Vietnam because of their cultural heritage, although, geographically, Vietnam is closer to Australia than is the United Kingdom). Besides these elementary media biases, a more profound, ideological and complex media bias is hidden in the content of news. Different authors (Baker, 1994; Nelson, 2003) describe methods for detecting this more subtle bias in content.

Researching media bias in the news is a demanding task because it has to identify semantic structures in adverse sources; simultaneously take into consideration the relations among owners, publishers, journalists, consumers and advertisers and finally extract meaning from all of it. Therefore, media bias research is hard to quantify. Successive problems are associated with it: complexity of data, information overload and data presentation. The problem of complexity of data is best addressed by a traditional social science approach, the information overload by the automated text mining methods and the data presentation by information visualization methods. However, neither of these disciplines is able to perform optimally media bias research on their own.

2. Proposal—Biasomic Approach

2.1. Proposal Aim

The aim of this research is to enable synergy between social science and computer science by developing a visual analytics approach as an interdisciplinary solution using the best approaches from the text mining, the best approaches from the social sciences and information visualization disciplines and become "the best of both worlds" (Keim Mansmann, Schneidewind, Thomas, & Ziegler, 2008). Keim et al. (2008) described visual analytics as an integrated approach combining visualization, human factors and data analysis where human factors (e.g., interaction, cognition, perception, collaboration, presentation and dissemination) play a key role in the communication between humans and computers, as well as in the decision-making process. Media bias research provides an excellent opportunity for both visual analytics and media bias research and their mutual enhancement.

The biasomic method is envisioned as a visual analytics method for the research of media bias in news that applies automated text analysis methods, information visualization and human gamers as annotators. Traditional media bias studies can be seen as linear and incohesive: social studies are limited by the scope and computer science studies by the data complexity. The biasomic method is conceived as a continuous, evolving loop of knowledge, in which news consumers are used to train the automated methods and the data analysts apply visual analytics methodology to perform exploratory data analysis (Širbegović, 2013).

2.2. Methodology

Methodology is divided into the following steps: preliminary analysis and development, system design, implementation and evaluation.

Preliminary analysis and development: Based on an extensive literature research, related established text mining, social science methods and information visualization methods will be identified and evaluated. Parallel to research of literature, news articles, news feeds and related content objects will be collected from relevant sources. Classification and categorization of news sources (conservative, liberal, geographical, etc.) and their content will also occur in this step.

System design: The identified methods will provide the basis for requirement definition and system design of a visual analytics software prototype. Its software specifications will depend upon the methods identified in the first step. This prototypical implementation will include text mining and information visualization methods identified during the first step and corresponding methods enabling user interaction.

Implementation: In the implementation step, the software prototype will be implemented and integrated with aggregated data collected by the agent developed in the beginning. Intensive testing will be performed during this step.

Evaluation: Both user evaluation and overall evaluation will be performed in this step. Within the user evaluation step, the software prototype will be evaluated by a set of experts from related social sciences fields: journalism and/or sociology. Besides user evaluation, the defined research question will provide criteria for an overall evaluation of whole research work.

2.3. Key Findings

The most important expected result of this research is the development of domain-specific visual analytics methodology, named biasomic, solely focused on research of media bias in the news. Beside this main result, the following research key findings/results are expected:

- Identification of the most suitable text mining methods for preprocessing of text corpora.
- Identification of most suitable information visualization methods that can be used to visualise related data.
- Development of an interactive workflow for visual analytics analysis of media bias.
- Construction of software prototype integrating all optimal methods for evaluation purposes of the whole research.
- Evaluation of optimal automated methods, information visualization methods and the evaluation of the framework prototype.

3. Predictive Scenario

The transcendental positive impact the biasomic approach will have on society at large is the empowerment of the individual in the media consumption process where the consumer stops being passive and becomes actively involved in the process of annotating news. In this case, one can envision development of various Web-based and mobile applications that filter news content, apply machine learning and enrich it by user contributions, thus transforming the consumer from a passive role into an active role. This shift will be made possible through user interaction and active involvement. This has important sociological and psychological effects because the human being stops being a passive news consumer and becomes an active actor, completely involved in the loop of knowledge, contrasting, analysing content and actively contributing through gamification to annotation of the same and on the end helps produce new value. Another positive impact of this research is the insight gained. Through the help of visual analytics, the user can more easily gain insight about events described in the news. A picture is worth a thousand words; therefore, visualization can help people gain insight about events that affect them thus empowering them.

In academic research, media bias was traditionally a research topic of diverse social science studies: media studies, cultural studies, journalism, political science, etc. The focus of such research was and still is on measuring the balance of media and on answering the question of whether the media are liberal or conservative. Furthermore, the traditional media studies analyse the deviations in international news, track certain issues and contrast them. There is also an ambiguity of terms that are used interchangeably to describe media bias such as ideological perspective, slant, spin, etc. The aim of this research is to enable synergy between social science and computer science disciplines and their sub-disciplines in order to study media bias from textual content. This leads to interdependence with those related disciplines. Evolution of this research is reciprocally dependent on developments in the mentioned related academic disciplines and emerging fields. Furthermore, one of the characteristics of the biasomic approach (Širbegović, 2013) is its elasticity that allows for continuous integration of any relevant methodology which serves the purpose of media bias research.

The aim in this first phase is to enable synergy between social sciences and appropriate sub-disciplines of computer science related to textual content, in particular visual analytics. In later stages, integration of other corresponding sub-disciplines (e.g., health informatics) could be involved in order to measure the influence of media bias on health. This could be performed on a large scale through the involvement of ubiquitous computing and mobile devices to produce health-related data (e.g., correlation of heart rate, blood pressure) and exposure to certain media content. The scope of this work could evolve over time to include various other data sources and corresponding disciplines that are able to deliver significant data to measure media bias and to involve it in everyday life. It will also include other media objects besides text such as audio, images and videos. The strongest interdependence this research has is with the field of computational media understanding. "Computational media understanding should do what our senses and cognition do: immediate understanding of events as diverse as watching a bird and listening to a speech" (Eidenberger, 2012).

Basically, this shows that a human being as a measure of effectiveness of an automated method is also in the center of biasomic methodology. It also shows that only what we can extract and understand from the content can we then visualise, present and analyse. Furthermore, because media bias is not only limited to the news but also to all other products, the scope of this research could eventually expand from the news to all products delivered to consumers. One could envision integration of augmented reality into such a task as shopping where a consumer is again transformed from a passive role into an active role, where he/she can scan a product in the store's aisle and simultaneously analyse it through a visual analytic application in order to learn about media bias behind it, ownership, its origin, production conditions involved in producing it, etc. A negative side effect and possible danger for the success of the biasomic approach is the fact that users themselves are biased (Gentzkow & Shapiro, 2006; Mullainathan & Shleifer, 2005). This fact has to be taken into consideration by careful user interaction design and studied in the future in order to avoid abuse and possible distortion of the whole loop of knowledge. Furthermore, even the question of causes of media bias is not answered yet clearly by social science. There is ongoing discussion on whether news outlets are responsible for media bias or if the people consuming particular news stories already have a set belief system. The so-called supply-demand discussion exists in the field of economics about the root causes of media bias. In economics, there is also an abundant pool of research concerning media bias. Here one can distinguish between theoretical and empirical research, where the theoretical research is framed by the supply and demand paradigm.

Consequentially, the research goals in economics concern primarily research of supply and demand forces in regard to their influence in causing media bias and influence on political actors and processes such as voting (Prat & Strömberg, 2011). These studies provide valuable insight for the biasomic approach (e.g., for modeling of semantic templates) or for simulation modeling because machine learning methods mirror methods applied in the social sciences. A good example of this is a study about the extraction of politically relevant information from news mentioned in the third section (Doumit & Minau, 2011). On the other side, these studies show the complexity of media bias research and the potential dangers awaiting the biasomic methodology.

4. Conclusions

Human involvement is critical for the successful implementation of a biasomic methodology. Computational media understanding has an inherent limitation which can be solved through involvement of human users. For an automated algorithm, cynicism, irony, and humour still represent formidable obstacles. On the other hand, humans can easily understand it and through interaction can improve the classification and categorisation of content.

Furthermore, the understanding of media bias and its decomposition could lead to user empowerment resulting in a loop of knowledge that changes the perception of facts taken for granted. Therefore, it is an imperative to design the interaction between users and learning algorithms, so that they can adjust themselves. On the other side, we have seen that users themselves are biased and that media bias as a topic is very controversial and represents a challenge that has to be researched with great judgment and understanding. Future work related to biasomic research will focus on the development of the first biasomic software prototype.

5. References

Baker, B. H. (1994). *How to identify, expose and correct liberal media bias.* Alexandria: Media Research Center, Davis Library, USA.

Doumit, S., & Minau, A. (2011). Online news media bias analysis using an LDA-NLP approach. *International Conference on Complex Systems.* NECSI.

Eidenberger, H. (2012). *Frontiers of media understanding,* at press. Vienna, Austria.

Gentzkow, M., & Shapiro, J. M. (2006). Media bias and reputation. *Journal of Political Economy, 114*(2), 280–316.

Heinrichs, A. (2005). *The printing press, inventions that shaped the world* (p. 53). Franklin Watts.

Keim, D. A., Mansmann, F., Schneidewind, J., Thomas, J., & Ziegler, H. (2008). Visual analytics: Scope and challenges. *Visual Data Mining,* S, 76–90.

Mullainathan, S., & Shleifer, A. (2005). The market for news. *American Economic Review, 95*(4), 1031–1053.

Nelson, R. A. (2003). Tracking propaganda to the source: Tools for analyzing media bias. *Global Media Journal, 2*(3).

Prat, A., & Strömberg, D. (2011). *The political economy of mass media.* London School of Economics, Stockholm University.

Širbegović, E. (2013). Biasomic—Visual analytics approach for media bias research. *Proceedings of the IADIS International Conference ICT, Society and Human Beings* (pp. 151–154). Prague.

17

MOBILE SOLUTIONS FOR THE NEW WAYS OF WORKING ERA

Mari Ylikauppila, Antti Väätänen, Jari Laarni, & Pasi Välkkynen

VTT TECHNICAL RESEARCH CENTRE OF FINLAND, FINLAND

1. Introduction

Knowledge workers are no longer bound to a traditional personal desktop and computer combination; therefore, they need flexible and configurable workspaces designed for diverse needs. This also sets new requirements and possibilities to the way mobile ICT devices are used in work environments. In addition, social media services offer new ways of communication between employees, information sharing with partners and public visibility and interaction with companies or public bureaus. Future knowledge work can be characterized by an increased independence from traditional office facilities and traditional ways of working.

Mobile work can be defined as a distributed work or multilocational work, meaning that a mobile worker need not possess a fixed workstation, and work can take place in multiple locations. Mobile workers can be divided into five categories based on the number of workstations in use and the type of mobility. On-site-mover is on the move all the time, but the movement happens inside a limited area (e.g., factory environment). Pendulum works, in turn, at two fixed workstations. Yo-yo is on the move all the time, but the geographical area is wider than for on-site-mover. Nomad works in a number of fixed workstations, and his/her working area is wide. Carrier has no fixed workstation at all, and all the work is done while moving from one place to another (Vartiainen, Hakonen, Koivisto, Mannonen, Nieminen, Ruohomäki, & Vartola, 2007).

A mobile tool can be defined as technology that supports mobile work. Mobile technology is wireless, portable and can be used anywhere and anytime. Mobile tools provide: (1) an easy access to the information systems of the organization, (2) information processing in real time and (3) Internet connection (Alahuhta, Ahola, & Hakala, 2005).

The benefits of mobile work have been recognised in a number of studies (e.g., Palvalin, Lönnqvist, & Vuolle, 2013; Vartiainen et al., 2005; Vuolle, 2011; Wigelius, Markova, & Vainio, 2007). These benefits can be considered from a worker's, an organisation's or a customer's point of view. Mobile work has been found to increase efficiency and flexibility of work. Due to the availability of updated and real time information, the quality of decision making is improved and work processes are optimized. When the information can be processed and shared in real time, there is less need for double work. Also, the number of human errors may decrease, since there is no need to handle information twice. Appropriate tools can also enhance subjective job satisfaction and motivation. From the organisation's point of view, the use of mobile technology makes possible more effective and efficient work processes. The benefits consist of the improved user experience and more efficient work processes. A higher customer satisfaction level has also been identified as a positive impact of mobile work.

New concepts for work settings have been developed. The flexible and configurable work environment can be defined as office facilities which can be divided in on-demand changeable sections and in which the employees do not have a personal office room, but instead work areas and rooms are dedicated for different kinds of work tasks and processes (e.g., teleconference, customer meetings, high-intensity work and internal meetings).

There is a need for mobility inside facilities when employees change the workstation based on the current work task and go outside the office when work is done in the field (e.g., at the customer meeting locales). When the work is divided into different locations, there is a need for tools that support this kind of multilocale work. If an employee frequently moves from one location to another within the office, it is important to guarantee fluent and uninterrupted work processes. This can be realized by providing employees with suitable tools which efficiently support both on- and off-site mobile work.

We have developed and tested a new ways of working (NewWOW) mobile demonstrator in the Finnish national NewWoW study, which focused on understanding the changing nature and needs of knowledge work. These new challenges in supporting and enabling appropriate work environments for future workers have effects on facility management and productivity of work organisations.

2. Mobile Tools for New Ways of Working

2.1. Aims of the Study

As a part of the new ways of working project, future mobile solutions for multilocational work environments were studied. The main goals of the study regarding mobile work and new work domains are the following:

- How do mobile solutions affect working in different contexts?
- What features of the NewWoW mobile demonstrator can support working in flexible and configurable workspaces?
- What are the main barriers for utilization of mobile devices in an office environment?
- Is it possible to substitute paper for tablet devices in judicial administration?
- What are the most suitable mobile devices for supporting working and customer meetings in future working environments?

2.2. Methodology

First, a number of scenarios describing mobile work were developed. Then, one of them—the judicial administration scenario—was selected for further study. Finally, a demonstrator application was developed, and then its use was studied.

2.2.1. Scenario Work

Scenario writing is a popular way to incorporate and generate design ideas for new systems and products and to identify the possible users and contexts of use for the systems or products to be. It is well suited to the design of new prototypes and concepts, where the context of use may vary a lot. Descriptions of people using technology help different participants in discussing and analysing how new technologies, applications and services could influence the everyday lives of the people involved and communities and society in general (Rosson & Carroll, 2002).

Scenarios describe users in particular usage situations, and they are not meant to describe the whole functionality of a system. The value and benefit of scenarios are that they concretise the new technical solutions to such a degree that they can be analysed and discussed with the participants. The descriptions enable designers and users to deal with complicated and rich situations and behaviours in meaningful terms, and to understand better the implications of particular design solutions for performing tasks (Carroll, 1995).

Overall, five different scenarios were prepared for the NewWoW mobile solutions study. They all described mobile working, new easily modifiable workspaces and professional mobile solutions for supporting knowledge work. The scenario that focussed on ways of knowledge work and customer service solutions in a district court was further developed. The main idea of the scenario was to describe how mobile devices and applications can be used in a Finnish judicial administration bureau and how utilisation of the mobile solution can support work practices. The scenario considered points of view of district court employees and customers.

2.2.2. Demonstrator Development

Based on the content of the modified judicial administration scenario, the mobile demonstrator was developed. The main goal of the demonstrator was to illustrate possibilities and features of future mobile solutions in employees' daily activities in judicial administration offices such as district courts. The demonstrator was developed to be used primarily with tablet devices, but it can also be used with Internet browsers of other mobile devices such as smartphones or laptops. The demonstrator was not meant to be a commercial prototype, and it was not integrated to the judicial administration information systems, although it included features and examples of realistic cases and forms.

The demonstrator includes a main page and five subsections (Figure 17.1). Other pages provide information on an employee including his/her status and background information (*Työntekijä*). The case page (*Tapaus*) presents documents of ongoing judicial processes. The calendar and facilities page (*Kalenteri & tilat*)

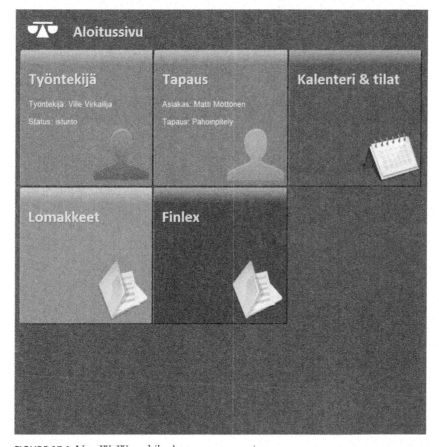

FIGURE 17.1 New WoW mobile demonstrator main page.

enables users to check and reserve available rooms by using the interactive floor plan map feature (Figure 17.2). The idea is to visualise the utilisation of an office environment (i.e., where meeting rooms and other shared workspaces for different needs are located). The form section (*Lomakkeet*) includes typical judicial administration forms. The *Finlex* section is a link to the online Finnish database of legislative and judicial information.

2.2.3. User Studies

The NewWoW mobile demonstrator was tested and evaluated together with end users. Overall, seven participants from the judicial administration departments were interviewed. The interviewees were recruited from a prosecutor office and from a criminal sanctions agency office. The participants worked in different positions, and their ages varied from 26 to 53 years.

The purpose of the interviews was to gather information on the acceptability, usefulness and usability of the demonstrator. One of the main aims was to evaluate how well the demonstrator can support mobile work and future flexible work facility usage. In addition, the participants filled in the background form that included questions of demographic factors and usage of mobile devices and applications in work. The interview sessions were based on the semi-structured interview method.

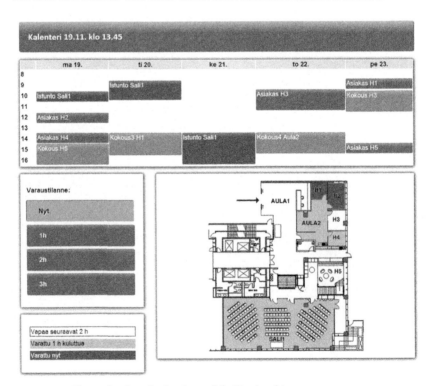

FIGURE 17.2 Floor plan based calendar and facility booking page.

2.3. Key Findings

Productivity of work and job satisfaction in general are believed to increase when new tools for improving the flexibility of work practices are introduced. According to the interviewees, the amount of double work and challenges that the employees are facing will increase when access to real time information is limited. For instance, in the current situations when the work is done outside the office (e.g., at customer meetings), information can be gathered in the field setting, but documentation has to be finished with a computer at the office. Time-saving benefits are immediate, if some of the tasks can be completed already when working in the field or while travelling.

In on-site mobile work, features such as an electronic calendar and a room booking system were considered to be especially useful. Since in the future the employees we studied would not have personal rooms, and the office is shared with other employees, it is important that suitable rooms are available for different kinds of work tasks and offer an employee an efficient and easy way to use tools to manage these facilities. The availability of materials independent of time, place and device would provide the employee with better possibilities to work more flexibly and effectively.

Both possibilities and challenges are evident when substituting paper prints for tablet devices. First, it was found that a mobile device with an appropriate screen size would make it possible to manage a large amount of documents effectively. Second, the material would always be available when needed. As a challenge, the importance of fluent management of documents was emphasized. When a great amount of paper documents are handled daily, fluent browsing and navigation and the ability to organise documents, make notes and add extra information become mandatory.

In addition to possible benefits, the challenges for adoption of mobile tools were discussed. Physical dimensions, security issues and suitability of the tool for completing tasks were seen as the main barriers for effective use of mobile tools. In addition, subjective attitudes and employees' technical skills influence their willingness to adopt new technology. Some of these may require changes in working practices, whereas others can be fixed with careful technology and service design.

3. Future New Ways of Work Enablers and Scenarios

The study showed that use of mobile technology could enhance work in many cases, but the situations when and for what kind of work tasks the mobile tool is suitable have to be identified and carefully considered. Usefulness and usability of the mobile tool are correlated with the employees' work tasks and characteristics of work. Some tasks do not require a possibility for mobile work outside the fixed workstation. The mobile work practices should be targeted to those tasks that will benefit more from off-site work.

While we are technically able to implement new flexible working environments and professional off-site mobile solutions, barriers to use should be taken into account. Employees may not be skillful enough or willing to utilise mobile solutions in their work. Physical dimensions, such as size of the device or absence of a physical keyboard, may limit the usage and usefulness of mobile tools. Regular work with a mobile device and reading from a small screen may frustrate the user in the long run. Also, age-associated changes influence the user's ability to read small texts and handle objects and devices which require precise actions from the user. The common uncertainties of reliability and stability of mobile technology may influence employees' willingness to adopt new mobile tools.

Also, large public offices such as government or community bureaus typically have traditional ways of managing different types of work tasks. Security issues can be a main challenge especially in public domains where employees are handling confidential client information. Usually, these offices handle all kinds of personal and confidential information, which set high demands for wireless networks in use. Since information security risks are a reality even inside an office, the risks are likely much greater when work is done outside an office. In order to reduce these risks, all kinds of malpractices of mobile systems must be prevented, and employees should be educated properly.

We should see all types of mobile devices as platforms for the information systems of offices and companies. Mobile device trends have shown, for example, that touch screen devices cannot be categorised into smartphones and large tablet devices. Smartphones include much larger and higher resolution displays than they did some years ago, and small tablet devices may now have phone features. When mobile and safety technology is mature enough, seamless and continuous online connectivity to public office documents will be as natural in the future as the ability to handle and read paper documents is now. In the future, we may not pay any attention to using mobile technologies in the same way that we do not think about the features of printed paper when we are reading now. As Mark Weiser put it: "The most profound technologies are those that disappear," referring to the ubiquitousness of text, the first information technology, which we do not even notice any more (Weiser, 1999).

One interesting idea that was raised is to loan tablet devices to customers in public offices. The loan tablet devices can be used for checking personal information of a case when visiting in a certain bureau. This makes possible real time and open information and document sharing between officers and customers so that they both have access to the case information in real time and in the same form. Officers could also wirelessly control customer loan devices and give guidance if necessary. The use of on-demand customer devices reduces or removes the need for printing documents and for filling in and signing paper forms. Digital signatures must be implemented in a commonly accepted and understandable way.

Despite the fact that instant loan devices could be available for everyone, customers may not be motivated or capable of using such devices. For example, visitors in judicial department offices or in the health care sector are not typically early adopters of new information technology solutions or services, and they may have physical or mental disabilities that reduce their ability to use new technology. In judicial administration offices and in health sector work environments, the safety of employees and theft protection must be addressed, since customers may have criminal backgrounds, or they may behave in an unexpected way.

Flexible and alterable workspaces should have integrated technologies and features that support instantly changing purposes of use. Different rooms and work areas may be used for personal and confidential customer meetings or for informal internal office meetings, or an office can offer bookable rooms for personal workstation use. The facility technology should also be integrated to the personal mobile devices. Wireless and reliable content sharing and presentation would be profitable in meetings.

As has already been mentioned, the nature of working is changing; the amount of knowledge work is increasing, and the trend seems to be that work independent of location is now increasing in popularity. When work is done in multiple locations and the possibility for face-to-face communication decreases, smooth interaction with information systems and communication between employees must be ensured.

4. Conclusions

Effective and user-friendly mobile devices and applications play a key role when enabling configurable workspaces in the future. Mobile solutions need to be integrated seamlessly to existing office information systems. Privacy, safety and security should also be taken into account. Our study indicates that employees of Finnish judicial administration can be potential users of professional tablet device solutions. Two features of the demonstrator, the floor plan-based calendar and the room reservation system, appear to be profitable in the context of flexible and shared office environments.

Knowledge work highlights the need to rethink how work is done and to rearrange work environments. Especially in a public sector, customer meeting situations, interoperability between public actors and required safety levels should be taken into consideration. The change from personal workstations to on-demand flexible workspaces and mobile work is one of the key challenges for knowledge work organisations. More research is needed to define this new era of knowledge work and to design and develop user-friendly tools for knowledge workers.

5. References

Alahuhta, P., Ahola, J., & Hakala, H. (2005). Mobilizing business applications—A survey about the opportunities and challenges of mobile business applications and services in Finland. *Tekes, Technology Review, 167/2005.*

Carroll, J. M. (Ed.) (1995). *Scenario-based design: Envisioning work and technology in system development.* New York: Wiley & Sons.

Palvalin, M., Lönnqvist, A., & Vuolle, M. (2013). Analysing the impacts of ICT on knowledge work productivity. *Journal of Knowledge Management, 17,* 545–557.

Rosson, M. B., & Carroll, J. M. (2002). *Usability engineering. Scenario-based development of human-computer interaction.* San Francisco, CA: Morgan Kaufmann.

Vartiainen, M., Hakonen, M., Koivisto, S., Mannonen, P., Nieminen, M. P., Ruohomäki, V., & Vartola, A. (2007). *Distributed and mobile work. Places, people and technology.* Helsinki: Otatieto.

Vuolle, M. (2011). Intangible benefits of mobile business services. *International Journal of Learning and Intellectual Capital, 8,* 50–62.

Weiser, M. (1999). The computer for the 21st century. *Scientific American, 265,* 94–104.

Wigelius, H., Markova, M., & Vainio, T. (2007, May 21–24). Successful mobile services for mobile work. In A. Toomings et al. (Eds.), *Proceedings of WWCS 2007, Computing Systems for Human Benefits from the 8th International Conference on Work with Computing Systems.* Stockholm, Sweden.

SECTION VII

Gaming

18

THE ROLE OF INTERACTIVE TECHNOLOGY IN PROSOCIAL MOBILE GAMES FOR YOUNG CHILDREN

Lynne Humphries

DAVID GOLDMAN INFORMATICS CENTRE, UNITED KINGDOM

1. Introduction

Designing interactive, digital games for preschool children can be a challenge as the children arrive at school at an early stage in their cognitive, physical and social development (Gelderblom & Kotzé, 2009). They are pre-literate and therefore any interaction instructions must be basic and used in an intuitive way. There are also challenges in evaluating the success of an interaction design as the children lack the metacognitive skills for think-aloud techniques (Edwards & Bendyk, 2007) because of their developmental age. As well as considerations of these cognitive limitations, there are physical limitations such as the lack of fine motor control (Gelderblom & Kotzé, 2009). Preschool children in mainstream schools arrive with a range of social skills and some may lack skills to interact socially and may yet be diagnosed with problems with interacting socially (e.g., those with autism spectrum disorder, ASC. The lack of these skills may affect their ability to cooperate with peers in playing games.

Many children are already familiar with cartoons and interactive games such as those provided on the cBeebies website (Joly, 2007) where a multimodal design provides interest and motivation. A design approach for children who have social problems but are developing normally may be adapted from designs for young children with ASC. Porayska-Pomsta et al. (2011) adopted an interdisciplinary methodology for designing interactive multimodal technology. They believe that using approaches from developmental psychology, the creative arts and artificial intelligence are the key to developing technology in this context. In their digital world, success can be rewarded using sounds. An advantage of technology compared to analogue methods of teaching emotions to children is that feedback with sound is very engaging and immediate.

One issue for the use of technology with preschool children is social boundary conditions for the use of mobile media. For example, Näsänen, Oulasvirta, & Lehmuskallio (2009) investigated the complex interaction of stakeholders, namely the children, teachers and parents in a study to use mobile technology to enhance their socio-emotional relationships. The authors' aim was to use technology to communicate children's day-to-day kindergarten experiences by the teachers and children using proprietary digital media to capture images. This allowed the sharing of experiences in near real-time situations. They classed their study as an intervention and reported a level of success, but observed that some children were more proficient with the camera than others. Teachers act as intermediaries and need to be trained in the use of mobile media as an educational tool to encourage those children with less exposure to media prior to starting school. However, there is an issue about the advantage that normally developing children with an advantaged background have compared to those arriving at preschool not having had exposure to and experience with some expensive devices. This situation may be compounded when this consideration is extended to children with autistic spectrum conditions where they may be adept with the use of technology but not in a social context.

Lack of access to technology for some young children leads to different levels of prior engagement with technology with income, ethnicity and education identified as some of the complex factors driving the digital divide (Wartella, Lee, & Caplovitz, 2002). The lack of experience with or exposure to digital technology may further confound children's readiness for school learning and socialising if they lack the requisite social and emotional skills to engage successfully in learning (Bulotsky-Shearer & Fantuzzo, 2011; Denham, 2006). One of the key developmental skills in interacting socially is to be able to recognise emotions, and some preschool children enter school having difficulties recognising the major group of emotions (McClure, 2000). Work with children with ASC in the field of emotion recognition has been done by the Autistic Research Centre at the University of Cambridge. Their work with The Transporters (trains with emotion expressions) with four- to seven-year-olds showed that this intervention had a positive effect on the learnability of emotion expressions, supporting their argument that children can be taught this affective component (Baron-Cohen, Golan, & Ashwin, 2009). The Transporters is based on a DVD intervention, but increasingly children have access to engaging, persuasive mobile technology which offers the possibility of more control and interaction by the children.

2. Designing Cooperative, Interactive Emotion Games as a Preschool Social Intervention

2.1. Aims

An important component of the social competencies needed when a child arrives at school is the child's ability to recognise the basic emotions of happiness, anger, fear, surprise and sadness. This study aimed to design and develop a game to test emotion recognition and also to be used as a fun, touch screen tablet game for cooperative play among preschool children. The design concept was based on recognising emotion faces for five of Ekman's (1971) six basic emotions: anger, sadness, happiness, surprise and fear. Disgust was omitted because evidence (Widen & Russell, 2010) suggests that children up to the age of nine confuse the facial expression of disgust with anger and link explanations of this emotion to anger. An important consideration in drawing the digital cartoons was to make the faces engaging and age-appropriate with characteristics of real emotions according to Ekman & Friesen's (1978) Facial Action Code System (FACS). The design process was iterative, and evaluation took place in school as part of observations of normal play activities. The children in Year 1 took part in activities to simulate emotion faces by playing emotion statues (a variation on musical statues) and an emotion faces photo shoot. Still photographs were taken (with permission) and used as a basis for the artist to draw the emotion face cartoons. The photographs were also analysed for children's level of expressivity as some children showed a low level of expressivity for certain emotions. Figure 18.1 shows the emotion game with emotion faces developed digitally by an illustration artist.

2.2. Methodology

The research took place over two weeks in the first year with 30 children from the preschool Foundation stage (Nursery, aged 3–4 years) and over another two weeks a year later in the same primary school when 18 of the same children were in Year 1 (Reception, aged 4–5 years) of the Foundation stage. The images were designed and used to form a set of 40 emotion images (5 emotions × 4 female faces and 4 male faces). A set of 20 of the most recognisable emotion faces (tested on two children aged 3 and 5) was used for the test cards and the full set of 40 for the randomly generated game images (Figure 18.1). Twenty-six of the children, now in the Reception class, were tested on emotion recognition using cartoon emotion face cards before playing a revised emotion game in same-sex and mixed sex pairs, and retested after the game. The collaborative play was evaluated using an adapted model of paired play with analogue games (Dewey, Lord, & Magill, 1988). The novelty of the emotion game is in the use of the specially designed cartoon emotion faces and the design that allowed the use of emotion sounds as feedback and a game that could be played both intuitively (without adult intervention) and collaboratively. Data were collected to test how the game was played collaboratively and whether playing the game improved the children's ability to recognise emotion faces from the emotion cards.

Two hypotheses were tested:

H_1 There is a difference in preschool children's emotion recognition scores after using the touch screen emotion faces game.

FIGURE 18.1 Emotion Game showing the "angry" emotion in play.

H_2 There is a difference in how children cooperatively play together using digital technology.

A child clicks on a chosen image which then drops into the centre. A red background signifies an incorrect choice. Choosing the four correct choices results in the emotion sound being played. The remaining emotion icons appear so the child can select the next set of emotions.

2.3. Key Findings

2.3.1. Gender Differences in Expressivity and Emotion Recognition

The first emotion face parts game (a prototype used in the initial study by Humphries & McDonald, 2011) worked well, and interesting observations were made about the differences in the ability of children to express emotions. Some of the children in the present study showed a relative lack of appropriate emotion expression when playing the classroom emotion games and were also reluctant to take part in the activities and play the game. In an analysis of the emotion expressions from the photo shoot and emotion statues game from the first phase of the study, a T-test of the mean scores of boys and girls in the photo shoot showed the girls were significantly better than the boys at expressing pretend emotions $[(16) = 3.398, p < .05]$. There were no gender differences in the overall ability to express pretend emotions, but boys were significantly worse at recognizing negative affect (sad, frightened and angry) faces.

2.3.2. Gender Differences in Collaborative Play with Digital Technology

A year later, the children's emotion recognition scores were tested using the cards before and after playing the game to give the pre- and post-test scores. The mean scores for emotion recognition increased but not significantly overall [pre-test M(18) = 14.39, post-test M(18) = 15.22]. There was no significant correlation between overall cooperation scores and emotion recognition scores. The maximum score that can be obtained on the adapted cooperation scale is 45. The boy-boy pairs scored M(4) = 34.5, the girl-girl pairs obtained a mean score of M(6) = 36.33 and the mixed pairs M(8) = 33.63. There is no significant difference between the mean individual scores, but there were differences with the children with low expressivity scores (0 and 1) depending on how the game influenced their post-test emotion recognition scores. When playing in mixed pairs, the girls scored significantly lower [M(4) = −.18, p > .05] than when playing in single-sex pairs [M(6) = 2, p > .05]. Conversely, the boys scored significantly higher when playing in mixed pairs [M(4) = 2, p > .05] than in single-sex pairs [M(4) = −.75, p > .05] (see Figure 18.2). A study into the link between children's emotional expressions and emotion and empathy development by Strayer & Roberts (1997) found a link between emotional expressiveness, emotional insight and role taking with empathy. It appears that girls with higher emotion recognition scores demonstrate more empathy in helping others when playing collaboratively.

When tested a year later, the most expressive children in the photo shoot scored higher in the emotion recognition card test. The children who had posed more emotion in the photo shoot gained a significantly higher mean score a

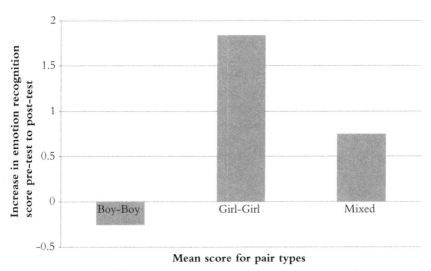

FIGURE 18.2 Results of the pair type on the increase in emotion recognition score.

year later for their post-test emotion recognition [M(10) = 16.6, p < .05] than those children who did not take part or could not pose accurate emotion faces [M(8) = 13.5, p < .05]. Conversely, the less expressive children gained a significantly higher score in the cooperation scale [M(8) = 42.29, p < .05] than the more expressive children [M(10) = 29.91, p < .05]. The initial exploratory study was designed to test the emotion game as a research instrument as well as an opportunity to immerse researchers in children's normal activities, and it was a natural progression to ask them to do the emotion activities. They saw all the activities as play. In this study, H_1 was supported in part. This supports McClure's (2000) meta-analysis of the literature on children's ability to recognise faces that finds mixed results on whether there is a gender difference. The results of the cooperation scores for the pairs suggest that children played with attention and fun for over 10 minutes at a largely self-directed multimodal game with emotion as a domain. It seems that boys learn from the girls in mixed pairs, but the girls gained more when playing with other girls than in mixed pairs. This supported H_2. The touch screen device made it easy for children to share the play without passing the mouse between them. The position on a desk in a play area, as opposed to where many desktop computers are placed, usually on a shelf or in an alcove, made sharing activities more accessible. The design with sound as a reward and one where they could choose their own strategies seemed to have been successful both in the fun element and from the perspective of increasing their emotion recognition scores. This small study resulted in some rich data that were successfully analysed using an adapted psychology scale designed for observing pairs of children playing nondigital games.

The results from the main study suggest that there may be gender differences in the skill at pretending emotions, recognising some emotions and also in strategies used when playing with technology with girls showing more empathy in helping their less-confident peers. The game design reduces complexity of emotion in faces (by using 2D cartoon faces based on realistic proportions and features) and uses sound as a feedback. The game was successful in increasing recognition of the emotion face cards. It has now been developed into an iOS app, and the new platform will be used in future research. Children may see the app as commercial as it will be available via mainstream download applications and it may have more credibility and appeal to children with ASC as a tool for practising emotion recognition while having fun. Mintz (2013) gives three guidelines for designing persuasive technology interventions for children with ASC: work with the children to identify needs, identify which children will benefit the most and consider use on different platforms. Although his study was aimed at older children, the advice for teachers to consider not what "teacher knows best" but to work collaboratively with the child is a good principle, even for preschool children.

3. Predictive Scenario (Future Research)

3.1. Aims

During the discussions with stakeholders about the design and application of the emotion game, teachers from a Key Stage 2 (children aged 6–11) local authority intervention unit suggested that the game would be valuable to children with ASC. Observations of preschool children playing on a preliminary visit to a primary school catering solely to children with ASC revealed a class of four-year-olds where the children were playing quietly in parallel with no shared communication. When asked whether the children shared when playing with technology, one teacher remarked that they had to use a timer to allow turns when children played with the desk-based digital games as they had little or no concept of turn-taking.

The next stage of this research will be to work with the staff at the specialist school to evaluate the emotion game in a larger cohort of ASC children, to assess the children's needs and preferences when using interactive technology. The aim is to assess the impact of the use of persuasive, mobile technology with young children with ASC to allow fun and control using a social skills domain (i.e., recognition of emotion). The scope will be to test the hypotheses on preschool children and possibly older children as some may have younger developmental ages than their actual ages. One consideration is empowering children and parents to use technology as a fun activity with social benefits rather than treating the game as an intervention with all the restrictions that the term may imply as the game is not strictly a clinical intervention. It is intended as a fun application to "nudge" improvements in social skills. The intended market is for teachers and parents. There is evidence (Mintz, 2013) that children with ASC react more positively to the reduced cognitive demand of playing a digital game. They are sometimes overwhelmed by verbal instructions from their teacher. Evidence from studies comparing cooperative play with children with ASC, behaviour-disordered children and typically developing children (Dewey et. al., 1988) shows that being able to correctly read people is a skill that children need for playing cooperatively. Their evaluation took the form of video observations of fun and complexity of interaction with rule-governed games scoring higher on the measures for all types of the pairs playing the games.

The future aim of this research is to use a mixed methods approach to collect rich qualitative data and quantitative performance data from children with ASC at a specialist local primary school. The game will be tested as a single-player game and with peers and a teacher. It is anticipated that the sharing activity shown by the typically developing children may not be evident. The research question for this study will be whether the motivation, attention and learning in children with ASC are better after playing on a tablet, singly or in pairs. The emotion game will be used as a research instrument. The built-in data capture will collect quantitative data when they play the game (percentage of selecting correct emotion faces).

A latin squares design will be used to avoid bias through practice effects. Ethical considerations are important with these vulnerable children, and care will be taken when setting length and timing of sessions. Interviews with stakeholders such as teachers and parents will elicit qualitative data on whether they see technology as a help or a hindrance for their children.

4. Conclusions

Increasing attention is being given to the design of mobile, tablet games for preschool children, including groups such as children with social problems and those on the autistic spectrum who above all need to have the same rich experience that their normally developing peers have. Efforts are being made to provide games that engage them and at the same time may help enhance their socialisation skills. Evidence from working with the emotion game indicates that you can design engaging games for tablets for preschool, pre-literate children that allow them control and fun. There is also evidence for some gender differences in the level of help given by children to their peers during cooperative play and the success in increasing emotion recognition scores after playing the game as an intervention. Outside school, children and parents will be downloading apps for fun, and children with ASC need to be involved in this activity as this is a normal part of their lives. If more apps are developed that can be accessed directly through the App Store or an equivalent, then these stakeholders can access suitable games rather than using only the games at school that teachers choose for them. Perhaps the ubiquity of mobile devices and apps will blur the social boundary conditions for the use of mobile media in schools and allow parents, children and teachers to find resources for fun and possible informal learning. Children learn by social interaction, and children with ASC have impaired social communication. Boys make up the majority of children with ASC, but they may overcome any deficit in emotion recognition skills if they can be motivated by persuasive digital technology to play and learn attentively with technology that has a social competency focus.

5. References

Baron-Cohen, S., Golan, O., & Ashwin, E. (2009). Can emotion recognition be taught to children with autism spectrum conditions? *Philos Trans R Soc Lond B Biol Sci, 364*(1535), 3567–3574. doi: 10.1098/rstb.2009.0191.

Bulotsky-Shearer, R. J., & Fantuzzo, J. W. (2011). Preschool behavior problems in classroom learning situations and literacy outcomes in kindergarten and first grade. *Early Childhood Research Quarterly, 26*, 61–73. doi: 10.1016/j.ecresq.2010.04.004. ISSN: 0885-2006.

Burger, K. (2010). How does early childhood care and education affect cognitive development? An international review of the effects of early interventions for children from different social backgrounds. *Early Childhood Research Quarterly, 25*, 140–165. doi: 10.1016/j.ecresq.2009.11.001.

Dawson, G., Toth, K., Abbott, R., Osterling, J., Munson, J., Estes, A., & Liaw, J. (2004). Early social attention impairments in autism: Social orienting, joint attention, and attention to distress. *Developmental Psychology, 40*(2), 271–283.

Denham, S. (2006). Social-emotional competence as support for school readiness: What is it and how do we assess it? *Early Education and Development, 17*(1), 57–89. doi: 10.1207/s15566935eed1701_4.

Dewey, D., Lord, C., & Magill, J. (1988). Qualitative assessment of the effect of play materials in dyadic peer interactions on children with autism. *Canadian Journal of Psychology, 42*(2), 242–260.

Edwards, H., & Bendyk, R. (2007). A comparison of usability evaluation methods for child participants in a school setting. In *Proceedings of the 2007 Conference on Interaction Design and Children* (pp. 9–15).

Ekman, P. (1971). Universal and cultural differences in facial expressions of emotion. In J. Cole (Ed.), *Nebraska Symposium on Motivation* (pp. 207–283). Lincoln: University of Nebraska Press.

Ekman, P., & Friesen, W. (1978). *Facial action coding system: A technique for the measurement of facial movement.* Palo Alto: Consulting Psychologists Press.

Gelderblom, H., & Kotzé, P. (2009). *Ten Design Lessons from the Literature on Child Development and Children's Use of Technology.* IDC, 52–60.

Humphries, L., & McDonald, S. (2011). Emotion faces: The design and evaluation of a game for preschool children, CHI EA '11. *Proceedings of the 2011 Annual Conference Extended Abstracts on Human Factors in Computing Systems.* ACM, New York, USA.

Joly, A. V. (2007, June 6–8). *Design and Evaluation of Interactive Cross-platform Applications for Pre-literate Children, Proceedings: Doctoral Consortium, IDC '07.* Aalborg, Denmark.

McClure, E. B. (2000). A meta-analytic review of sex differences in facial expression processing and their development in infants, children, and adolescents. *Psychological Bulletin, 126*(3), 424–453.

Mintz, J. (2013). Additional key factors mediating the use of a mobile technology tool designed to develop social and life skills in children with autism spectrum disorders: Evaluation of the 2nd HANDS prototype. *Computers and Education, 63*, 17–27.

Näsänen, J., Oulasvirta, A., & Lehmuskallio, A. (2009). Mobile media in the social fabric of a kindergarten. In *Proceedings of CHI'09.* ACM, New York, NY, USA.

Porayska-Pomsta, K., Frauenberger, C., Pain, H., Rajendran, G., Smith, T., Menzies, R., Foster, M. E., Alcorn, A., Wass, S., Bernadini, S., Avramides, K., Keay-Bright, W., Chen, J., Waller, A., Guldberg, K., Good, J., & Lemon, O. (2012). Developing technology for autism: An interdisciplinary approach. *Personal and Ubiquitous Computing, 16*, 117–127.

Strayer, J., & Roberts, W. (1997). Facial and verbal measures of children's emotions and empathy. *International Journal of Behavioral Development, 20*, 627–649.

Wartella, E., Lee, J., & Caplovitz, A. (2002). *Children and interactive media: A research compendium,* prepared for the Markle Foundation (35-page manuscript). Retrieved from http://www.markle.org/news/_news_IMCresearch.stm and http://www.digital-kids.net/

Widen, S. C., & Russell, J. A. (2010). The "disgust face" conveys anger to children. *Emotion, 10*(4), 455–466.

19

LOCATION-ENABLED STAMP-RALLY SYSTEM FOR LOCAL REVITALIZATION

Akira Hattori (1), Haruo Hayami (2), & Tasuku Kobayashi (3)

(1) KOMAZAWA UNIVERSITY, JAPAN, (2) KANAGAWA INSTITUTE OF TECHNOLOGY, JAPAN, AND (3) KANAGAWA INSTITUTE OF TECHNOLOGY, JAPAN

1. Introduction

Activities such as orienteering or scavenger hunts, or in Japan stamp-rallies or walk-rallies, have been conducted in a variety of fields. For example, such activities in the field of education have the potential to satisfy the objectives of orientation at universities by delivering useful information to students and enhancing their levels of engagement and motivation (Gray, Lindsay, & Walraven, 2011). They are also often conducted during tours around local areas in Japan to entice and entertain participants at events (Kichiji, 2011). People visiting various locations at such events can lead to local revitalization in the area.

Mobile devices such as smartphones and tablet computers have recently continued to evolve, and more features are constantly being added to them (Ellul, Gupta, Haklay, & Bryson, 2013). There are a growing number of applications for such devices. Their useful functionalities also hold promise for educational and fun activities such as orienteering or scavenger hunts (Cerny & Holcomb, 2012).

However, it is important for members of the public to participate in community activities to address real-world social issues, many of which are inherently location-based (Wilson, Rice, & Fraser-Rahim, 2011). The functionality of mobile devices with built-in location sensors can facilitate the use of location data. Therefore, the ability to take advantage of location-based/enabled systems and services forms one of the most fundamental features of such community activities.

This chapter first presents a system for conducting a stamp-rally and then proposes a combination of the system and location-based systems. We also present a special system for collecting location information with Twitter.

2. System for a Stamp-Rally Combined with Bingo

2.1. Purpose

Orientation at universities is an essential program to introduce new students to many aspects of their departments (Hassanien & Barber, 2007). The purpose of orientation is to acclimate students to their new university communities and to enable them to make friends and create social groups. Scavenger hunts have the potential to meet these objectives, and stamp-rallies are often one of the events most widely held for new students in Japan (Miyagawa, Yamagishi, & Mizuno, 2011).

People go to certain locations to have their booklets stamped with rubber stamps at stamp-rallies. Each location has a unique stamp. There is also a stamp-rally combined with bingo where participants can enjoy playing bingo by collecting stamps from separate locations to make the rally more fun. However, since the number of locations specified in an event may differ depending on the day it is held, organizers must have stamps for the maximum number of possible locations. In addition, some locations, such as bus stops or bulletin boards within a campus, make it difficult to have booklets stamped. We developed a system for conducting a stamp-rally combined with bingo to explore the use of mobile devices in such areas (Hattori, Kobayashi, & Hayami, 2013).

2.2. Overview

Figure 19.1 outlines the structure of our system. Participants at an event visit various locations across the university and read quick response (QR) codes there

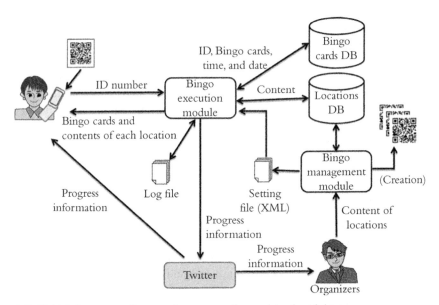

FIGURE 19.1 Structure of system for stamp-rally combined with bingo.

1	31	12	25	27	3
10	7	34	13	14	19
4	16	35	2	36	30
9	15	21	5	8	26
33	32	22	28	20	29
11	24	23	18	17	6

stamp-rally combined with bing

Library

t ID card. The total number of items you ca
uate can borrow up to 15 items, but can on

FIGURE 19.2 Bingo card and information about location displayed on mobile phone.

using their mobile phones. When they are read, the QR codes introduce their bingo cards and information about the locations (see Figure 19.2). Each grid of a bingo card has an ID number assigned to each location by our system. When a participant reads a QR code at a location, the corresponding ID number on his or her bingo card is marked off.

As can be seen from Figure 19.1, our system consists of a bingo management and a bingo execution module. The bingo management module has functions to set up a bingo card and manage information that corresponds to individual locations. The bingo execution module has functions to register participants, mark off numbers on their bingo cards, determine if they have achieved a specified pattern from the numbers marked off and offer information on the progress of the bingo game to the participants. When organizers of an event set up a bingo card, the bingo management module outputs an extensible markup language (XML) document that describes the configuration information of the card. The bingo execution module creates and manages the bingo cards of all participants according to the XML document. Each time a participant reads QR codes at a location, the module determines if he or she has achieved a specified pattern. It also posts the progress of the bingo game on Twitter.

3. Evaluation

We conducted stamp-rallies at our university orientations for the new students in 2011 and 2012 using our prototype to evaluate the system's potential. We grouped the new students into teams of three or four in 2011. Each team used one of its member's mobile phones. The bingo card had 16 squares, and the winning combination was a simple line. Each student used his or her mobile phone in 2012. The bingo card had 36 squares, and the winning combination was two lines.

In 2011, a total of 108 students took part and were grouped into 44 teams, 33 of which achieved the specified pattern. The number of locations visited to achieve the specific pattern ranged from six to 13 and was nine on average. About 70% of the 108 students indicated that they enjoyed the stamp-rally. Only 25 students looked at Twitter during the rally. Two hundred students, on the other hand, participated in the stamp-rally in 2012, 40 of whom achieved the specified pattern. The number of locations that were visited to achieve the specific pattern ranged from 19 to 27 and was 23.8 on average. Two-thirds of the 183 students positively answered the question about whether the stamp-rally provided an opportunity to talk with others in their classes. About half of them answered "agree" to the question about whether the stamp-rally should be repeated for future students.

4. Discussion

On the whole, the students had positive attitudes toward the prototype. In both years, we received many positive comments such as "It was a good opportunity to make friends" and "I became interested in the laboratories." These comments suggested that our system provided new students an opportunity to make friends and to become interested in university life. We also received many comments such as "I went to various locations on the campus," "I had fun visiting some locations that I did not know," and "It was interesting to play a game around the campus." These positive comments suggested that our system could support new students in finding their way around the campus. These results also revealed that our proposed system could potentially foster a sense of community and familiarize new students with their new university life.

The bingo execution module posted information in 2011 about the progress of bingo on Twitter. However, only 20% of students checked such tweets. As the most important thing for students was to achieve a specified pattern, they wanted to visit various locations as fast as they could. Some students simply misunderstood that they had to sign up for Twitter to check the tweets posted by the module. We also received some comments such as "I did not know that the system offered information about the progress of the bingo game." However, it was necessary to incorporate mechanisms to actively use Twitter in our system.

These comments also suggested that our system could make it possible for students to visit every location and know about the place. For example, students could explore history, environment and culture near their university through lecture and field work using our system. In that case, the system provides them with such field data. We think that it would be useful to provide students with information in accordance with their learning abilities. To do that, we need to understand their learning statuses. Providing questions in each location would be useful for that.

We called the system described in this section the "stamp-rally system."

5. Combination with Location-Based Systems

5.1. Background and Purpose

We plan to contribute to revitalizing local communities through a combination of the stamp-rally system and location-based systems in the future and by using them in practice in local communities.

Because of the widespread use and growing popularity of mobile devices, such as smartphones and tablet computers that have built-in sensors to obtain location data, we are seeing the emergence of a number of social network services that can share users' location data with others (Lindqvist, Cranshaw, Wiese, Hong, & Zimmerman, 2011). Social media such as Facebook and Twitter have also launched location-enabled functions (Marcus, Bernstein, Badar, Karger, Madden, & Miller, 2012). The convergence and combination of geo-referencing information and location technology built into information and communications technology (ICT) are expected to make important contributions to social issues in community settings, such as economic recovery, strengthening disaster preparedness and local revitalization (Ellul, Gupta, Haklay, & Bryson, 2013). Understanding and participation by members of the public are essential elements for such combinations to produce an effect. It is very important to make proper use of specific information that individuals and community groups have who participate in volunteer activities. Much of this information is location-based because most of their voluntary activities are designed and carried out to meet the needs of their local communities. They can also find town charm and resources through these activities. Therefore, using their information could promote participation by members of the public and create local communities in which everyone can take part in community activities. It is also important for people to actually walk the streets to revitalize the local communities.

We intend to explore the possibility of making active use of information that individuals and community groups gain through volunteer activities for local revitalization. This makes it possible to share and take advantage of town charm and resources with which they are familiar. In addition, it is possible to continuously collect information about the progress of bingo on Twitter when our stamp-rally system does not post such information because people who took part in stamp-rallies in community settings using the system can post information about town charm and resources that they found during the event. People are expected to walk the streets both in terms of collecting and utilizing town charm and resources which can lead to local revitalization.

We have developed a system to obtain the history of user check-ins to contribute a better understanding of the availability of location-based social networking services in local communities using Foursquare's application programming interface (API), which is one of the leading location-based social networking services using the location data obtained from the global positioning system (GPS) in mobile devices (Hattori, Fukumoto, Yokoi, & Hayami, 2012). This gives him or her the system's original badges depending on how many specified places he or she visited in a town walking event. The system also visually displays the history on a map and a timeline. Applying the mechanism of check-ins to the stamp-rally system, in which QR codes are used to confirm that users visited locations, makes it possible to use location data obtained from GPS as well as QR codes. It is also possible to notify of visits to a location by posting a tweet with the location data of the place.

Foursquare's API and our stamp-rally system are similar in terms of focusing on the consumption of information about locations. However, we have also developed a system to collect information about town charm with pictures using Twitter and to display it on a map. The next section presents this aspect of our system in detail.

5.2. System to Collect Information on Town Charm Using Twitter

It is essential for people to actually walk the streets to revitalize local communities. We have developed a system for town walking events on the basis of this premise. When participants in a town walking event take pictures with their mobile phones that feature town charm and resources that they found along the streets and post tweets with pictures and the location data obtained from GPS on the phones with which they took the pictures, the system collects the tweets and displays them on a map in real time.

Figure 19.3 outlines the structure of the system, which has two main functions. The first is to add tweets posted on Twitter to the database of our system, and the

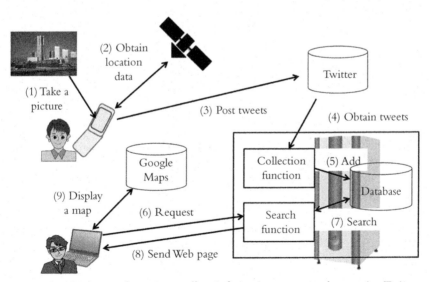

FIGURE 19.3 Structure of system to collect information on town charm using Twitter.

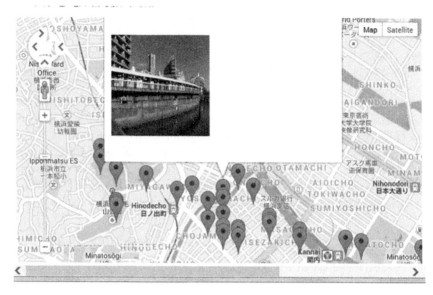

FIGURE 19.4 Example of map displaying tweets as points.

second is to display them as points on a map based on the location data related to the tweet, which is a set made up of the latitude and longitude. Participants in town walking events post tweets containing pictures of town charm and resources, location data obtained from GPS and specific hashtags to be identified during events. The system then collects such tweets based on hashtags using Twitter's API and extracts the uniform resource identifiers (URIs) of the pictures, the location data and the text from each tweet to add them to the database. The collected tweets are displayed as points on a map using Google Maps API. The pictures and text of tweets corresponding to markers are shown (see Figure 19.4) when users of our system click a marker on the map.

We held a town walking event five times using our system in Yokohama to confirm its effectiveness in cooperation with a community group called "Yoko-hama Action Planner," which consisted of university students and young working adults in their 20s and 30s. The main purpose of the events was for them to learn about the area and to become attached to the town. The participants in the town walking event were grouped into teams of three or four and walked around the town for three hours. Over 500 tweets were posted during the town walking events to show them the town charm and resources that they found. Someone replied to a tweet posted by the participants during the events. This communica-tion suggested that social media could disseminate information on town charm and resources and provide an opportunity for people who were not able to take part in the walking events to become interested in the area. They discussed town charm and resources while looking at the tweets and the map after each event.

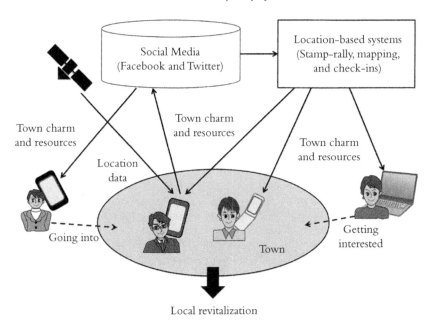

FIGURE 19.5 Combination of stamp-rally system and location-based systems.

We intend to use posted tweets containing town charm and resources as information on locations in the near future and conduct a stamp-rally with our stamp-rally system in community settings. However, specifying too many locations in the stamp-rally can create various problems. For example, it would be difficult to complete a bingo pattern when an event opened because the batteries of mobile phones would go dead before participants achieved a specified pattern. Thus, we need to add a function to the stamp-rally system to support organizers of events in selecting tweets from a number of them to use as information on locations for the stamp-rally. To do that, we plan to introduce mechanisms such as a "Like" button on Facebook so that people can become interested in the town and easily become involved in selections. In addition, we intend to provide opportunities for them to share new town charm and resources by letting participants in the stamp-rally post tweets with their photographs and location data during the events. As outlined in Figure 19.5, we believe the combination of the stamp-rally system and location-based systems that we have developed will lead to an increased number of people being interested in the town and local revitalization in the future.

6. Conclusions

This chapter described a system for conducting a stamp-rally combined with a bingo game and presented the results and findings from field trials using our prototype at our university orientations. We also explained the combination of a stamp-rally system and location-based systems that we developed. Further, we described a special system to collect tweets containing town charm and resources posted during town walking events. We intend to conduct field trials with this combination in Yokohama in the future. However, as there is room to further develop and enhance our systems, we would like to advance our studies in cooperation with community groups.

7. References

Cerny, J., & Holcomb, J. (2012). Using a QR code scavenger hunt (iHunt) to promote library services to teens. *Virginia Libraries, 58*(1), 39–42.

Ellul, C., Gupta, S., Haklay, M., & Bryson, K. (2013). *A platform for location based app development for citizen science and community mapping. Progress in location-based services* (pp. 71–90). Springer.

Gray, S., Lindsay, E., & Walraven, J. (2011). ORIENTHUNT: The development of a scavenger hunt to meet the needs of a first year engineering orientation. *Proceedings of the 2011 AAEE Conference* (pp. 543–549). Fremantle.

Hassanien, A., & Barber, A. (2007). An evaluation of student induction in higher education. *International Journal of Management Education, 6*(3), 35–43.

Hattori, A., Fukumoto, T., Yokoi, S., & Hayami, H. (2012). A study of a system for town walking event using a location-based social networking service. *Proceedings of the International Conference on e-Commerce, e-Administration, e-Society, e-Education, and e-Technology 2012* (pp. 854–867).

Hattori, A., Kobayashi, T., & Hayami, H. (2013). Development and practice of a system for conducting stamp rally combined with bingo using mobile phones. *Proceedings of the IADIS International Conference Web-Based Communities and Social Media 2013* (pp. 13–21).

Kichiji, N. (2011). Network analysis of the traffic lines of the tourists visiting Kamikawa Central District in Hokkaido, Japan: Based on the data from the 'Kamui Mintara' Stamp Rally. *Economic Journal of Hokkaido University, 49*, 89–112.

Lindqvist, J., Cranshaw, J., Wiese, J., Hong, J., & Zimmerman, J. (2011). I'm the mayor of my house: examining why people use Foursquare—a social-driven location sharing application. *Proceedings of the SIGCHI Conference on Human Factors in Computing Systems* (pp. 2409–2418).

Marcus, A., Bernstein, M. S., Badar, O., Karger, D. R., Madden, S., & Miller, R. C. (2012). Processing and visualizing the data in tweets. *SIGMOD Rec, 40*(4), 21–27.

Miyagawa, T., Yamagishi, Y., & Mizuno, S. (2011). A walk-rally support system using two-dimensional codes and mobile phones. *Proceedings of the 6th International Conference on e-Learning and Games, Edutainment Technologies* (pp. 71–77).

Wilson, S. M., Rice, L., & Fraser-Rahim, H. (2011). The use of community-driven environmental decision-making to address environmental justice and revitalization issue in a port community in South Carolina. *Environmental Justice, 4*(3), 145–154.

20
TECHNOLOGY ENHANCED LITERACY LEARNING IN MULTILINGUAL SUB-SAHARAN AFRICA

The Case of Graphogame Kiswahili and Kikuyu Adaptations in Kenya

Carol Suzanne Adhiambo Puhakka, Heikki Lyytinen,& Ulla Richardson

UNIVERSITY OF JYVÄSKYLÄ, FINLAND

1. Introduction

Kenya's literacy rate was estimated to be approximately 87% in the year 2011 according to UNICEF. Nonetheless, approximately 70% of third grade Kenyan children cannot read basic second grade stories (UWEZO Assessment Report, 2012). Poor literacy levels are often due to a low level of teacher education, over-sized classrooms and lack of reading materials at home or at school. Most teachers in Kenya lack necessary training to teach early reading skills as depicted in the Kenya Primary Math and Reading Program Report (PRIMR, 2013) that highlights results from Early Grade Reading Assessment (EGRA, 2010), the (UWEZO, 2010) initiative and the National Assessment System for Monitoring Learner Achievement (NASMLA, 2010) which show that a large percentage of Kenyan children are unable to read simple texts or to understand what they read. These early literacy problems affect many Kenyan children and are worse for the children who are at risk for developing reading disabilities.

2. Background

For a review of the results of the Jyväskylä Longitudinal Study of Dyslexia (JLD), see Lyytinen, Erskine, Ahonen, Aro, Eklund et al. (2008). A digital training game called GraphoGAME[TM] has been developed to help children learn to read (for description of the game and its development, see Lyytinen, Erskine, Kujala, Ojanen, & Richardson, 2009). GraphoGAME, which is known in Finland as Ekapeli, was originally intended as a research tool into reading acquisition in the Finnish language because it offers an efficient way in which the basics of reading can be observed by focusing on the main issues in learning to read (i.e., the learning of connections between spoken and written language). Research indicated that the game had the potential to prevent reading difficulties in children. The game uses phonics, which is agreed to be the most effective method to teach reading skills in both nontransparent English (e.g., Ehri, Nunes, Stahl, & Willows, 2001) as well as in transparent writing systems such as German (e.g., Landerl & Wimmer, 2008). The game was developed for use by children from 6.5 years of age as research shows that children below this age tend not to be mature enough to benefit from phonics instruction that is based on systematic building of connections between sub-lexical written and spoken units. It systematically introduces spoken sounds (phonemes) with the written counterpart first, and then syllables which are followed by words. The child should ideally play the game for 5- to 15–minute periods several times a day until the child learns the letter-sound connections (spoken communication by Heikki Lyytinen). More than 200,000 children have played the game in Finland and successfully learned the letter-sound connections (Lyytinen et al., 2013). GraphoGAME is the name given to all other language adaptations of this Finnish literate game. In principle, GraphoGAME should be effective in providing support in teaching reading also in African local languages which are similar to the Finnish language, consistent on grapheme-phoneme correlations (i.e., each grapheme—letter or letter combination—corresponds to one phoneme and each phoneme has its own grapheme, consistent at grapheme-phoneme level in both reading and spelling). In Africa, the GraphoGAME research was previously piloted in Cinyanja, a Bantu language commonly spoken in Lusaka Zambia. First grade children who received at least two hours of intervention improved in spelling and orthographic skills according to research conducted by Chilufya (2008) and Ojanen, Kujala, Richardson, & Lyytinen (2013).

2.1. Objectives of the Investigation

1. To explore whether GraphoGame-Kiswahili and GraphoGame Kikuyu adaptations help children improve orthographic processing skills in Kiswahili and Kikuyu, respectively.
2. To explore whether GraphoGame-Kiswahili and GraphoGame Kikuyu adaptations help children learn letter sound knowledge in Kiswahili and Kikuyu, respectively.
3. To explore whether GraphoGame-Kiswahili and GraphoGame Kikuyu adaptations help children learn syllable sound knowledge in Kiswahili and Kikuyu, respectively.
4. To explore whether learning letter-sound knowledge affects other literacy skills (e.g., spelling).

2.2. Methodologies

The participants were first grade pupils (N = 111) from one Kiswahili-speaking school and (N = 85) pupils from one Kikuyu-speaking school. Eighteen children received GraphoGame Kiswahili intervention, and 16 children received Grapho-Game Kikuyu intervention. However, due to absenteeism, not all the data were available for analysis and comparison. In the orthography test, the children were presented with a total of 80 items in the Kiswahili adaptation and 107 items in the Kikuyu adaptation. The children were required to draw a circle around all items they considered orthographically appropriate items in the respective tests. The drawings started from legal/illegal letters and continued in small steps to word/nonword level. In the spelling test, the children were required to choose (by underlining or drawing a circle around) the items that corresponded to the sounds they heard. These sounds of increasing difficulty starting from single phonemes and ending with words were sounded out by the teachers who had received a total of three hours of training in sounding out prior to the tests. The children received one hour of orientation on the tests (30 minutes each day on two consecutive days before the assessments). The aim of the orthography test was to assess orthographic awareness of the children in print, and the instructions were to identify the items (letters, syllables, words) that were correct in the particular language (i.e., Kiswahili and Kikuyu). The orthography tests were scored as correct (C) = 1 and not correct (NC = −1) (i.e., the children were penalized for choosing an incorrect item because choosing an incorrect item meant they lacked orthographic awareness in the particular language). The absolute minimum score for Orthography Kiswahili was −52, and the maximum score 28. The absolute minimum score for Kikuyu was −67, and the maximum score 40. The Kiswahili and Kikuyu spelling tests had a total of 25 item rows: they started with letters, then progressed to syllables, then to CVCV (Consonant, Vowel, Consonant, Vowel) words and CVCVCV words and were scored as correct (C) = 1 and not correct (NC) = 0. From each item rows, the children were to choose one item from a choice of five items in print. The maximum score for the spelling tests was 25 and the minimum score was 0. The tests were correlated, in other words the Orthography tests 1, 2 and 3 and Spelling tests 1, 2 and 3 were measuring the same thing respectively (orthography test Kiswahili (p = .522), Orthography test Kikuyu (p = .584), Kiswahili spelling/dictation test (p = .522), Kikuyu spelling/dictation test (p = .910).

The orthography test and spelling test Kiswahili and Kikuyu were given to the Kiswahili (N = 111) and Kikuyu (N = 85) speaking children respectively. The children were given two pretests (Orthography and spelling tests 1 and 2), with a difference of only one day between these two pretests and the post test, Orthography and spelling tests 3, after the intervention period which took a total of 5 days (i.e., children gained at least 4 hours playing time). The tests were assessed and the low scorers (LS) based on the performance in the tests (1 and 2), (N = 73) for the Kiswahili study and (N = 54) for the Kikuyu study. The LS were determined by adding the total scores of each of the tests (Orthography tests separately and spelling tests separately) and then determining the means. A child who scored equal to or below 23.5 in the spelling test and a score equal to or below 12 in the orthography test was considered a low scorer in the Kikuyu study and respectively below 21.5 in the spelling test and equal to or below 4.5 in the orthography test was considered a low scorer in Kiswahili. In the Kikuyu study a group of Low-Low (N = 16) scorers were selected from the (N = 54) low scorers and respectively Low-Low (N = 18) scorers were selected from the (N = 73) low scorers for the Kiswahili group. The Low-Low scorers received the GraphoGAME intervention (via inexpensive mobile phones) while the Low-High scorers were in a waiting list to receive GraphoGAME later. The Intervention groups (GG players/ Low-Low scorers) played GraphoGame for 15 minute periods four times a day for five days; in total they played for at least four hours in both studies respectively. The playing time was organized in such a way that the children played during break times while the other children (all other children in the study including the Low-High scorers) were playing outside in the school playing field.

2.3. Key Findings

The pre-intervention results based on the selection criteria in the orthographic knowledge and spelling show that these children are at risk of developing reading problems that most probably stem from poor instruction and conflicting language codes. Using repeated measures MANOVAs the general results of a comparison of the means of the pretest 1 and 2 combined against the posttest 3 in the orthography test and spelling tests in Kikuyu and Kiswahili of (N = 49) Kiswahili non-players (N = 18) GraphoGAME Kiswahili players and (N = 38) non-players and (N = 16) GraphoGAME Kikuyu players show that the children who were exposed to the GraphoGame Kikuyu and Kiswahili adaptations improved in their orthographic skills based on the orthography test assessment (p < .001) for both the Kikuyu and Kiswahili studies, more than the non-players. In the Kikuyu and Kiswahili spelling tests, however, there was no significant change in the spelling test performance. In other words the GraphoGAME players did not catch up to the non-players in their spelling skills in the tests and there was no interaction between the players and non-players.

3. Predictive Scenario (Future Research)

Based on the findings of the previous research which show that GraphoGAME has the potential to assist children to acquire reading skills, it has been deemed necessary to conduct further research using more advanced devices, e.g., android tablets that will enable the researchers to gather more detailed information that will show how the player engages in the GraphoGAME. The GraphoGAME records all information which shows what items (letters, syllables and words) the player selected when they heard a specific sound. Because it records everything the player does, it gives the researcher an opportunity to analyse children's choices, error styles and general learning process all the way through. This analysis is done via gamelogs which can be analysed with several computer programs which each have different features and methods of measuring. The general way of interpretation is that 60% performance is equivalent to guessing and performance at or above 95% is considered to be a sign of real knowledge. The performance level is set this high because the items in the study are phoneme-letter correspondences which are in essence automatic. That way it is easier to identify the exact problematic areas for the player so that intervention can focus on these specific areas. Based on the fact that the development of the adaptations of the game is ongoing, the game can be tailored to focus on areas that are problematic for children of a specific language group.

The proposed research (which is now complete) involved Class 1 pupils in 2 Kiswahili (Kiswahili is the lingua franca of Kenya) speaking primary schools in Nairobi County. A total of N = 269 children participated in the research study. At least 130 children played the GraphoGAME Kiswahili adaptation and the other 139 who were the control group played another digital game. The children received three external assessment tasks (pseudo word spelling test, single word spelling test and short sentence multiple-choice reading test all in the Kiswahili language) immediately before and after the intervention period. The intervention period (playing Kiswahili adaptation) was 20 minute periods with 10 minute period breaks for two and half hours every day for 15 days in order to obtain at least 8 hours training time (exposure time). In addition, both groups of children (control group and player group) did the assessment tasks within the Grapho-GAME Kiswahili adaptation which include a letter/syllable sound assessment task and word recognition task.

It is expected that this validation study will provide such data to support scientific evidence on the efficiency of training with GraphoGAME so that the 1st grade pupils in the Kenyan public primary schools will be able to start to use the Kiswahili adaptation of GraphoGAME. In addition it will allow the GraphoGAME developers to understand the areas of the GraphoGAME that need to be developed so that they are more culturally sensitive to the African children (given that GraphoGAME was initially developed in Finland for the Finnish children). The proposed idea is that this will be done via a public procurement made by the Kenyan government so that the GraphoGAME is free for the end user (the grade 1 pupils). Through this validation research and the more extensive dissemination of GraphoGAME in Kenya, GraphoGAME will be promoting acquisition of early literacy skills in Kenya which is a children's right and addresses the basic element of the second Millennium Development Goal which is providing Universal primary education in an effective way that shows evidence based results. Moreover, teachers can use the GraphoGAME tool and the GraphoGAME-related content (e.g., providing information and practical examples on reading instruction) to receive the training they require in order to teach early reading effectively. In this way, their capacity as competent teachers will be increased. This process will broaden their understanding into the practicalities involved in doing collaborative research and implementation that involves two different continents and cultures (in this case Europe and Africa) and adapting products developed in one cultural environment to another. It will also enable their understanding of what is involved when working with African governments for public procurement in education.

One of the main challenges of this procurement model is that teachers need to embrace the GraphoGAME as a tool that will help them teach early reading skills efficiently and effectively given that in Kenya especially, as a result of the free primary education, the classrooms are large (with 60 to 100 pupils per class in some public schools). Some teachers may view the use of technology to teach pupils as a process that renders them redundant in their teaching profession. Second, education has not been given first priority by the government. In cases such as Kenya where there is now more emphasis on education (e.g., with the proposed laptop for schools project), the government faces so many challenges that it may not be in a position to afford the best products for school children. Hence, the government may not be willing to invest heavily in what it may consider only one component of learning (i.e., reading) at the expense of math and other sciences. It is important to note that in the African culture the importance of reading as a basic skill toward literacy has been undermined.

4. Conclusions

Given that the Kenyan situation is very complex due to its multilingual nature, it is important to understand how such a focused and theory-based technological tool as GraphoGAME can efficiently provide learners and teachers the necessary learning support in this type of environment where the children speak various mother tongues in their homes. It is also necessary to involve parents in the teaching of early literacy skills as this process will be more effective if the environment both at home and at school supports reading acquisition. GraphoGAME intervention studies have shown scientifically significant results on its effectiveness in teaching reading skills in several different language contexts (e.g., Finnish, English and German). It is important to further develop this tool to provide an appropriate learning environment for learners in different cultures, to make it a multiplatform application, to provide learning support beyond learning the basic reading skills and to find ways to disseminate it widely so that all learners who might benefit from playing have access to it. It could be that for its dissemination, a joint effort from various policymakers and stakeholders is needed in order to make it happen in the near future.

5. References

Aro, M. (2005). Learning to read: The effect of orthography. In R. Malatesha Joshi & P. G. Aaron (Eds.), *Handbook of Orthography and Literacy*. Mahwah, NJ: LEA.

Chilufya, J. (2008) The effect of computer-assisted letter-sound correspondence training on learning to read in Zambia. Unpublished Master's thesis. University of Jyväskylä.

Ehri, L., Nunes, S., Stahl, S., & Willows, D. (2001). Systematic phonics instruction helps students learn to read: Evidence from national reading panel's meta-analysis. *Review of Educational Research, 71*(3), 393–447.

Holopainen, L., Ahonen, T., & Lyytinen, H. (2001). Predicting delaying in reading achievement in a highly transparent language. *Journal of Learning Disabilities, 34*(5), 401–413.

Holopainen, L., Ahonen, T., & Lyytinen, H. (2002). The role of reading by analogy in the first grade Finnish readers. *Scandinavian Journal of Education Research, 46*(1), 84–98.

KNEC (2010) report. National Assessment System for Monitoring Learner Achievement (NASMLA): Monitoring of learner achievement for class 3 in literacy and numeracy in Kenya. Retrieved April 21, 2014 from http://www.knec.ac.ke/main/index.php?option=com_phocadownload&view=category&download=182:std-3-abridged-report&id=62:std-3-abridged-report

Landerl, K., & Wimmer, H. (2008). Development of word reading and fluency in a consistent orthography. An 8 year old follow up. *Journal of Educational Psychology, 100*(1), 150–161.

Linehan, S. (2004). Language of Instruction and the Quality of Basic Education in Background Paper for the EFA Monitoring Report, 2005, Paris, UNESCO.

Lyytinen, H., Erskine, J., Ahonen, T., Aro, M., Eklund, K., Guttorm, T., Hintikka, S., Hämäläinen, J., Ketonen, R., Laakso, M. L., Leppänen, P. H. T., Lyytinen, P., Poikkeus, A. M., Puolakanaho, A., Richardson, R., Salmi, P., Tolvanen, A., Torppa, M., & Viholainen, H. (2008). Early identification and prevention of dyslexia: Results from a prospective follow-up study of children at familial risk for dyslexia. In G. Reid, A. Fawcett, F. Manis, & L. Siegel (Eds.), *The SAGE handbook of dyslexia* (pp. 121–146). Sage Publishers.

Lyytinen, H., Erskine, K. J., Ojanen, E., & Richardson, U. (2009). In search of a science base application: A learning tool for acquisition. *Scandinavian Journal of Psychology, 50*, 668–675.

Ojanen, E. Kujala, J. Richardson, U., & Lyytinen, H. (2013). Technology-enhanced literacy learning in Zambia: Observations from a multilingual literacy environment. *Insights on Learning Disabilities, 10*(2), 103–127.

Piper, B. (2010, July) Early Grade Reading Assessment Findings Report. Retrieved April 21, 2014, from https://www.eddataglobal.org/reading/index.cfm/EGRA%20Kenya%20072910%20Final.pdf?fuseaction=throwpub&ID=275

USAID (2012, June). The Primary Math and Reading (PRIMR) Initiative Baseline Report. Retrieved April 21, 2014, from https://www.eddataglobal.org/documents/index.cfm/TechR_PRIMR-Kenya_Task13_Baseline%20report%20full%20060812.pdf?fuseaction=throwpub&ID=480

UNICEF Annual Report. (2011). Retrieved April 21, 2014, from http://www.unicef.org/publications/files/UNICEF_Annual_Report_2011_EN_060112.pdf

UWEZO Assessment Report. (2010). Are our children learning? Annual Learning Assessment Kenya 2010: Summary and key findings Retrieved April 21, 2014, from

http://www.uwezo.net/wp-content/uploads/2012/08/KE_2010_AnnualAssessment
ReportSummary.pdf

UWEZO Assessment Report. (2012). Are Our Children Learning? Retrieved October
27, 2013, from http://www.uwezo.net/wp-content/uploads/2012/09/RO_2012_
UwezoEastAfricaReport.pdf

INDEX